D1603540

MATTERING PRESS

Mattering Press is an academic-led Open Access publisher that operates on a not-for-profit basis as a UK registered charity. It is committed to developing new publishing models that can widen the constituency of academic knowledge and provide authors with significant levels of support and feedback. All books are available to download for free or to purchase as hard copies. More at matteringpress.org.

The work of the Press has been supported by: Centre for Invention and Social Process (Goldsmiths, University of London), European Association for the Study of Science and Technology (EASST), Hybrid Publishing Lab, infostreams, Institute for Social Futures (Lancaster University), OpenAIRE, Open Humanities Press, and Tetragon.

MAKING THIS BOOK

Mattering Press is keen to render more visible the unseen processes that go into the production of books. We would like to thank Endre Dányi, who acted as the Press' coordinating editor for this book, the two reviewers David Healy and Maggie Mort, Steven Lovett for the copy editing, Daniela Ginsburg for the proofreading, Alex Billington and Tetragon for the typesetting, and Will Roscoe, Ed Akerboom, and infostreams for formatting the html versions of this book.

COVER

Cover art by Julien McHardy.
Illustration by Nick Hayes.

GHOST-MANAGED MEDICINE

Big Pharma's
Invisible Hands

SERGIO SISMONDO

 Mattering Press

First edition published by Mattering Press, Manchester.

ISBN: 978-0-9955277-7-5 (pbk)
ISBN: 978-0-9955277-8-2 (ebk)

Mattering Press has made every effort to contact copyright holders and will be glad to rectify, in future editions, any errors or omissions brought to our notice.

CONTENTS

LIST OF FIGURES

I

POWER AND KNOWLEDGE IN DRUG MARKETING

PHARMACEUTICAL COMPANY INTERVENTIONS

DRUGS ARE AT THE CENTRE OF MEDICINE. MOST MEDICAL SCIENTISTS DO research on the effectiveness and safety of drugs. Most physicians working in modern scientific medicine focus on solving problems by providing drugs. The same is true of most patients: when we walk into the doctor's office, we usually hope to walk out with a prescription for drugs that promise to heal us, to improve our quality of life, or to keep us in good health. But which prescription? Why that one? What leads our doctor to write those particular words and symbols on her little square of paper?

Imagine this scenario: after seeing a TV ad for some drug (perhaps you can't quite remember which), you think that it might be time to get your cholesterol checked. Your doctor agrees, saying that adults should have their cholesterol checked every five years, and you head down to the lab. The results come back, and you learn that you have somewhat elevated LDL cholesterol levels, although not enough to panic. But considering that you're firmly in middle age and had an apparently healthy uncle who had a heart attack at 70, your doctor recommends that you take a statin. You start to ask a question, and he interrupts: 'These drugs are so safe they should be added to the drinking water.' There are various choices, but he recommends Zovachor [not a real drug name], one of the biggest sellers. He's been prescribing it for years, and he has just read an article that showed that, for people in your age group, Zovachor had the best benefit-to-risk profile of the major statins. He had heard one of his old medical school profs speak about it at a conference he attended last year, and that guy practically wrote the book on heart disease. He hands you a free sample, and a prescription. You leave, feeling safer.

How many times might drug companies have intervened in this scenario? Of course, a company placed the ad that convinced you to see your doctor. That's One. Should you have taken the test? What is an elevated cholesterol level? Drug companies have helped to fund research that has resulted in recommendations for regular testing and that has steadily lowered what physicians consider normal cholesterol. Two and Three. They've also funded the studies that identify risk factors like your uncle. Four. Who did the safety studies on statins, and years later have still not released all of the data? Five. Who has promoted the slogan 'so safe they should be added to the drinking water', which almost every doctor has heard? Six. Your doctor was probably given that article on Zovachor by a drug company sales rep. Seven. Chances are that the article itself was ghostwritten for the maker of the drug, given to some highly regarded professors of medicine to put their names on, and then submitted to a good medical journal. Eight, Nine, Ten. Your doctor was probably funded to attend that conference. Eleven. His former professor was also probably funded, and another company ghostwriter may have written his talk. Twelve and Thirteen. In fact, that professor's reputation as a whole has almost certainly depended on research and publication help from the industry at many stages. Fourteen. And then there's that sample, placed in your doctor's cabinet by a sales rep the week before, encouraging him to prescribe the drug. Fifteen, and counting.

Ghost-Managed Medicine is a study of the pharmaceutical industry and its agents, as they try to shape and spread the medical knowledge of value to themselves.

Pharmaceutical companies sustain large networks to gather, create, control and disseminate information. They provide the pathways that carry this information, and the energy that makes it move. Through bottlenecks and around curves, knowledge is created, given shape by the channels it navigates. Pharma companies create medical knowledge and move it to where it is most useful; much of it is perfectly ordinary knowledge that happens to support their marketing goals. But because of the companies' resources, their interests and their levels of control, they become key shapers of almost all medical terrains.

In this book, I shine a light on some important tactics and practices that drug companies use to influence medicine. I describe paths of drug information and knowledge from contract research organizations (which perform the bulk of pharma's research) to publication planners (who direct the production of ghostwritten medical journal articles) to key opinion leaders (who are deployed to educate physicians about drugs) and beyond. In describing these paths I am describing circumstances of the production, circulation and consumption of medical knowledge; as a result, my project is about political economies of knowledge.

In pharma's preferred world, research, education and marketing are fused. Our actual world is not so very far from that: when practicing physicians gain knowledge, they most often gain it from agents of big pharmaceutical companies, including local sales reps, researchers and educators sponsored to spread the word, and perhaps even journalists who needed a story to write. All these agents may aim to tell physicians the truth, but the truths they tell are drawn from streams of knowledge that have been fed, channelled and maintained by drug companies at every opportunity.

There is a 'ghostly' aspect to drug companies' actions. My co-option of the 'invisible hands' metaphor draws attention to that, and ties ghostliness to pharmaceutical marketing. Research on markets has shown the extent to which they are created by institutions and constituted by concrete actions. In the case of pharma companies, much of the work to establish and exploit markets, the work to coordinate the production and circulation of knowledge, is performed by invisible hands.

Let me explore these themes a little further.

THE MEDICAL KNOWLEDGE ECONOMY

We often hear the term 'knowledge economy' connected with pushes to increase countries' high-tech spheres, scientific output and participation in higher education. Usually, the term refers to a 'knowledge-based economy', where the production of goods depends heavily on technical knowledge. In a knowledge-based economy, knowledge itself becomes an object of investment, trading, and deployment. In this book, I treat knowledge not merely as a productive resource, but as a good connected to other goods. I explore the circumstances of the production, circulation and consumption of pharmaceutical knowledge – what we might call the 'political economy of pharmaceutical knowledge'.

Knowledge – and information more generally – doesn't move on its own through its environments. For this reason, we can treat it as a kind of substance, rather than as something purely ethereal. In mundane terms, the knowledge we care about most is rarely easy to come by and spread. To create and establish valued knowledge typically takes resources, infrastructure, tools, skilled labour and considerable effort. A claim only becomes an established fact when it has been picked up by enough of the right actors, and woven into the fabrics of what they do and say. To spread facts isn't much easier.[1]

I approach these topics from frameworks established in Science and Technology Studies. As a field, Science and Technology Studies does not provide a unified account of either the production or the distribution of knowledge, but it does always treat knowledge as something constructed, and not just waiting to be found.[2] The field is based in the recognition that it is possible to regard the construction of scientific facts – through actions in laboratories and elsewhere – as the upshot of careful rhetorical work, and of work to establish what can be taken for granted: scientific knowledge is something produced.[3] Science and Technology Studies also treats the movement of facts and would-be facts as something that could, in principle, be accounted for as the result of actions, rather than as a simple natural phenomenon.[4]

Because of this background, I am interested in *how* the pharmaceutical industry constructs and moves facts and claims, and this book will, I hope, provide some novel insights into that.

The quasi-substantiality of knowledge runs against the grain of some grand claims about new economies. Digital information can be easily reproduced and transmitted, and this makes it look as though new digital tools could create a very egalitarian political economy of knowledge, one in which the barriers to contributing to and accessing knowledge are modest. Wikipedia might serve as a good model of this egalitarian economy; it's easy to edit and easy to read.[5]

Egalitarianism when it comes to knowledge is a laudable ideal, but the fact that knowledge is a form of cultural capital, already unevenly shared and constantly exploited to create new inequalities, makes it an ideal that is difficult to live up to. Actors come to knowledge arenas with differing amounts of cultural, social, symbolic and economic capital. This capital can be converted from one form to another, and the accumulation of capital depends upon the conversion not being transparent. Actors develop and deploy their capital to establish and change their relative statuses.[6]

Not only do medical researchers and physicians try to establish themselves as particularly knowledgeable, but the pharmaceutical industry helps them to do so. Pharma companies use their considerable economic capital to create and distribute other forms of capital: cultural, social and symbolic. Pharma companies ghost-manage the production of medical research, they shepherd the key opinion leaders (KOLs) who disseminate the research as both authors and speakers, and finally they orchestrate the delivery of continuing medical education (CME) courses. In so doing, they position themselves as the ultimate sources of the information physicians rely on to make rational decisions about patient care. In this we can see the importance of pharma's hegemonies over medical knowledge.

Imprisoned by the Fascist government from 1926 to his death in 1937, the Italian philosopher Antonio Gramsci filled notebooks with thoughts about politics and culture. In his *Prison Notebooks*, Gramsci explores how a dominant actor doesn't need to use overt coercion when it has *hegemony* over key institutions – as the Fascist government developed over the press, schools, religion and popular arts. In Gramsci's thinking, hegemony establishes what is taken for granted or regarded as 'common sense' in different areas. In this book, I look at attempts to achieve hegemony over medical knowledge through contract research, publication in medical journals, the creation of medical culture via sponsorship of KOLs, and the continued dissemination of that culture via sales forces and patient advocacy organizations (PAOs). There are rough parallels between these institutions and those – like the press and schools – that Gramsci discussed.[7]

It is easy to talk about hegemony in hand-waving terms, finding some parallels or analogies between dominant interests and the actions or commitments of institutions – for example, between big business and elite newspapers.

However, it is a challenge to identify and describe concretely the mechanisms that shape institutions and the views attached to them. Perhaps emblematic of the challenge, Gramsci writes that 'Every social group ... creates together with itself, *organically*, one or more strata of *intellectuals*, which give it homogeneity and an awareness of its function, not only in the economic but also in the social and political fields.'[8]

If Gramsci is right, the organic creation of intellectuals and ideas in dominant cultural groups tends to be hidden from view, naturalized within cultures. In the more defined sphere of medical knowledge, the mechanisms of cultural control are also at least partially hidden, and pharma companies' roles have become naturalized. For many physicians, for example, pharmaceutical industry influence looks innocuous and ordinary, to the extent that they see the industry as the best source of medical information. The industry has achieved a level of hegemony over parts of medical education, and therefore over what physicians see as treatable diseases and how they should be treated.

However, the creation of intellectuals and the domination of institutions do not happen at all organically, but are instead the result of deliberate and careful actions. In this book, insiders describe in great detail how they and pharma companies aim for hegemony. They make their strategies and tactics visible to each other when they network and promote their services. They need to provide evidence to each other of the value of their tools and skills. Observers – like me – can eavesdrop by spending time at the perimeters of the industry.

This book is broadly about knowledge, but the issues at stake don't fit well within traditional epistemology, the branch of philosophy that studies knowledge. Epistemology chiefly studies justification, and in particular tends to focus on the justification of beliefs as held by individual people. It is beyond doubt that some of the claims that drug companies make and promote are poorly justified, and some are false in egregious ways. On occasion, there are major scandals about errors, falsehoods and gross manipulations circulated by pharma companies – the 'fake news' of the medical world.[9] But, by and large, these companies work within the medical mainstream, and produce data of reasonably high quality using the most valued of research tools; they go on to analyse it using standard statistical means, and construct articles that pass the scrutiny of peer reviewers at many of the best medical journals.[10] The problems of knowledge in the drug industry discussed in this book are not primarily problems of justification.

However, seen in terms of political economies of knowledge, there are serious concerns about the practices of pharmaceutical companies. Largely unnoticed influence and control permeate important areas of medical knowledge. Individual companies with stakes in specific medical topics can influence knowledge so that their preferred science becomes dominant. The medical world then focuses on what the companies care about most, using the terms that they establish. Pharma companies can achieve hegemony over understandings of particular diseases, symptoms, treatment options, trajectories and side effects. Through the enormous resources at their disposal, they have staked out dominant positions on the overall terrain of medical knowledge. The drug industry has concentrated power to make particular medical knowledge salient, and the interests guiding that power are narrow.[11]

Very closely related to all of this are questions about agency, the capacity to act independently. In my account, I describe industry actors' efforts to constrain and co-opt the agency of target physicians, patients and others. That is, pharmaceutical companies and their delegates try to persuade physicians and others to make decisions that align with the companies' goals. Pharma's efforts are successful enough that they invest in them over and over again.

The flood of knowledge that companies create and distribute is not designed for broad human benefit, but to increase profits. At least some of the time, broad human benefit and profits are in direct opposition to each other. Therefore, it is perhaps less pertinent to ask whether this or that piece of pharmaceutical knowledge is justified or true than to note instead that the structures that create and distribute pharmaceutical knowledge concentrate power in a limited number of entities with very narrow interests and defined goals.

THE INVISIBLE HANDS OF THE PHARMACEUTICAL INDUSTRY

Many otherworldly creatures occupy the dark spaces of human cultures. Ghosts, zombies, vampires and others – all not quite alive but feared for their attacks on the living – walk in shadows. Part of the mystique and terror surrounding these beings is rooted in the fact that we can't quite see them, or can't see them for what they are. Vampires, for example, can make themselves appear ordinary, or even, in some literary traditions, sophisticated, charming and aristocratic. They maintain their lifelike status by sucking the essence of life, usually in the form of blood, out of their victims.

Normally, the 'invisible hand' metaphor doesn't carry any occult connotations. Adam Smith used it (very infrequently) to describe how individuals promote the interests of others or of society by acting in their own self-interest. The 'invisible hand of the marketplace' has come to stand for the processes by which innumerable real or possible selfish choices are thought to stabilize markets and optimize local utility. As groups, producers and consumers of a good should arrive at a price at which all of the good is sold and all of the demand is met. The invisible hand of the marketplace is, then, an effect of many visible hands.

In a classic book of business and economic history, Alfred Chandler describes how, in the nineteenth century in the US, there arose a new 'visible hand' of the marketplace, in the form of middle managers in new medium-sized and large companies. The planning carried out by these professional managers replaced some of the coordination previously effected by the free market, because it was more efficient and created more stability for the firms. On Chandler's analysis, professional management allowed the largest of these companies to dominate sectors of the US economy and to reshape the larger markets of which they were a part.[12]

The pharmaceutical industry is immensely fond of invisible hands, but not Smith's kind. The hands I make visible in this book are more like Chandler's managerial hands. However, they try to maintain a ghostly status so that they cannot easily be seen, or cannot be seen for what they are. For pharmaceutical marketing to work best, it has to look like disinterested, unbiased, impartial medical knowledge. As a result, many of the hands doing the companies' marketing work need either to be invisible or to look as though they're doing something else. In this sense, *Ghost-Managed Medicine* is a study of the spectral in the pharmaceutical industry.[13] The book follows spectral elements of first the production and then the distribution and consumption of medical information, along the path described just below.

The industry provides roughly half of all funding for clinical trials – often randomized, controlled trials (RCTs), the most valued form of medical knowledge – and sponsors most of the new trials initiated each year.[14] The bulk of that funding goes to contract research organizations (CROs) and related firms. CROs plan and run clinical trials to get drugs approved and to make new cases for drugs to be prescribed. They recruit doctors, who recruit trial subjects, whose tissues, fluids and observable qualities can be transformed into data. CROs are the first of the phantoms in the drug industry, feeding on trial subjects' bodies, but mostly staying out of sight in the medical research world. In the end, CROs make no claim on the data they produce; they simply turn it over to the companies that hire them to use as they want.

Using this and any other available data, the pharmaceutical industry produces a significant portion of the scientific literature on in-patent prescription drugs. In the more prestigious medical journals, as many as 40% of the articles on recently approved drugs have been ghost-managed for companies.[15] I use the term 'ghost management' when drug companies and their agents control or shape multiple steps in the research, analysis, writing, publication and dissemination of science. Ghost management, I will show, is common. Some of the key ghosts are called publication planners, who design publication strategies, create teams of professionals to shape and write articles, select the journals they will be submitted to and choose KOLs to serve as the putative authors of these articles.

As a result of the work of CROs and publication planners, medical science is shaped to serve marketing goals. The drug companies' interests can be expected to influence any number of choices in the design, implementation, analysis, description, and publication of clinical trials. We can reasonably expect – and there is abundant evidence – that the companies make choices to support their commercial interests. Even if companies are not completely coherent actors, they are coherent enough in their goals that choices at all the different stages of research and communication generally point in the same direction. The result is still recognizably medical science, and may even be high-quality science, but it is science designed to help sell drugs.

This continues with the communication of medical science in the field. When they give talks, KOLs contribute to the enormous influence that the drug industry has on medical knowledge. KOLs are the zombies of the industry, the animated bodies sent out to do pharma's bidding – like the original zombies of Haitian folklore, who were created and controlled by sorcerers, and who served as slaves. Most KOLs are fully constrained; they present scripted presentations to other doctors and make the scientific and medical cases established by CROs and publication planners. The form of education in which KOLs participate is one thoroughly shaped by the companies that sponsor it. What KOLs communicate will often be sound medical science, and this is why they are willing to communicate it. Generally, they are fully committed to what they are doing; they believe their own talks and can easily justify their roles in marketing campaigns. The KOLs interviewed for this book defend giving promotional talks in idealistic terms: if physicians are 'not educated enough, the public will suffer', says one; 'oh, it helps other patients elsewhere, it's spreading the word – it's spreading the gospel', enthuses another. KOLs' brains and souls have been taken over. They are sent out to take over other brains and souls, to convince more doctors of the evidence base for specific prescriptions.

There is a sophisticated service industry around all forms of medical communication. Marketers broadcast their ability to do 'promotion through education', claiming that CME courses can be 'custom tailored to meet pharmaceutical marketers' needs'.[16] As agents of drug companies, medical education and communication companies (MECCs) create courses, plan conferences and seminars, conduct surveys and write articles and studies. All of this is then placed in the hands of the educators, researchers, and doctors who will use them to good effect. These firms feed stories to the journalists who write for newspapers and medical magazines, giving them technical details, journal articles, the names of experts to contact, and even narrative lines. They even provide video clips for television networks that then air stories about the latest advances.

Now for the boots on the ground: pharmaceutical sales representatives. These men and women work full-time to increase drug sales, which means convincing physicians to 'change their prescribing patterns'. Variants of this phrase come up over and over again in pharma circles. The reps convince doctors to change their prescribing patterns by subtly boxing them in, effectively draining their agency, their ability to act independently. Sales reps arrive at physicians' offices already knowing what their targets prescribe, how they see themselves, and a host of other small facts that might help to establish rapport. They are also armed with sets of scripts for most occasions, so they are prepared for doctors' evasive moves. The result is that even if doctors see themselves as making their own decisions through the interactions, the sales reps are well placed to make those decisions lead to fresh prescriptions of the drug under discussion. Doctors feel that they are in control of the situation and their actions, while sales reps are stealthily 'changing prescribing patterns'. These sales reps make good use of the scientific studies that drug companies commission and shape. Medical science sells drugs by allowing doctors to make justifiable decisions.

Patient advocates and patient advocacy organizations are further important nodes in the shadowy marketing of drugs. Two-thirds of PAOs in the US receive industry funding, and the organizations within that group receive 45% of their funding from pharmaceutical, medical device and biotechnical companies.[17] Some 93% of PAOs that make presentations before or participate in discussions within the US Food and Drug Administration (FDA) receive industry funding.[18] The situation is similar in other high-income countries such as the UK.

In extreme cases, PAOs are creatures *of* the industry. They are fully funded by one or more companies, staffed by professionals, and find patients to be members after the fact. They, like many other funded PAOs, serve as lobbyists and do public relations work, promoting drugs and diseases and defending pharma against negative publicity. They are sirens for the industry, singing passionately about better futures with better drugs. And as for pharma's other phantoms, invisible hands are busy manipulating other actors, working diligently to disguise motives and interests.

Overall, then, pharma companies rely on systematic pressure on the circulation of scientific knowledge and the resulting medical practices. This is a system of influence made more effective by being shadowy and spectral.

Because I focus on ghostly marketing within and immediately around medicine, I won't address more overt kinds of marketing in this book. For example, in 2016 in the US – the large country most open to drug ads – pharma as a whole purchased more than $3 billion in television advertising, and spent nearly as much on ads in magazines, newspapers and other media. Of that, $300 million went to ads in medical journals.[19] It may be that ad spending gives companies some leverage over television networks and other media, including medical journals, and thereby expands pharma's influence. However, to limit the areas I address, I don't explore that leverage here.[20]

Pharma companies have many agents over which they have direct control, such as the companies, firms, agencies and consultants they hire for specific purposes or to create specific products. By outsourcing to these agents, the companies take advantage of external expertise and resources, and extend their reach. The agents I describe in this book, which include the ones on which companies spend the most money, are hired to produce or transmit information to be taken up by other elements of the market, including regulators, physicians and patients. The companies and their agents influence those other elements by shaping what they know and believe. Regulators, physicians and patients then act in ways that seem rational, obvious or easy. To the extent that the companies are successful, they constrain the agencies of their targets in much the same way that an expert chess player can constrain the agency of a more novice opponent across the table.

AN EXPANSIVE VIEW OF MARKETING

Total drug sales rise nearly 10% per year, through good times and bad.[21] This suggests that we still need some large stories about the efficacy of marketing and the demand for drugs.

The 'market' of neo-classical economics is a metaphor. Markets were once physical spaces, where sellers and buyers would meet to exchange goods and money. Of course, all sorts of other things happen in traditional markets besides buying and selling: carting goods in, setting up stalls, socializing, theft, and pretty much anything else that happens when people gather. But the original metaphor has almost always been used with a narrow focus on planned buying and selling.

In the tightly packed physical market that is the source of the economists' metaphor, goods of the same kind sold by different vendors quickly end up fetching the same price, because anybody charging too much is unable to

compete with vendors in the next aisle, and anybody charging too little realizes that they could make more money by closing the gap between themselves
and their competitors in the stand across the way. Profits should tend to drop,
because whenever there are opportunities for high profits on one kind of good,
multiple sellers should switch to making and selling more of that good, bringing
the price down. Overall, the logic of the metaphor points toward an efficient
price mechanism that balances supply and demand. Today, actual markets are
mostly regulated to make them behave like the markets of economists' metaphor.

The modern corporation, company or firm is an institution for evading
the market of neo-classical economics. Obviously, firms have no interest in
seeing their profits drop to zero, so they are engaged in continuous wars on free
markets. Activities such as branding and advertising attempt to make products
incommensurable, to establish monopoly control and to increase the number
of buyers and the price for a particular product. For example, to the extent that
different strains of rice are broadly comparable, that new sellers can enter the
rice market, and that there isn't a tremendous imbalance of resources among
buyers, eventually rice prices should tend toward a level equal to marginal costs
and profits should drop. Enter Nishiki brand 'New Variety' rice, advertised as
superior to other rice brands and of a consistently high quality. If consumers
agree that Nishiki is not strictly comparable to other rice, then the Nishiki
company will be able to maintain profits.

Firms arise and evolve to avoid free markets, using a variety of strategies
more available to corporate bodies than to individuals – such as having managers
dictate employees' actions, thereby reducing 'transaction costs'.[22] In this book,
I emphasize one set of reasons based on firms' abilities to marshal resources to
shape or control markets for their own benefit.[23]

While some people might be temperamentally comfortable living with
uncertainty, firms engage in careful planning to limit the effects of uncertainty at
every turn. Economist John Kenneth Galbraith identified a number of strategies
that modern corporations use to deal with uncertainties in supply and demand.
In the extreme case, they can simply take control over uncertainty. Galbraith
writes: 'This consists in reducing or eliminating the independence of action of
those to whom the planning unit sells or from whom it buys.'[24] In other words,

firms depend upon the coordination and delegation of both inside and outside actions, rather than the rational actions of independent actors.

Pharmaceutical companies would control all the actions of market gatekeepers and customers if they could, but they can't. Instead, they do the next best thing and engage in campaigns of influence, subtly reducing the independence of the actors they need to sell their products. Because of a number of unusual features of the drug business, this can be a very successful strategy.

We might see pharma companies as engaging in 'channel marketing', influencing various 'channel partners' in order to access customers.[25] A company controls or influences channel partners, which then influence either customers or still more channel partners. With strong enough bonds, the company will eventually control the whole channel between itself and the customers. Figure 1.1 provides a highly schematic image of the interactions involved.

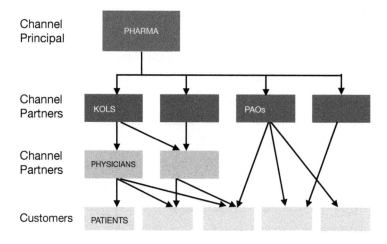

FIG. 1.1 Channel marketing

One unusual feature of the drug business is that the most profitable products are available only by prescription. As a result, pharmaceutical companies focus their marketing attention much more on prescribers than on end consumers. They want physicians to make favourable diagnoses, and then to write prescriptions for their products. Health and medicine are forbiddingly complicated subjects, and drugs are dangerous. Consumers – that is, patients – typically lack the knowledge to be considered competent stewards of their own treatment, and also lack the knowledge to evaluate or challenge their doctors' assessments and recommendations. Patients have limited choices when it comes to many drugs; usually they are allowed to decide only whether to fill the prescription and whether to take the drug.

Health, medicine and drugs are such complicated subjects that even many physicians lack the knowledge to independently evaluate or challenge claims that appear in medical journals or clinical practice guidelines. Many doctors are in the position of having to choose primarily whom to trust, rather than what to trust.[26]

In addition, end consumers of the most profitable drugs often don't fully pay for them. In wealthy and middle-income countries, different kinds of public and private insurers provide the bulk of the funding for expensive treatments. These insurers are gatekeepers of a different kind than are physicians, and so become another marketing target for pharma companies. They are increasingly important targets, because healthcare costs keep increasing and insurers appear to be trying to contain their spending – including on drugs.

In its everyday use, 'marketing' is a term for actions to promote products, perhaps by advertising and branding. The American Marketing Association has a much broader concept of marketing, defining it as 'the activity, set of institutions, and processes for creating, communicating, delivering, and exchanging offerings that have value for customers, clients, partners, and society at large'. In this definition, not only have the traditional physical markets of the original market metaphor disappeared, but so has the narrow focus on planned buying and selling.[27] The modern world is leaving the market of neo-classical economics behind.

In the 'marketing era' captured by this expansive definition, products (or services) don't simply arrive at a marketplace to be sold. Companies don't merely try to satisfy pre-existing needs, but identify opportunities to shape needs and the means of satisfying them.[28] In the ideal case, every step in the trajectory of manufacture, advertisement, transportation, sale, delivery and consumption will have been shaped by every other step. Products should be designed with their future paths in mind, and consumers should be created with products' paths to them in mind. Products, pathways and consumers should all be shaped so that they meet in pre-arranged harmony.

In the context of the pharmaceutical industry, the American Marketing Association's definition would include anything that drug companies – or any body or person used by the companies – do to get their products into consumers' bodies.[29]

I find the American Marketing Association's definition of marketing useful, because the activities pharmaceutical companies engage in to create sales are not neatly bounded. Take clinical trials, for example. Early clinical trial work simultaneously identifies good candidates for drugs and defines potential markets – most of the time, these tasks are identical. A clinical trial can serve to convince regulators to allow a product onto the market, and to allow it to be advertised as useful for certain medical conditions; without that permission there will be no sales. A trial can serve to provide evidence that will help convince doctors to prescribe drugs and insurers to pay for them. A trial can help create a buzz around a product, through reports on it placed in medical journals and the popular media. A trial can suggest new, unapproved uses for a drug. A trial can put a drug in the hands of physician-investigators, who will then prescribe it more frequently. A trial can establish relationships with investigators, who can later be called upon to speak on behalf of the studied drug and others. A trial can enrol patients, who may continue to use the studied drug after the trial is over. An ongoing or future trial can serve to delay answers to questions about a drug. Every single one of these uses of trials contributes to marketing drugs.

Marketing in the marketing era is still essentially a set of intentional activities. It is done by companies and their agents, but not by independent actors, who merely happen to increase sales. My focus on marketing in this book is also a focus on some of the marshalled forces at work.

Pharmaceutical companies outsource a great many of their tasks. The vast majority of clinical research, one of the companies' largest costs, is outsourced to CROs and private site management organizations, and to a lesser extent to academic researchers and the academic research organizations that universities have set up to compete with CROs.

Although companies still do some of their own drug discovery and development work, an increasing number of the drugs in their pipelines are first developed by biotechnology companies and startups of one kind or another. They then move into larger companies through licensing arrangements or the acquisition of the smaller companies by the bigger ones. Small companies just don't have the capacity to market anything other than the most specialized drugs.

Pharma companies also outsource to medical education and communication companies (MECCs) much of the development of publication plans, the writing of medical science articles, other articles, promotional presentations, medical education programmes, and more. The companies even outsource parts of their marketing planning, and may make agreements with other companies to hire or share sales forces for particular projects.

So, what is a pharmaceutical company, if so much of its work is done by outsiders? The companies keep core competences in all of their functions, so that they can intelligently manage all of their projects. Some of them have internal strengths – for example, some maintain expertise in the development and production of vaccines. But most importantly, the companies engage in high-level planning, both long- and short-term. They create, stake out and defend positions.

A company engages in marketing by pushing different agents, groups and entities together to create a unit that works well and is much stronger and more powerful as a result. I call this 'assemblage marketing'. The ideal result is a market that not only buys the company's drugs, but is permeated through and through by acceptance of and interest in those products. It is a market designed so that to purchase particular drugs is rational, or the path of least resistance.[30]

Figure 1.2 sums up the central narrative of this book. Through various agents, a pharmaceutical company creates a market by producing, shaping and transporting research and medical journal articles, as well as key opinion leaders and patient advocates. It pushes these in the expectation of influencing regulators, physicians, patients and other useful actors.

In this picture, markets are made, not born.[31] The idea of assemblage marketing suggests that a market can be created for any product, given enough

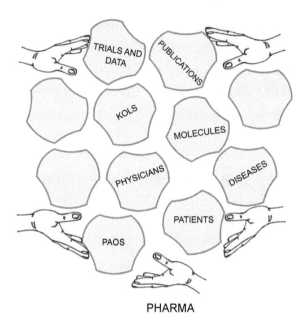

FIG. 1.2 Assemblage marketing

resources. This point suggests that the less obvious the initial assemblage of elements for the eventual market, the more resources a company must put into shaping and moving those elements. Eventual demand is a product of initial demand and marketing effort.

For the company, the result of assemblage marketing is much more than the sum of its parts, because – to the extent that it is successful – the assemblage is constructed with the company's interests in mind, these interests being expressed through its preferred medical knowledge, assumptions and practices.

SHAPING PATIENTS AND DISEASES

Tucked into the bottom-right of my diagram of assemblage marketing is a tile labelled 'diseases'. Like the elements on all of the other tiles, diseases can be shaped and adjusted to make a stronger and more profitable market.

In the 1960s, critics railed against the authority of physicians, who were seen as medicalizing intimate events and processes. Criticism of medicalization was especially prominent in challenges to psychiatry by scholars such as Michel Foucault and Thomas Szasz. Their work was later picked up and applied in different realms, especially by feminist scholars. As a result, there have been challenges to, in particular, mental health diagnostic categories ranging from schizophrenia to anxiety and depression, and also to the medicalization of ordinary life events and stages, such as childbirth and menopause.

The focus on professions has more recently lost some of its traction, and physicians today look like only one set of actors in the struggle for control over bodies, health and illness. Today, medicalization looks as though it is merely grease for the wheels of pharmaceuticalization – the objects of most critics' attention, for example anxiety, depression, and menopause, are closely associated with new classes of drugs.[32]

To increase their sales, pharma companies try to 'sell sickness'. They work to expand awareness of diseases for which their drugs can be prescribed, and to increase the likelihood that people will see themselves as having those diseases.[33] Sometimes this work is subtle and long-term, accomplished by building a corpus of medical science on a condition and systematically promoting disease labels and products. In other cases, however, it is more focused, as when pharma companies create defined 'disease awareness campaigns' to have an immediate impact.

An announcement for one conference on disease awareness campaigns states that it is intended 'for representatives from pharmaceutical, biotechnology, and medical device companies and advocacy groups with responsibilities in the following areas: disease area marketing, patient experience, patient engagement, integrated marketing, health system engagement, public relations, digital marketing, communications, multichannel marketing, content strategy, patient strategy, product development commercial strategy' and so on.[34] Almost all of the responsibilities listed appear to be aspects of marketing and communications, and it isn't obvious that the medical affairs side of pharmaceutical companies is represented anywhere on the list.

Depression is one of the most obvious and important diseases affected by the availability of drugs. Until the 1960s, depression was a relatively uncommon diagnosis, and tended to be associated with the elderly.[35] It became slightly more prominent in the 1970s, promoted by makers of the first generation of antidepressants.[36] Since the arrival on the market of Eli Lilly's drug Prozac in 1987, however, ever-increasing numbers of people have been diagnosed with depression. The number of people disabled by depression has increased, diagnostic criteria for depression have continually broadened, and estimates of the prevalence of depression have gone up dramatically.[37] It is now the 'common cold' of mental disorders.

Prozac, or fluoxetine, was the first successful drug within the Selective Serotonin Reuptake Inhibitor (SSRI) family, now often called simply 'antidepressants'. Companies selling SSRIs have marketed both the drug and the disease. They have invested heavily in research on depression and antidepressants. They have widely promoted a serotonin-deficiency theory of depression, followed by a chemical imbalance theory, for neither of which there is much evidence. They have established close connections with psychiatrists and other physicians who write textbooks, articles, and clinical practice guidelines. They have sponsored awareness and anti-stigma campaigns. The companies have successfully established the disease both medically and culturally, helping physicians to recognize and diagnose it often, and helping patients to interpret their feelings and experiences in terms of it – perhaps even to shape their identities around it. The World Health Organization predicts that within twenty years more people will be afflicted with depression than with any other health problem.

Depression may seem like a special case, both because it is a mental illness and because the boundaries between the disorder and sadness are imprecisely defined. However, there are many examples of more 'bodily' illnesses that have been strongly affected by marketing efforts, including common chronic diseases such as hypertension, diabetes, high cholesterol and osteoporosis.[38]

To take one of these examples, when the company then known as Merck Sharp & Dohme introduced an anti-hypertensive drug, Diuril (chlorothiazide) in 1957, hypertension (high blood pressure) was a sign associated with underlying poor health. At that time, high blood pressure wasn't itself generally seen as a problem, and therefore wasn't something to be controlled. Even defining high blood pressure was difficult, since blood pressure was represented within populations using a bell-shaped curve, so any dividing line between high and normal was artificial. Diuril dramatically lowered blood pressure, apparently only in people with elevated levels, suggesting that it might address some root problem. Together with an amazingly successful marketing campaign, its effects established hypertension as a disease.[39] The mild side effects of Diuril and other diuretic drugs made it straightforward for companies and their agents to argue for diuretic use to treat ever-broader populations with ever-lower blood pressures. Recommendations followed suit, and blood pressures that were once judged as within a normal range became perceived as high. People came to understand themselves as hypertensives or at least as disposed to hypertension; in one case, that of hypertensive African-Americans, the condition has become linked to racial identity.[40] The pharmaceuticalization process has continued as new antihypertensive drugs have been found.

Chronic conditions like hypertension neatly fit a new model of health and illness. Once upon a time, people generally considered themselves healthy unless they felt ill, or had unusual frailties or symptoms. But two major changes have resulted in a new model of health. First, in the past half-century we have seen the rise of risk factors: familiar things such as diet, age and sleep patterns, and unseen and unfamiliar things such as cholesterol levels, positive BRCA1 and 2 genetic tests, and PSA (prostate specific antigen) readings. We are all at risk, differing only in degrees. Second, and partly as a result of the first change, we can be normal and unhealthy at the same time, at least when there is some hope for treatment. For example, the unfortunate results of ageing used to be just that, but now we look for medical means to stave them off or treat them. As a result, there is no contradiction in the thought that most of us are less than healthy in this or that respect. In addition, there is no limit to the potential demand for health. We are all always unhealthy. Most of the ways in which we are unhealthy are chronic, so treatments can extend for life. And since we are all unhealthy in so many ways, treatment – even successful – of risk factors or conditions allows us to focus on new problems.[41]

Drugs don't define diseases by themselves. But drugs affect diseases, as do pharmaceutical companies through disease awareness campaigns. The companies change categories and the material ecologies of diseases, and in the process sometimes make people diseased who weren't before.

THIS BOOK'S SOURCES

The pharmaceutical industry is secretive about many things. It is extremely difficult to get inside drug companies, and especially difficult to get information about the research and marketing of particular current and recent drugs. Researchers who have managed that task have often relied heavily on documents becoming publicly available through lawsuits.[42] Where it makes sense to do so, I will draw on such documents. But there are also other ways to dig deeper into the industry and its practices.

As I've mentioned, drug companies outsource many activities to outside agencies. This creates a need to communicate. The agencies need to promote and advertise their services. People in the agencies communicate amongst themselves and with drug companies about the services they offer, the tools they use, and best practices. And all the people involved, both inside and outside the drug companies, need to network. As a result, there are newsletters, workshops and conferences focused on different aspects of pharma. I think of these as penumbral, sitting in an imperfect shadow of the industry. In these partial shadows, we can see some of the industry's phantoms talking about and displaying what they do.

Writers in these publications and speakers at these events describe the practices of the drug companies and agencies they are allied to. They often speak candidly about the goals they are expected to meet, the problems they face, and the solutions they've found, though they almost always disguise the products in question. From their accounts, I have gained a picture of how drug companies attempt to construct, shape and spread medical knowledge. I have to be cautious about what these writers and speakers claim, because they are always promoting themselves, and are apt to exaggerate their influence.[43] However, they often provide case studies with revealing details, give evidence of their effectiveness, and corroborate each other's accounts. As a result, it's possible to form a reliable impression of drug company work.

To put together this book, I attended thirteen of these penumbral meetings, listening to several hundred presentations on a variety of topics; my research associates attended four more such meetings. Three of the meetings took place in Europe (in Berlin, London and Vienna) and the rest in the US (in cities from New York and Philadelphia to San Diego). As a result, I have more US examples than European ones, though I have tried to reduce the imbalance in this book by selecting good European examples wherever appropriate. Most of the structures I discuss are international in nature and apply similarly to most wealthy countries, though on some issues there are important local legal and regulatory differences. I do, however, start with one long and (so far) peculiarly North American case, a story of the marketing of the painkiller OxyContin. This case is derived from the secondary literature, rather than my primary sources, but it illustrates the processes and the stakes of pharma's marketing efforts.

As much as possible, I tried to be a fly on the wall at pharma conferences. Even wearing a badge with my name and university affiliation, this was easier than it might sound. At the coffee and pastry tables, at lunches and receptions, people would ask some version of 'What is an academic like you doing here?' I would reply by saying something about my field of Science and Technology Studies, and how it studies knowledge production and knowledge management. Before I had finished a few sentences, most interlocutors' eyes were glazing over: they were at the conference to network, and I was going to be of absolutely no value to them.

Meetings are useful events, where you can learn a lot about the structure of work. At the meetings that my colleagues and I attended, speakers talked about goals, problems, conflicts and organizational structures.[44] I recount only things that were said in public, mostly from the podium, though occasionally in a question from the floor. I don't report on catty hallway conversations, but rather present the part of the pharmaceutical industry that is public – albeit within its own shadows.

Because these were public meetings, it is difficult to fully ensure the anonymity of speakers. Nonetheless, I don't refer to them by their own names. Moreover, I take the views of almost all of these speakers to be representative of their colleagues more generally, so there is no need to highlight their identities. I give them pseudonyms that reflect their work. For example, I assign people working in the medical side of pharma – in medical affairs departments or as medical science liaisons – common names that begin with M, such as Mr Moore or Ms Morales (see Fig. 1.3). I try to reflect very roughly the range of ethnic origins of actual names in my pseudonyms.

PRIMARY FOCUS	INITIAL	EXAMPLE
Patient Adherence	A	Mr Anderson
Communication/Marketing	C	Ms Cruz
Editor of Medical Journal	E	Dr Evans
Key Opinion Leader	K	Dr Klein
Legal, Compliance and other Consultants	L	Ms Lee
Medical Affairs/Medical Science Liaison	M	Mr Moore
Publication Planning	P	Ms Patel

FIG. 1.3 Pseudonym system used in this book

In addition, I draw on anonymized interviews with a small number of industry actors and with more than a dozen physicians and researchers who have worked as speakers for drug companies. For additional material and to corroborate what I learned elsewhere, I have read widely in the parallel newsletters and magazines – the 'grey' literature of the industry. When I quote from printed sources rather than meetings, I attribute words to their actual authors, either in the text or the endnotes; given the citations, anonymity is not possible.

In most of the chapters of this book, I give space to these many speakers, the spectral hands of the industry. They often speak in idealized terms, outlining goals and the tools with which they hope to achieve them. When they speak about achievements, they tend to focus on successful cases, rather than fully successful campaigns. As a result, this book presents pharma's aspirations and strategies, and does not portray a fully achieved hegemony. Nonetheless, especially when we put the different phantoms' accounts together, what they present is chilling.

CODA: AN AMERICAN NIGHTMARE

In the rest of this chapter, before turning to the different agents who shape and move information for the pharmaceutical industry, I present a cautionary tale. It is an extended example that includes almost all of the elements of the rest of this book. For the most part, it is a very ordinary tale of drug marketing, except for the inherent dangers of the particular drugs and the scale of the disaster they created.

The number of drug overdose deaths in the US and Canada has been increasing by approximately 20% per year since the year 2000.[45] In that period, more than 200,000 North Americans have died from prescription opioids.[46] Prescription opioid abuse has cost the affected economies billions of dollars.[47] The situation is only getting worse, because in recent years users have increasingly been forgoing prescription opioids for heroin and, latterly, illicit fentanyl and carfentanyl – the last two of which are extremely powerful painkillers now often mixed in with other street drugs to increase potency.

How did millions of North Americans become addicted to opioids, leading not just to deaths but also to huge numbers of devastated lives and much pain for the family members and friends of those addicted? The story is complicated, and has elements that range from the US invasion of Afghanistan in 2001 to the anomie felt by too many North Americans. But a central part of the story is particularly important for this book: the pushing of prescription painkillers, especially OxyContin. My short account here makes connections with most of the themes of this book: the marketing of OxyContin was in most ways exactly the same as the marketing of any other major drug. However, the story of OxyContin is different, because of the devastation that followed.[48]

The US Food and Drug Administration (FDA) approved OxyContin for sale in 1995. The painkiller in OxyContin is oxycodone, an old – invented in 1916 – morphine derivative, similar to heroin in its structure and overall effects. The selling point of the new drug was high concentrations of oxycodone in each pill combined with a continuous-release mechanism, which its maker, Purdue Pharmaceuticals, called 'Contin'. The Contin mechanism, which had been patented in 1980, was supposed to moderate euphoric and similar effects, and provide pain relief for twelve hours. The result, it was claimed, was a minimally addictive opioid. For Purdue, OxyContin was a good replacement for its previous slow-release opioid, MS Contin, which had a record of being abused as a recreational drug.

The FDA set the rules for the marketing of OxyContin, making it possible to produce, promote and distribute the drug. The initial 'label' for OxyContin approved it for the treatment of pain associated with musculoskeletal conditions, and later expanded it to include other conditions. At any time after the drug's approval, doctors could prescribe it for whatever conditions they saw fit, but Purdue could not promote it for anything beyond the label. As it happened,

Purdue exceeded its mandate, but stayed close enough that it was not caught for a few years. Curiously, the initial label noted that, when properly prescribed, addiction was 'very rare',[49] a claim that was quickly challenged. But the FDA had established the framework for the promotion of OxyContin. Meanwhile, the US Drug Enforcement Agency, which authorizes production quotas of potentially addictive painkillers, allowed the production of oxycodone to increase nearly forty-fold from the early 1990s to today.[50] There has been a twenty-fold increase in the opioid family of drugs during this time. Purdue made huge profits, and the Sackler family that owns the company became enormously wealthy; the Sacklers are known for their philanthropy, making highly visible donations to art museums and universities.[51]

Early promotion of OxyContin, often known on the street as 'Oxy', involved recruiting doctors, pharmacists and nurses to the cause of aggressive pain treatment. Purdue's Oxy marketing plans from 1996 to 2001 included inviting more than 5000 attendees to over forty lavish, all-expenses paid conferences in pain management and speaker training.[52] These conferences established a prescriber base for Oxy, and more importantly, a base of key opinion leaders (KOLs) to sit on Purdue's speaker bureau, to give paid presentations to other prescribers. The company's speaker bureau list included 2500 doctors, of whom 1000 were active.[53] With this KOL force, Purdue sponsored more than 20,000 educational events to make the case for using opioids to treat pain aggressively.

Purdue made an arrangement with the Joint Commission on Accreditation of Healthcare Organizations, which had issued pain standards for hospitals. By sponsoring the work of the Joint Commission (an 'independent, not-for-profit organization'[54]), Purdue gained the exclusive right to distribute educational materials, which gave the company access to hospitals seeking accreditation.[55] In one analysis, the Joint Commission's new standards for pain management in the year 2000 was one of the two most important events driving the opioid epidemic, the other being the introduction of Oxy itself.[56]

Purdue didn't have a large enough sales force to market OxyContin, so it established an agreement with Abbott, a much larger drug company with a broad array of products. Abbott had the foresight to include in its initial agreement a clause stating that the company would have no legal responsibility for the drug, making Purdue the drug's sole legal and public face. (Still, Purdue's legal costs so far have been relatively small, in light of the effects of the drug and the profits that the company has raked in.)

Both Abbott and Purdue worked their Oxy sales force hard. The average bonus for Purdue sales reps in 2001 was $71,500, an amount considerably higher than their $55,000 average salary. Abbott offered cash prizes and luxury vacations to top sellers. Meanwhile, sales reps were coached on how to woo doctors with food, how to connive their way to getting three or five minutes of doctors' time to make pitches, and how to position the product. Digging through internal Abbott documents, David Armstrong reports 'an almost religious zeal' to sell the drug:

> Sales reps were called 'royal crusaders' and 'knights' in internal documents, and they were supervised by the 'Royal Court of OxyContin' – executives referred to in memos as the 'Wizard of OxyContin', 'Supreme Sovereign of Pain Management', and the 'Empress of Analgesia'. The head of pain care sales, Jerry Eichhorn, was the 'King of Pain' and signed memos simply as 'King'.
>
> 'As you continue to carry the OxyContin banner onto the field of battle', it's important to keep highlighting OxyContin benefits to your doctors', Abbott urged its sales staff in a memo contained in the court records.[57]

In addition to free samples left at doctors' offices, in 1998 Purdue created a patient starter coupon programme for OxyContin, to provide a number of patients with free initial prescriptions of between seven and thirty days. As part of the programme, doctors were given coupons they could pass on, thereby helping disadvantaged patients. Purdue exhibited all the generosity of a neighbourhood drug dealer with a potential new customer.

In the years following the introduction of OxyContin, a number of medical journal articles made the case that very few opioid prescriptions led to addictions. Strongly suggestive of a promotional campaign in the medical literature is the fact that a 1980 letter to the editor of the *New England Journal of Medicine* that claimed that fewer than 1% of hospitalized patients treated with opioids became addicted was cited more than 600 times, with citations spiking after 1995. Most letters to the editor are lucky to be cited even one-tenth as often.[58]

Purdue and other drug companies have intervened more broadly in the medical science of opioids. As of 2017, the nine most cited reports of randomized controlled trials of oxycodone in medical journals were all funded by Purdue or one of the network of international companies spun off by Purdue. A majority of the many authors on these articles – most have six or more authors – are apparently independent medical researchers, though corporate authors are sprinkled around. None of these nine influential OxyContin trial articles describes in any detail who conducted the research, who did the statistical analysis, who wrote the article, or who did the shepherding necessary to submit it to a journal, make the needed revisions, etc. In other words, these reports were almost certainly ghost-managed. These are only the most cited reports of randomized controlled trials; many more articles, including reviews, commentaries and less cited reports, may also have been ghost-managed for Purdue.

One of these influential medical journal articles failed to report some cases of withdrawal symptoms, cases that could be argued away.[59] Whereas the article reported withdrawal symptoms in only one of 106 patients, an internal review found that eleven others reported negative experiences on the drug, these being at least possibly due to withdrawal symptoms. An 'agreed statement of facts' from a legal action included an account of the following episode:

> [A] PURDUE employee emailed a PURDUE supervisor regarding the review of withdrawal data …: 'Do you think the withdrawal data from the [osteoarthritis] study … is worth writing up [an abstract]? Or would this add to the current negative press and should be deferred?' The supervisor responded: 'I would not write it up at this point'.[60]

The journal article was reprinted 10,000 times, to be given to doctors.

There is a widespread belief (vigorously denied by Purdue) that the pills don't provide pain relief towards the end of their twelve-hour dosing period, creating a 'cycle of pain and euphoria that fosters addiction'.[61] In the face of this and other increasing concerns about addiction, the industry latched onto a convenient and somewhat speculative concept: pseudoaddiction. Pseudoaddiction is not a genuine addiction, but is instead a condition in which patients receive inadequate doses of opioids to manage pain. These patients display the signs of addiction, but only because they are suffering from their underlying pain. Therefore, runs the inescapable logic, rather than attempting to wean patients off opioids, the medical community should prescribe them more! Purdue has indeed recommended responding to inadequate treatment with bigger doses, though critics suggest that in the context of the twelve-hour problem bigger doses create 'higher highs [and] lower lows'.[62]

There is little evidence for the existence of pseudoaddiction. However, lack of evidence has not stopped a great many medical articles from using the concept in an uncritical way, especially review articles, clinical guidelines and commentaries.[63] We cannot know how many of these were strongly influenced by pharma companies. However, a small number do acknowledge pharma support: nine of those twenty-two acknowledge support from ... yes, Purdue.[64]

Purdue and other companies producing opioids have also contributed generously to education about pain – producing a book often given away to medical students[65] – and to organizations such as the American Geriatrics Society and the American Academy of Pain Medicine. On an American Geriatrics Society panel that wrote guidelines for the treatment of chronic pain in seniors, more than half of the members had been paid for consulting or speaking by one or another of the companies that manufacture opioids.[66] More recently, organizations that have received funding from manufacturers of opioids have tended to oppose precautions about prescribing.[67]

The promotional efforts were extremely successful in some areas. For example, between 2007 and 2012, more than 200 million doses of Oxy were shipped to pharmacies in West Virginia, a sum that amounts to more than 100 pills for every adult and child in the state. Purdue had found its markets, based on presumed epidemics of untreated pain. During that period, there was a steady increase in sales of the higher-strength pills, consistent with a growing rate of addiction.[68] Drug distributors, which knew exactly to which towns and pharmacies the pills were being sent, didn't raise the alarm, even when they were legally required to; they made billions of dollars in profits.[69]

In 2007, three of Purdue's executives were convicted on criminal charges for misleading doctors, and the company paid $600 million in fines.[70] There have been a great many more lawsuits since then, some of which have involved settlements, and some of which are ongoing. However, the total amounts that the company will pay out in fines and settlements are trivial compared with the amounts it has earned.

OxyContin's sales were disproportionately rural. Taken recreationally, Oxy became known as 'hillbilly heroin'. Why was Oxy so strongly associated with places such as Kentucky, West Virginia, Ohio and Maine, or in Canada, with rural Ontario and Newfoundland?

Purdue, followed closely by its competitors, had put much more effort into promotion and sales in rural than in urban areas.[71] Purdue consistently targeted those doctors who were the highest prescribers of opioids; this skewed the company's marketing toward areas with a history of opioid use, such as the Appalachian area, and in general toward rural areas with older populations. Although the eventual users of OxyContin cut across generations, older people dealing with pain were the first market.

Drugs always have cultural aspects, and these are especially obvious for illegal drugs.[72] As the use of OxyContin spread, it became part of the fabric of a number of local cultures, perhaps including cultures of sharing medications, and certainly as a way of dealing with social and economic problems. Oxy flourished where it first became common. The original safety warning on OxyContin advised patients not to tamper with the pills:

> Warning: OxyContin Tablets are to be swallowed whole, and are not to be broken, chewed, or crushed. Taking broken, chewed, or crushed OxyContin Tablets could lead to the rapid release and absorption of a potentially toxic dose of oxycodone.[73]

As observed in a 2004 US General Accounting Office report on problems with OxyContin, this label may have 'inadvertently alerted abusers to possible methods for misuse'.

Finally, there were larger issues of distribution. Once Oxy and other prescription opioids became common street drugs, they had to compete with other street drugs. Most pharmaceuticals only have to compete with each other, with alternative treatments, and with other approaches to health. In this case, however, prescription opiates were going head-to-head with heroin and other drugs that produce euphoria.

Oxy and its kin had a built-in advantage, though. The main distribution system for prescription drugs is usually entirely legal, going from manufacturers to wholesalers to pharmacies to patients with prescriptions. The drugs only become illegal if pills are stolen, the prescriptions are fake, or patients sell or give pills to other users. Drugs like heroin, on the other hand, are illegal at every step of the distribution system. With heroin arriving in North America at major cities and ports, the first points of its distribution are in those high-density centres. Through the first decade of the twenty- first century, the price of heroin and Oxy was similar enough that distribution systems made the difference: heroin sold better in major cities and on the coasts, and Oxy sold better in rural areas and the interior.

One of the most effective forms of distribution of Oxy was through 'pill mills'. Doctors would set up offices, often in the form of stand-alone pain management clinics. They would see patients for a minute or two, prescribe a month's worth of high doses of painkillers and other popular drugs, and collect a fee in cash. The most successful pill mills dispensed the drugs through their own pharmacies, making a profit on both the prescription and the drugs. There was so much cash and drugs flowing through pill mills that they had to hire heavily armed guards.

The balance started shifting in 2012 and the following few years. The US and Canadian governments started taking the opioid addiction problem seriously. They closed pill mills, passed new regulations for prescriptions of opioids, and in some cases banned OxyContin altogether. Purdue didn't fight back, because its patent on OxyContin was running out anyway. The company had developed a new product, OxyNeo, which is more resistant to tampering. Purdue took a high road, appearing to help authorities solve the problem of the diversion of prescription drugs to the street.

The industry as a whole did fight to protect itself. The US Drug Enforcement Agency (DEA) saw what was happening, and started insisting on its power to combat not just street drugs, but the pill mills, the wholesale distribution companies, and even the pharma companies themselves, which were the largest participants in the drug trade. Over the course of a decade, the pharmaceutical industry created legislative momentum for a bill that it wrote, eventually to be known as the 'Ensuring Patient Access and Effective Drug Enforcement Act'. The Act, which was passed in 2016, established routes by which the DEA could consult and communicate with pharma companies, but prevented the agency from following prescription drugs up the chain. This ensured that the DEA couldn't investigate distribution or pharma companies. Although the DEA was vehemently opposed to the Act, it was muzzled by a two-part strategy: DEA employees were systematically offered jobs working directly or indirectly for the industry – altogether, fifty employees moved – and well-funded legislators made their more general support of the agency contingent on its staying silent about the Act.[74] Most legislators who voted for the Act didn't understand its implications. The lead Congressman sponsoring the Act, Representative Tom Marino of Pennsylvania, was briefly President Trump's choice to be 'drug czar', until the story of his work against the DEA was revealed.

The situation also changed because of the Sinaloa Cartel in Mexico. The cartel saw its revenue from marijuana plummeting as a result of efforts to legalize the drug. The Cartel, led by Joaquín Guzmán Loera, better known as 'El Chapo', needed to change its business model. Since marijuana had become less profitable, it replaced that crop with another: poppies. Leveraging its experience in the marijuana trade, it set out to dominate the US heroin market.[75] The result was a 75% drop in the price of heroin, previously sourced from such places as Afghanistan and Pakistan. As the price of Oxy rose and that of heroin fell, users made the switch en masse. Purdue, Abbott and the other companies selling opioids had established their clientele, and the Mexican cartels simply took their customers. Other Mexican cartels soon followed the Sinaloan lead, and also moved into the fentanyl trade.

Although pharma has ceded a large share of the opioid trade to the Mexican drug cartels, some pockets of the industry continue to compete for – and thereby increase the size of – segments of the market. US annual sales of OxyContin peaked in 2011 at nearly $3 billion, but Purdue is vigorously expanding internationally to make up for declining US figures. The company's owners have an international consortium of companies, Mundipharma, and are working to convince doctors in Southern Europe, Latin America and Asia not to fall into the trap of 'opiophobia', an affliction of doctors that leaves patients suffering from chronic pain.[76] The campaign is following some standard paths by recruiting KOLs to speak about pain management and the available drugs. Purdue has also pursued the youth market, by testing OxyContin on children – a move that also briefly extended its US patent on the drug. As one commentator writes, 'OxyContin for kids: What could possibly go wrong?'[77]

Other pharmaceutical companies are looking for ways to compete in the North American market, too. In late 2016, seven executives and managers who had worked for Insys Therapeutics were arrested in connection with an alleged programme to bribe doctors to prescribe Subsys, a spray that includes fentanyl; in addition, three of the top Subsys prescribers have been convicted of felonies. The supposed bribes were disguised as consulting and speaking fees.[78] For their part, some doctors have been happy to profit handsomely. Two Alabama doctors were convicted in 2017 on a raft of charges connected with enormous numbers of prescriptions of Subsys and another fentanyl product, Abstral. The doctors had been accepting kickbacks from Insys for prescribing Subsys for a variety of unapproved conditions. They were also attempting to manipulate the stock price of the relatively small company Galena Biopharma, the maker of Abstral, in the process becoming the top two prescribers of Abstral in the US.[79] Meanwhile, in a familiar move, Galena has established a coupon programme to give away the first month's worth of Abstral.[80] What could possibly go wrong?

2

DATA EXTRACTION
AT THE MARGINS OF HEALTH

THE EUROPEAN MEDICINES AGENCY (EMA) APPROVED FORTY-EIGHT CANCER drugs between 2009 and 2013. A study found that, at the point of approval, there was no evidence for improvement in either survival or quality of life in 65% of the different uses for which those drugs were approved. It seems that the EMA approved those drugs on the basis of hope, not evidence. As it turns out, hope was vindicated in only a minority of cases, because even after five years of follow-up studies, there was no evidence of improvement in either survival or quality of life in 53% of the different approved uses.[1]

There is nothing unusual about cancer drugs. For example, cholesterol-lowering statins are among the most widely prescribed of drugs, but meta-analyses have shown that they are only marginally effective at preventing heart attacks. Given the drugs' relative weakness, in 2013 the American College of Cardiology and the American Heart Association released new guidelines aimed at increasing the drugs' successes ... by increasing the number of people taking them![2] In this context, it might be useful to remember that the ancient Greek word *pharmakon* can be translated as either 'cure' or 'poison'. Or, in an adage attributed to the sixteenth-century alchemist and physician Paracelsus: 'The dose makes the poison.'

Across almost all areas of medicine, close studies of recently approved drugs show that most drugs offer negligible new benefits. Prescrire, an independent healthcare evaluator, found that of ninety-two new drugs it evaluated in 2016, there were no breakthroughs, one 'real advance', five that 'offer an advantage', nine that are 'possibly helpful', fifty-six that offer 'nothing new', and sixteen that were 'not acceptable'. Prescrire reserved judgment on five others. The 2016 results were not very unusual.[3]

The small benefits are connected to the high costs of trials. One doctor puts it this way: 'Since [the pharmaceutical companies] anticipate that the drug will have little efficacy at best, affording slight benefit to most or more benefit to very few, the licensing trials are expensive, large, and sloppy.' With so much at stake, these '[l]arge sloppy trials seeking small effects lend themselves to all sorts of data massaging and data torturing.'[4]

'If you have to enrol a ton of people into your trial, that's a sign the drug has a very small effect', writes analyst Alan Cassels.[5] Small expected effects push the companies to run ever-larger trials, enrolling ever more people. Estimates of the number of participants in clinical trials vary widely, but the number sits somewhere between three and six million annually.[6]

For pharmaceutical companies, extracting a statistically significant but small effect from a trial is much more important than shooting for a large effect. Most of the time, a small apparent effect in the data – usually in as few as two of the trials – is all that regulators demand for drug approval, and approval is the most important step in marketing the product. Most of the time, a small apparent effect is also all that pharma companies need to successfully sell their products.

'A drug is a molecule surrounded by information', I was told at a workshop for industry medical science liaisons that I attended in 2012. I would go slightly further: The right information surrounding the molecule *makes it* a drug. In particular, the right clinical trial information allows companies to make distinctions between their molecules and less effective ones, which brings regulators' approvals and endorsements. Moreover, the right information allows companies to make strong claims about the drugs, which brings doctors' buy-ins and recommendations.

As a result, running clinical trials has itself become an industry, one that serves pharma companies. I see it as a resource extraction industry: the trials extract fluids, measurements and observations from experimental bodies, to produce data. The data, after being heavily processed, becomes one of the key ingredients of a drug, crucial to bringing it to market and to making it circulate in that market. But the drug industry has evolved to be able to take advantage of very small effects, so most of the data extraction and processing happens at the very margins of health.

THE RISE OF EXPENSIVE RESEARCH

In the background of the pharmaceutical industry's enormous influence over medical knowledge sit fifty-year-old changes in the importance of different kinds of medical research. Pressures from both government regulators and internal medical reformers have led to the rise of the randomized controlled trial (RCT) as the most valued and important kind of medical research. This change in the most important style of scientific reasoning[7] in medicine has had huge effects. And the change is one that pharma companies have been well positioned to use to their advantage.

Medical Pressures

The RCT as a central plank of medical knowledge is relatively recent. In the English-speaking world, credit for the first real RCT in medicine is usually given to the UK epidemiologist Austin Bradford Hill, for his 1946 trial of the effect of streptomycin on tuberculosis, and for his advocacy of RCTs in medicine. One can find forerunners, such as Germany's Paul Martini, who advocated for and performed RCTs on drugs starting in the 1930s, and gained influence in the 1940s.[8] The RCT rose in importance over the following few decades to become the 'gold standard' of clinical research by the 1990s, in the wake of extensive advocacy by statisticians and medical reformers.[9]

For statisticians, random sampling in an experiment is the key requirement for making data amenable to statistical analysis. A well-designed and well-conducted RCT, by randomly assigning subjects from a population, produces results that have a defined probability of applying back to the population. Perhaps more important as a reason for the rise of RCTs, random sampling, especially combined with double blinding, has addressed widespread concerns in medicine about researcher bias.[10] Since the 1950s, attempts to make RCTs the foundation of scientific medicine have been fairly successful, and since the 1970s physicians have been repeatedly told that RCTs are the only kind of reliable information on which to base clinical practice.

The rise of what is known as 'evidence-based medicine' has further promoted the idea that the practice of medicine should be based on RCTs – multiple RCTs, if possible. Evidence-based medicine started in the medical curriculum of McMaster University in Canada, based around practical clinical problem-solving. The clinical epidemiologist David Sackett led the way by developing courses on critical appraisal of the medical literature, which turned into a series of articles published in 1981.[11] A decade later, on the invitation and patronage of *Journal of the American Medical Association* editor Drummond Rennie, those articles were updated and republished as a manifesto. The approach rejected doctors' reliance on intuition – which had long been attacked – and even physiological reasoning and laboratory studies. The manifesto begins:

> A new paradigm for medical practice is emerging. Evidence-based medicine de-emphasizes intuition, unsystematic clinical experience, and pathophysi-ologic rationale as sufficient grounds for clinical decision making and stresses the examination of evidence from clinical research.[12]

With this dense prose, the reformers were chronicling, applauding and promot-ing a revolution.

RCTs are not perfect tools, though. The artificialities of RCTs lead to knowl-edge that doesn't map neatly onto the real world as we find it – the rigorously managed treatments in trials are rarely repeated in ordinary treatments, and populations studied are never exactly the same as the populations to be treated.[13] In a related vein, RCTs tend to promote a standardization of treatment that does not fit well with the variability of the human world – in other words, the most effective standardized treatment may not be the most effective treatment for a particular patient in a particular context.[14] In addition, most RCTs are worse at identifying uncommon adverse events than at showing drug effectiveness. Though RCTs are held up as a gold standard, poorly designed or executed RCTs may be of less value than sound versions of other kinds of studies.[15] Illustrating all of the different ways in which RCTs are less rigid than they appear is the fact that studies supported by pharma produce much more positive results than do independent ones,[16] showing that the method does not prevent bias.

Regulatory Pressures

Medical reform was one of the reasons why RCTs moved toward the heart of medicine. A second reason was the fact that government regulators made RCTs central to the approval process for drugs.

Much of modern drug regulation descends from the US Kefauver-Harris Act of 1962. Sponsors of the Act were responding to two sets of problems, though the Act did not actually address either of them. In the years leading up to the Act, Senator Estes Kefauver had put his energies into challenging the pharmaceutical industry on terrain where the US consumer had the most complaints: high prices stemming from patent-based monopolies. His efforts at reform were largely failures. Pharmaceutical companies and their industry association were able to deflect Kefauver's attacks on drug patents and prices.[17] The 1962 Act was spurred more directly by the compelling story of how the US had narrowly avoided disaster by not being quick to approve thalidomide – an episode used by the Kennedy Administration to push regulation forward.[18] Dr Frances Kelsey of the Food and Drug Administration (FDA) had consistently questioned the safety of the drug, and had delayed its approval. Meanwhile, in Europe and elsewhere, thousands of babies had been disfigured by the use of thalidomide as an anti-nausea remedy and tranquillizer.

While the Act was supposed to improve the safety of drugs, in fact it added little to existing regulation of safety in the US. New was a requirement that drug companies show the efficacy of their drugs before they could be approved. Evidence of efficacy had to involve 'adequate and well-controlled investigations' performed by qualified experts, 'on the basis of which it can fairly and responsibly be concluded that the drug will have its claimed effect'.[19] The FDA structured its regulations around phased investigations, starting with laboratory studies and culminating in multiple similar clinical trials, which would ideally be RCTs.

It was only on the basis of the evidence from these trials that a drug could be approved for sale in the US and that claims for that drug could be made. The key provisions of the Kefauver-Harris Act concerned the appropriate and necessary scientific knowledge for the marketing of drugs. The FDA was already an obligatory point of passage for getting drugs to possible markets in the US.[20] After the Act, though, approval also meant setting out the conditions for more marketing, by establishing what the companies could say about their drugs. The apparatus of approval, including laboratory and clinical research, became all about creating possibilities for advertising and otherwise promoting particular drugs.

The FDA had become a guarantor of sorts, offering a stamp of approval to assure doctors and patients that new drugs worked and weren't too harmful. For the companies, this turned out to be a gold mine. Essentially, the FDA was vouching for the drugs it approved, and simultaneously limiting the competition. The approval system dramatically increased the value of patented drugs by adding layers of exclusivity.

Over the following few decades, regulators around the world followed the FDA's lead, especially in using phased research culminating in substantial clinical trials as a model. For example, Canada's regulations followed swiftly, in 1963. The United Kingdom established new measures that same year, and followed them up with a framework similar to the FDA's in 1968. European Community Directives issued in 1965 required all members of the European Community to establish formal review processes, which they did over the next decade. Japan introduced its version of the regulations in 1967.

Especially since the expansion of drug regulation in the 1960s and 1970s, in-patent drugs have been promoted – and generally accepted – as more powerful than their older generic competitors. The result is that the drug patent has become a marker of quality, even though versions of most of the competitors were once patented, and often recently.[21]

In general, the drug industry has opposed new regulations, which increase costs, hurdles, and sometimes uncertainties.[22] It also has challenged aspects of regulators' authority in court.[23] Drug companies and industry associations continually lobby regulators and legislators in quieter ways, to shape regulation in their interests around the globe.[24] We can, for example, see industry interest in shaping regulation in the International Conference on Harmonization of Technical Requirements for Registration of Pharmaceuticals for Human Use (ICH). It is strongly in pharma companies' interest to bring a new drug to market as quickly as possible, which increases the amount of time it can be sold while still under patent protection. Differences in the regulations for different major markets slow the process by requiring that the companies do tailored research to meet those different demands. For this reason, the International Federation of Pharmaceutical Manufacturers' Associations created the ICH, bringing together the regulatory agencies of the European Union, Japan and the US.[25] In a series of meetings beginning in 1991, the ICH standardized testing requirements, keeping the structure of phased investigations running from laboratory studies to RCTs, but ensuring that one set of investigations would be enough for these three major markets. There are many other ways, too, in which regulations are being standardized around the world. The many countries interested in pieces, however small, of the enormous pharmaceutical business bring their rules into line with those in place in North America and Western Europe, to make it easier for pharma companies.[26]

Though the industry complains about the costs of this research, and actively challenges the regulations that increase them, high costs have the unintended effect of preventing many non-industry researchers from contributing to the most valued kinds of medical knowledge: the RCTs of the kind that regulators require. Meanwhile, drug companies sponsor most drug trials, and in so doing affect their results. The companies fully control the majority of the research they fund, and to some extent they can choose what to disclose and how. Recent studies show that these companies don't (despite being mandated to do so) publicly register all of the trials they perform, and don't publish all of the data even from the trials that they do register.[27] As I'll show in the next few chapters, the articles they publish rarely make clear the full level of control the companies have had over the production of data, its analysis or its presentation; for example, company statisticians are rarely acknowledged, meaning that their contributions aren't flagged.[28] This allows the companies to use RCT data selectively to quietly shape medical knowledge to support their marketing efforts. At the same time, drug companies' integration into medical research allows them to participate more overtly and broadly in the distribution of their preferred pieces of medical knowledge. The result is that drug companies have considerable control over what physicians know about diseases, drugs and other treatment options.[29] So, while pharma companies have generally opposed new demands by regulators, they have also benefitted enormously from those demands.

Phased Research: An Outline

Bringing a drug to market involves many different kinds of research. Typically, it starts with a mixture of company strategizing, market research and biochemistry, where a company identifies a disease area in which it would like to have one or more products, and identifies some lines of biochemical or physiological research that look promising for that disease area.

Companies might identify initially promising substances – a process often given the somewhat misleading name 'drug discovery' – in any of a number of different ways, though the most common is by high-throughput screening. With a target human receptor in mind, the companies create an assay, a highly repeatable test for activity on the receptor. At that point, robots take over. Trays with between several hundred and several thousand copies of the assay are fed through a machine, which applies a different substance, from huge libraries of substances, to each copy of the assay. A good library might have nearly a million different substances, derived from soils, scraped from plants and moulds, or taken from anywhere else. The robot measures the effect of each of these substances on the assays, and promising candidates are marked for further rounds of testing, and eventually for pre-clinical studies.

With a smaller number of molecules in hand, the company begins learning about what they are, how they can be expected to act in human bodies, and how toxic they are likely to be. Laboratory studies follow, on both tissue samples and live animals. These lab studies are focused on learning how toxic and carcinogenic the molecules are, and so whether they are worth pursuing further. The choice of animal models – always including mice or rats, and one of dogs, pigs or primates – for different tests depends on the molecule's expected form and effects, and is intended to gather information likely to be relevant to humans. Tests at this stage are structured by the ICH agreement, and results from these tests will be submitted to regulatory agencies as part of the application to pursue clinical tests in humans, and for eventual drug approval.

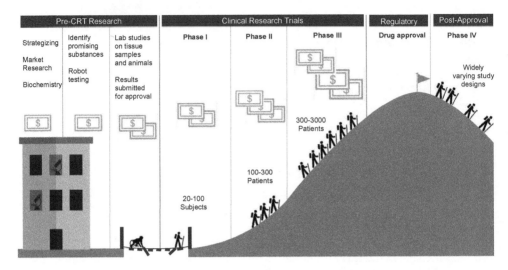

FIG. 2.1 Stages of drug development

There are four different official phases of clinical trials for most drug applications (see Fig. 2.1). Phase I trials are tests on twenty to one hundred healthy human subjects. These trials, which I describe in more depth towards the end of this chapter, are designed primarily to determine the short-term safety of the candidate drug, but along the way the company will learn about its side effects, about comfortable dosage levels and tolerability, and perhaps something about efficacy.

Phase II trials bring in roughly one hundred to three hundred patients who have the targeted condition or disease. These trials are, therefore, to establish whether the candidate drug has biological effects that map onto medical treatment in a large enough percentage of the patients to make the drug worth pursuing – they should be RCTs, to allow for comparisons of treatment and placebo groups. Phase II trials also continue with the process of fine-tuning the dosage and monitoring safety.

At Phase III, the companies are running full trials designed to provide evidence of efficacy. They recruit populations that roughly match the ones for which they will be seeking market approval, and run trials that bear on how the candidate drug would officially be used, if approved. Depending on the condition to be treated, and the expected size of the drug's effects, trials might recruit small or large numbers of patients, usually in the range of a few hundred to a few thousand. On the one hand, some conditions are too rare to recruit many patients, but on the other, if the drug is likely to show only marginal benefits, the number of patients in the trial has to be large enough to produce usable data. Phase III trials provide the key data feeding into applications to approve drugs, because if they are successful these trials provide evidence that the drug works, without causing too many negative effects. The evidence might not be in the form of cured patients, because many trials have only surrogate endpoints, markers taken to stand in for successful treatment – such as tumour size reduction in cancer, rather than extra years lived.

Finally, Phase IV trials include any clinical studies that take place after a drug has been approved. They might mimic trials of any of the earlier phases, depending on the purposes for which they have been designed. They might look like Phase I trials, if, for example, the goal is to provide evidence of whether a drug can be taken on an empty stomach. They might look like Phase III trials, if the goal is to provide fresh evidence to convince doctors to prescribe the drug. Or they might take yet different forms – for example, 'seeding' trials recruit doctors to prescribe a drug, to familiarize doctors with the product and to gather commercial information.

How Much Does Drug Development Actually Cost?

Industry-allied organizations – patient advocacy organizations, academic research units, think-tanks – can serve as a part of a larger echo chamber for the industry. One of the most important occupants of that chamber over the past forty years has been the Center for the Study of Drug Development (CSDD), located at Tufts University in the US. The CSDD was founded in 1976 by Dr Louis Lasagna, a prominent clinical pharmacologist known for his revision of the Hippocratic Oath. Lasagna was a key opinion leader who frequently worked closely with the pharmaceutical industry and had good connections with important US conservative figures.[30] The CSDD is funded through grants from the industry, and gathers some its data directly from the industry, maintaining strict secrecy:

> Data are collected from the people who create it – pharmaceutical and
> biotechnology companies. They cooperate because they know Tufts CSDD
> will generate a comprehensive and objective picture of the drug develop-
> ment process, while strictly ensuring that individual company data are not
> disclosed.[31]

The CSDD has had an enormous impact on the pharmaceutical industry, in
particular through its regular estimates of the cost of developing a drug.[32] By
2001, the estimate was a whopping $800 million, and by 2014 the CSDD had
increased its estimate to an even more whopping $2.6 billion.[33] Figures like these
can be easily put to use to justify reduced regulation, longer monopolies, and
especially high prices. In the face of $2.6 billion in costs, the industry contends,
innovation could easily grind to a halt.

These figures are extremely controversial, to put it mildly. The data was
provided by pharmaceutical companies on conditions of strict secrecy, so there
is no way of knowing how representative it is. The studies included only drugs
that the companies had 'self-originated', though probably the majority of drugs
stem from publicly funded research. Research costs may include work that was
unnecessary for approval. The figures take no account of tax incentives and
other government subsidies. And the largest cost in the study – nearly half the
total – is the opportunity cost of capital, calculated circularly, as if the companies
invested in their own stocks (which have tended to increase in value enormously
in recent decades, presumably in part because of drug development).[34]

Though competing estimates vary widely, and there is a fair amount of uncertainty about any estimate, a number of plausible figures come in at 10% to 25% of
the CSDD ones.[35] One recent study of publicly available data from US Securities
and Exchange filings for firms developing cancer drugs, which duplicated the
CSDD assumptions as closely as possible, came up with a figure of $648 mil-
lion, still a hefty sum, but almost exactly 25% of the CSDD's bloated figure.[36]

It may be that specific kinds of focused and efficient drug development
projects can be much less expensive yet. The Drugs for Neglected Diseases
Initiative, a non-profit originally founded by Doctors Without Borders, has
developed seven new treatments for a mere $290 million.[37] That works out at

less than 2% of the industry's claimed cost per drug. Because of this, and because the initiative is non-profit, it has been able to deliver treatments, including an antimalarial drug taken by 500 million people so far, at minimal costs. In 2013, when Andrew Witty, then CEO of GlaxoSmithKline, said that the CSDD figure was 'one of the great myths of the industry', he was suggesting that there were real efficiencies to be gained by focusing on projects more likely to be success-ful[38] – the Drugs for Neglected Diseases Initiative seems to have taken that advice as far as possible. The projects it chose were unlikely to be profitable enough for any pharma companies to take on, so they were low-hanging fruit.

INTEGRATION OF THE INDUSTRY INTO MEDICAL RESEARCH

Novelty, patents and regulation are bound up with an intensification of bio-medical research. This has led to the accumulation and leveraging of what some scholars are calling 'biocapital',[39] which involves the mutual cultivation of invest-ment funds, biomedical infrastructure, and biological products and knowledge. We can see this even in public-private partnerships for drug development in the service of global health, with parties contributing in order to maintain claims on the circulating capital, materials and knowledge.[40]

Because of the expense of RCTs, companies and researchers have had to develop new formal structures to manage large trials.[41] With large costs and overheads, the emphasis on RCTs has shifted the production of this most highly valued medical knowledge from independent medical researchers to pharma-ceutical companies. The drug industry has steadily become more integrated into the medical research community, both because it produces important medical knowledge itself (generally through subcontractors) and also because it provides important funding for studies by more-or-less independent medical researchers.

Contract Research Organizations

Here is a standard image of pharma-sponsored research. First, a researcher designs and proposes a study. Then, looking for support, that researcher approaches one or more drug companies. A company may choose to fund the research, either out of interest in the results or to buy goodwill, or both. Then, the researcher performs the study, writes up a few articles on it and submits them to journals.

Journal articles stemming from industry-sponsored trials are likely to report conclusions favourable to the sponsors, as shown by multiple studies, systematic reviews and meta-analyses.[42] For some areas within medicine, articles from industry-sponsored research are nearly certain to come to positive conclusions. In the standard image of sponsored research, then, we have to assume that more-or-less independent researchers align their studies with funders' interests, through design, implementation, interpretation and/or publication. There are many ways they might do this. For example, the experimental drug can be tested against an inappropriate comparator or in an unrepresentative population; or, perhaps, the statistical tests are chosen with success in mind.

Though conflict of interest is a powerful force, it seems odd that conflicts of interest stemming merely from research funding could produce industry-friendly results in independent research, at least with the consistency that we see. Whether they are industry-friendly or not, we don't have to believe that independent researchers are so easily influenced – because the standard image of sponsored research is wrong about what's standard.

Pharma companies outsource almost all of their clinical research, some to academic groups but mostly to for-profit contract research organizations (CROs), which perform 70-75% of industry-sponsored research on drugs.[43] The industry has been growing rapidly, at an average rate of 34% annually between 1997 and 2007, and at 15% annually in the years following. The growth is large enough that there are now trade associations for CROs; the UK-based Clinical & Contract Research Association, for example, boasts roughly thirty members, most of which are small or mid-sized CROs with primary offices in the UK. Since they produce research for hire, CRO science can represent drug company interests from the outset.

In 2014, I visited the European meeting of the Drug Information Association in Vienna. That conference is large, needing a convention centre to house the several thousand participants. At the Vienna meeting, speakers included drug company representatives, executives from CROs, regulators from a variety of different kinds of national and EU agencies, and patient advocates. It was an opportunity for these various stakeholders in bringing new drugs to the market to hear each other out – albeit in a formal setting, given the size of the meeting. Up for discussion was a broad array of issues about the design and regulation of clinical research, including issues about how to design regulations for testing and approving novel products, issues about how to plan clinical research so that it would feed into both approval and post-approval needs, and issues about transparency and disclosure. Although it was clear that there were divergences, almost everybody at the meeting had interests in the enormous project of the commercialization of drugs.

What struck me most was the exhibit hall, where CROs and other agencies working for the drug industry had set up slick booths to promote their services. There were many more CROs than I had known existed. Perhaps because the meeting was in Vienna, a number were emphasizing their abilities to run trials in Eastern Europe and the former Soviet Union, but their overall reach was global. Some CROs are specialized in other ways, like PaediaCRO, a German company that performs only paediatric research, or The Regulatory Affairs Company, an international firm that only handles drug approval submissions and the planning that goes into them. Many are full-service firms, ready to take on almost anything that drug companies don't see a need to do themselves. Especially for small drug companies, outsourcing multiple functions makes sense, because they can then rely on CROs' specialized knowledge and know-how.[44]

CROs can be involved at all stages of research: doing analytic and synthetic chemistry, performing in vitro and in vivo toxicology studies,[45] providing laboratory services related to trials, running the trials themselves, analysing data, doing health economics research, pharmacovigilance (monitoring effects of drugs after approval), interfacing with regulators, and even handling the full drug approval application process.

Trials represent the core of the business, though. CRO-conducted trials are designed either for the drug approval process or for the further development of data to support the marketing of drugs, or for both. CROs, in turn, typically contract with clinics and physicians to do the hands-on work of clinical studies. They recruit patients in a variety of ways, through public advertisements, networks of specialists, or just through physicians' practices.

Companies are becoming more sophisticated about populations, as well. In an interview in a study of offshored trials, a former Chief Executive of a CRO says, 'Companies can now pick and choose populations ... in order to get a most pronounced drug benefit signal as well as a "no-harm" signal.'[46] This requires access to larger populations, often populations in multiple countries.

So, while CROs need to perform research of high enough scientific quality to support the approval and marketing of drugs, and they need to do so inexpensively and efficiently, they also need to serve other goals of the pharma companies that hire them.

CROs' orientation to their clients leads them to make choices in the implementation and execution of the RCT protocol that are more likely to produce data favourable to those clients; they might, for example, skew the subject pool by systematically recruiting certain populations, or they might close some sites for breaches of protocol, especially if results from those sites are throwing up red flags. Given the enormous complexity of protocols for large RCTs, it would be no surprise if these choices contributed to the relationship between sponsorship and favourable outcomes.

Unlike the academics who are occasionally contracted to run clinical trials, CROs offer data to pharma companies with no strings attached. Data from CRO studies are wholly owned and controlled by the sponsoring companies, and CROs have no interest in publishing the results under their own names. The companies can therefore use the data to best advantage, as we will see in the next chapter. Company scientists and statisticians, publication planners and medical writers use the data to produce knowledge that supports the marketing of products.

Trials with and without Borders

CROs tend to work in multiple countries both within and outside North America and Western Europe, including poorer, 'treatment naïve' countries where costs per patient are considerably lower.[47] However, North America and Western Europe still have more than 60% of the market share for drug industry trials. Of trials registered in the largest database, ClinicalTrials.gov, between

2006 and 2013 there were nearly ten times as many trials per capita in high-income countries as in middle-income ones.[48] In terms of sites registered in this period – large trials are conducted at multiple discrete sites – nearly 70% of the nearly 460,000 were in North America and Western Europe.[49] Nevertheless, an increasing number of sites are in Asia, Africa, South America and Eastern Europe; significant West-to-East and North-to-South shifts appear to be underway.[50] The costs of trials, in terms of fees paid to physicians and subjects, and the cost of medical procedures, are much lower in the Global South, even in locations that have sufficient medical infrastructure to serve as good locations for trials.

India, for example, is well positioned to provide subjects. India's *Economic Times* wrote in 2004, 'The opportunities are huge, the multinationals are eager, and Indian companies are willing. We have the skills, we have the people.'[51] India has invested heavily to establish the material, social and regulatory infrastructure needed to bring clinical trials to the country, for example, by providing education in the running of trials and establishing ethical standards.[52] It is estimated that the costs per patient are from 30-50% lower in India than in North America or Western Europe.[53]

Government structures and incentives play a variety of roles. Seeing clinical trials as a major business, India has offered tax incentives to CROs and pharmaceutical companies for their local Research and Development (R&D), has dropped a requirement that clinical trials must have 'special value' to the country, has not insisted that experimental drugs later be marketed in India, and has invested in the training of clinical trial workers[54] – key human resources in addition to trial subjects. As a result, all of the major international CROs have established operations in India, and there are also a large number of local CROs. For pharma companies looking for trial sites, there is a developing infrastructure in places like India.

Ethical variability is a further reason for the globalization of trials. Different standards apply even between established members of the European Union and newly admitted members in Eastern Europe. Even when participants in lower-income countries try to apply basic international ethical standards, circumstances still make for differences in practice. There have been cases of enormous differences in protocols between higher- and lower-income countries, which have sparked considerable debate; these extreme cases, though, are exactly that. CROs take more modest and careful advantage of ethical variability to lessen the cost and increase the efficiency of trials.[55] CROs also compete with each other, creating downward pressure on the implementation of ethical standards; in this context, for example, industry actors complain about 'floater sites', pop-up research clinics whose short life expectancies create difficulties for CROs working with more established clinics.

To return to the case of India, Sonia Shah claims that the ethics infrastructure is weak in the country. She quotes health activist Sandhya Srinivasan as saying that ethics committees reviewing trial applications meet not to thoroughly review those applications, but 'in order to enable clearance'.[56] On the other hand, Kaushik Sunder Rajan argues that ethical frameworks and ethics committees are key to capacity-building for clinical trials in India; international companies operate on international standards, need trials to meet those standards and are ensuring the existence of ethics committees.[57]

There may also be public relations and liability pressures to move trials away from North America and Western Europe.[58] Deaths and other severe adverse events are likely to attract more unwanted media attention in pharma companies' core market areas than if they occur elsewhere. Legal liabilities tend to be much higher in North America and Western Europe, and especially in the United States, than in the rest of the world.

Why hasn't pharma moved more quickly to lower-cost, lower-risk environments? Historical reasons are important. For example, before the ICH, the FDA insisted that the majority of trials used for a drug application be conducted in the US, resulting in the national development of material and social capital for running trials. In particular, Phase I trials are generally in-patient exercises, conducted in clinics with beds and other facilities; some of the older material infrastructure continues to be used. Just as there are in lower-income countries,[59] there are even a number of established US and European populations of 'professional guinea pigs'.[60] Also, many countries are trying to attract trials: Denmark and others see their strong healthcare systems and ability to track individuals as offering good infrastructure for both recruitment and the running of trials.

But a significant part of the reason for the continued dominance of North America and Western Europe for Phase II, III, and IV trials is the importance of contacts with doctors in large markets. Clinical trials create and maintain those contacts. A large trial will often involve more than a hundred doctors, each of whom recruits a dozen or more patients. The doctors are paid both for recruiting patients and for all procedures that they, as investigators, perform as part of the trial. While they are earning that money, they are also becoming familiar with the drug and developing a stronger relationship with the company sponsoring the trial. Clinical trials can provide opportunities to sell drugs.

Investigators can also be enrolled to further help sell drugs once they are approved. As I describe in later chapters, they can become speakers for the company, giving talks to other doctors. If they are seen by the company as having the right kind of status, investigators can become authors on ghost-managed articles stemming from the trials. They can, in effect, become nominally independent advocates and salespeople for the drug being studied.

Investigator-Initiated Trials

If CROs take 70-75% of pharma's trial business, what about the other 25-30%? What about the trials run by independent medical researchers but supported by drug companies? To find out, I set off to a large new Colonial Revival hotel in suburban New Jersey for a conference on these 'investigator-initiated trials' (IITs). Roughly a hundred pharma employees working on IITs attended, with a smaller number of people interested in selling services to the industry tagging along. This was a poor cousin of the Drug Information Association meeting I had attended in Vienna.

The companies support IITs both to further relationships with doctors and to contribute to positive scientific publicity. Sometimes, resonating with the term 'IIT', investigators will actually design trials and simply seek funding from companies with which they have established relationships. But more often, IITs are only partly independent. Mark Schmukler of Sagefrog Marketing, a general marketing firm with expertise in the health sector, writes that the goals of any IIT programme are:

- Adding to the base of knowledge for a product.
- Generating abstracts and publications to be shared with the medical community at congresses or meetings.
- Increasing the familiarity of key physicians with the use of a product.
- Producing advocates for the use of a product.[61]

Most importantly, 'the IIT process itself, which derives from the Clinical Development Plan, should be timed carefully. For pre-launch trials, results and publications should come forward within 6 months of the anticipated launch'.[62] All of this suggests that while IITs may be 'investigator-initiated' in some senses, they are still expected to fit neatly into the company's marketing plans.

In fact, drug companies are inconsistent on these issues. At the meeting on IITs that I attended, panellists discussed technicalities of putting out requests for proposals for trials, starting from regulatory and marketing needs. Speakers and audience members explicitly recognized that if companies started from needs, especially regulatory needs, the trials couldn't be fully independent – which ran afoul of some people's ideas of what they were doing. One participant asked, 'Doesn't using a trial for drug approval mean a level of company involvement that means that it is a sponsored study?'

A senior medical affairs director for one company, Dr Moore, described how medical science liaisons need to 'interact with investigators to get the right studies submitted to meet your corporate needs – without crossing lines!' The trick is to make sure that investigators propose exactly what the companies need. 'Say you need IITs in order to commercialize in a country ...', then you can work with influential doctors in the country, the relevant KOLs. Moreover, an advantage of IITs is that they tend to be much less expensive than CRO-run trials, especially when the trials take place 'overseas'. Dr Macar, a vice president for medical affairs of a specialized drug company, referred to this as 'outsourcing'. For Macar and Moore, these partly independent trials are a necessary part of commercialization.

Other drug company speakers, including one who had been working on IIT programmes for a number of years, were indignant about issuing requests for proposals and working closely with investigators to shape the trials. 'We shouldn't be doing any of these things', insisted Mr Mayer, who went on to say that they can get the companies in trouble: 'The last CIA [Corporate Integrity Agreement payment] for Pfizer was 3.2 billion [dollars]. It's not funny anymore.' Making sure that IIT programmes aren't just a kind of 'outsourcing' helps to keep the companies safe from charges of manipulating evidence. Although the disagreement clearly wasn't settled, Dr Macar tried to finesse a way through the uncomfortable problem. The distinction between control and independence in trials 'still seems to be a pragmatic distinction, where it's mostly grey'.

The Integration of Marketing and Research

John LaMattina, former President of Pfizer Global Research and Development, writes that 'EVERY clinical trial carried out by the biopharmaceutical industry always has input from the company's commercial division.'[63] LaMattina doesn't mean to say that the marketing department intervenes in a nefarious way, to turn good science into bad. Instead, he points to the fact that all clinical research is ultimately in the service of marketing drugs. Commercial goals shape the science:

> Yes, biopharmaceutical companies have the goal of making profits. To achieve this, the billions of dollars that are invested in clinical trials must be judiciously spent. Companies draw on all experts in their organization (research, clinical, regulatory and commercial) to maximize the chances that the clinical trial, should it successfully meet its goals … will show the full value of the new medicine.[64]

The 'full value of the new medicine' is its maximum potential return for the companies. Research has to provide information that will define drugs and their markets, and will help move those drugs to their customers. To repeat a claim I made earlier in this chapter, a drug is a molecule surrounded by information. As a result, for pharmaceutical companies there is never a sense in which research is separate from marketing.

There are many ways in which drug companies can shape trials to make commercially useful outcomes more likely. Trials might involve advantageous comparator drugs, unusual doses, carefully constructed experimental populations, clever surrogate endpoints, trial lengths unlikely to show side effects, and definitions likely to show activity or unlikely to show side effects. In addition, companies can shape their publications of trials by including only some clinical endpoints, doing subgroup analyses, choosing advantageous statistical tests and presentations, heavily promoting positive results and burying negative ones, speculating about reasons for ignoring negative results or simply emphasizing positive results through the craft of writing. When Merck was testing its ill-fated painkillers, rofecoxib (Vioxx) and etoricoxib (Arcoxia) – these are COX-2 inhibitors, which should offer pain relief without the negative gastrointestinal effects of many traditional painkillers – it used every single one of these techniques to improve one or another of its published trials.[65] We have more insights into these cases than most others, because of legal actions against Merck, but there is no reason to think that the company was doing anything out of the ordinary.

For example, when Merck ran a trial of its drug rofecoxib against an established painkiller, naproxen, it found more cardiac problems in the rofecoxib patients than in the control group. The company claimed that this was understandable, given that naproxen offered protection to the heart – even though naproxen's heart benefits were entirely speculative. The initial journal article presenting that same trial's results neglected to mention three of the heart attacks that occurred among the rofecoxib patients, because those heart attacks happened after the cut-off date for reporting them. Curiously, the cut-off date for cardiac adverse events was different from the cut-off date for gastrointestinal adverse events, which were expected to play out in favour of Merck's drug, rather than the comparator drug. The resulting positive article was as heavily promoted as any piece of medical science could have been, because the company bought 900,000 reprints of the article to distribute to doctors.[66]

In the opening section of this chapter, I quoted a critical doctor accusing the industry of running 'sloppy' trials. The trials are only sloppy in the eyes of critics. For the companies, the trials can be very carefully designed to produce favourable results that can be used for market approval and then broader marketing efforts.

EVERYBODY IS A BOOK OF BLOOD[67]

Many of the participants in Phase I trials – trials on 'healthy volunteers' – have been through many such trials. Some even label themselves 'professional guinea pigs' or 'professional lab rats', because payments from trials make up most or all of their incomes. Typical studies pay between $2000 and $4000, though longer-term studies can pay significantly more. As a result, frequent participants hustle to be in the better studies.[68]

Most Phase I trials follow very similar protocols. The clinics recruit subjects by advertising, and the advertising is amplified through networks of experienced healthy volunteers. Subjects are screened to ensure that they are indeed healthy enough to participate, that they haven't participated in another trial too recently, and that they aren't taking any drugs that might interfere with the trial drugs. Frequent Phase I participants may lie in order to be eligible, and prepare their bodies so as to pass the screening tests – they can't afford long washout periods between trials. The selected participants arrive on the first day of the trial and begin a daily regime of drug-taking, eating, sleeping and being subjected to a battery of tests: biopsies, drawing of blood, collection of urine and faeces, taking of vital signs, physical exams, and so on. Participants are restricted to the clinic, stay in dorm-like rooms, and move only from their beds to the cafeteria to common rooms to examining rooms. The food is standardized and measured out, and the days are routinized. Trials typically last from one to a few weeks, though there are shorter ones and the occasional much longer one. Sociologist Jill Fisher observes that risk is made 'banal' by the routines of Phase I trials, which are familiar to the frequent participants and clinic staff. Even the variations among trials follow familiar patterns.

Participants' bodies are production sites. The participants ingest or are injected with novel substances, and then the clinic staff collect their tissues and fluids, and make less intrusive observations and measurements, to be turned into data. Blood is the key fluid: in addition to more routine draws of blood, many trials involve pharmacokinetic measurements that might involve ten, or as many as twenty, small draws on a single day, leaving the participants dizzy and nauseous.

Clinic staff monitor negative reactions to the drugs, including ones that pose real risks to participants. Fevers, nausea, vomiting, hallucinations and sleep paralysis would all be human events if they occurred outside the clinic; inside the clinic they are bodily reactions, and become data.[69] Clinical trials are clinical in that they treat and observe actual bodies, but they are also clinical in their detached and unsentimental relationships with those bodies.

T.S. Eliot said, 'The purpose of literature is to turn blood into ink', and the same applies to clinical trials.[70] Indeed, clinic staff refer to many Phase I trials as 'feed 'em and bleed 'ems' and there are routine references to 'feeding and bleeding', tasks that structure the days of staff and participants alike.[71] Besides rhyming, the two tasks are related, because the feeding is a crucial step to allow bleeding. On the path toward the creation of medical facts, manipulated bodies are turned into marks on paper (and in computer files), allowing the unwieldy materials to be left behind and this newly created data to be neatly juxtaposed with other data.

Phase II-IV trials are quite different from Phase I trials, because they recruit subjects with the targeted health conditions or in the targeted markets, rather than 'healthy volunteers'. They don't pay participants more than honoraria, but they do offer some hope of treatment. They are more often outpatient trials than inpatient ones. They tend to be larger, sometimes much larger. And they follow much more varied protocols, so varied that it would be impossible to canvass them in a list.

But the vampiric experimental logic still applies to later-phase trials. Subjects' bodies are still production sites. Subjects ingest or are injected with substances, and then their bodies are monitored for reactions. Blood is drawn, measurements are taken, outcomes are recorded. Negative outcomes and adverse events become data, treated clinically by the trial apparatus.

CONCLUSIONS

In the second half of the twentieth century, medical reformers successfully demoted the art of medicine in favour of the science of medicine. Meanwhile, policy reformers successfully focused drug regulators' attention on scientific evidence of efficacy and safety. In both settings, the science in question has become dominated by clinical trials, preferably randomized controlled trials.

To work with these new regimes, pharma has become increasingly dependent on science. Large RCTs provide the data that regulators demand, data to show that a would-be drug has at least some more efficacy than a placebo, and that it isn't too dangerous. Parallel and harmonized regulations around the world define bars for drugs to clear, and the industry invests exactly the resources needed to clear those bars. In return, national and international regulators – the most important elements of the market – vouch for the drugs and maintain a low-competition environment.

The pharmaceutical industry cannot, in general, rely on academics and academic institutions to run its growing numbers of clinical trials. Too much rides on timely success. For that reason, the industry turns to companies that often sit unnoticed in its shadows: contract research organizations. The CROs running most of the industry's trials draw fluids, measurements and observations from the bodies of millions of participants to create one of the industry's most precious substances, namely the data that, when processed, can turn an experimental substance into a marketable drug.

But much of this resource extraction sits at the margins of health. Most new drug applications show that only a few of the trials conducted find a statistically significant difference between the drug and a placebo. Most applications aren't able to show a consistent medically meaningful effect. However, most of the time that small apparent effect in the data is all that's needed for approval and to make positive cases to doctors.

3

GHOSTS IN THE MACHINE: PUBLICATION PLANNING 101

THREE PUZZLES

I was looking at the CV of a distinguished professor of medicine, and saw that he had authored (generally co-authored) approximately 800 articles in peer-reviewed journals, an average of nearly thirty per year over his career. His publication rate has accelerated, and he has been authoring forty articles per year in the past decade. How can a scientist publish forty articles in a year? Year after year? In the fields in which I work, five peer-reviewed articles in a year is respectable.

I was looking at the articles published on a blockbuster drug (i.e. sales over $1 billion per year). The PubMed database contained over 700 articles in the 'core clinical journals' that showed that drug's generic name as a keyword. There were over 3200 articles on the drug in medical journals as a whole. Other blockbuster drugs have very similar profiles. Why do these drugs merit such attention?

I was part of a research project that systematically compared industry-sponsored published studies with apparently independent ones. We did a statistical summary – a 'meta-analysis' – of previous efforts to compare sponsored and independent medical research; the comparison involved nearly four thousand different medical studies. The industry-sponsored publications were significantly and strikingly more likely to arrive at industry-friendly results than were the apparently independent publications.[1] How could mere sponsorship lead researchers to come to results that favour their sponsors? Can research funding really have such strong effects?

THIS TRIPLE MYSTERY HAS A SINGLE SOLUTION. THE PHARMACEUTICAL industry produces an abundance of targeted knowledge, flooding its important markets. To gain the largest scientific impact and market value from research, drug company articles are often written under the names of independent medical researchers. Pharma company statisticians, reviewers from a diverse array of company departments, medical writers, and publication planners are only rarely acknowledged in journal publications, and company scientists only sometimes acknowledged. The public knowledge that results from this ghost-managed research and publication is a marketing tool, providing bases for continuing medical education, buttressing sales pitches, and contributing to medical common sense and further research. In the world of pharma, knowledge is a resource to be accumulated, shaped, and deployed to best effect.

THE GHOSTS BEHIND PHARMA'S MEDICAL PUBLICATIONS

When I first became interested in pharmaceutical research and marketing, a number of people in medicine were talking about ghostwriting. It was common, it seemed, for medical journal articles to be written by professional writers working for pharma companies. Those writers' names did not appear on the articles themselves, which were instead 'authored' mostly by medical researchers. Clearly, this was a scandal.

It is an understatement to say that university researchers can be competitive. Since published articles are one of the main currencies of prestige for academics, many medical researchers first see the scandal of ghostwriting in terms of injustice, the injustice of guest authors taking credit for work that they didn't do. It is only on further reflection that they extend the blame to include ghostwriters and the pharmaceutical industry.

Surprisingly, the people talking about medical ghostwriting are rarely curious about the larger structures in which ghosts appear. It is as if ghostwriting is something that happens frequently, but on a purely one-off basis. This can't be right, especially since pharma companies are large organizations and so must have structures to handle ghostwriting. When I became interested in pharma's publications, I immediately became curious about background questions, such as: Who hires the writers? How do they know what to write? How is the work planned and executed? How many articles are ghostwritten? In trying to answer these questions, I quickly stumbled across 'publication planning', and started to study who publication planners are and what they do.[2] When we focus on publication planning, the guest authors and ghostwriters start to seem like a bit of a distraction from more important ghosts.

Publication of drug company research in medical science journals, and its presentation at conferences and meetings, is governed by 'publication plans'. These plans extract scientific and commercial value out of data and analyses, sometimes by designing studies with that value in mind, and always by carefully constructing articles that establish consistent profiles for drugs. As we've seen, most sponsored clinical trial research is handled by contract research organizations (CROs). The data these CROs produce is typically analysed by pharma company statisticians, and then articles are written by hired medical writers. Much of this process is guided and shepherded by publication planners and planning teams.

The manuscripts are 'authored' by academic researchers, whose contribution may range from having been on a company advisory board related to the study, to having supplied some of the patients for a clinical trial, to editing the manuscript, to simply signing off on the final draft. The publication planners then submit the manuscripts to medical journals, where they are generally well received and are published. While these published articles contribute to accepted scientific opinions, the circumstances of their production are largely invisible. When they are useful, they form the basis for presentations by hired doctors and researchers. Marketing departments of the companies involved may buy thousands of reprints, which sales representatives can give to practising doctors.

It is worth quoting at length one publication plan's description of planning itself:

Strategic publication planning provides the tactical recommendations necessary to develop a scientific platform within the biomedical literature to support the market positioning of an established product or the launch of a new product. The process of publication planning includes:

- An analysis of the characteristics of the market into which the product will be launched
- An analysis of competitive issues
- The expected product profile
- Identification of issues relevant to the disease state or primary indication for the product
- Development of a series of key communication messages addressing the major issues
- The availability of clinical and preclinical data to support the key communication messages
- Recognition of appropriate target audiences for each of the recommended publication tactics
- Recommendations for publication vehicles (e.g., journals, meetings, congresses, etc.) for each publication activity.[3]

This very direct description encapsulates much of the rest of this chapter, hitting on all of the major goals and aims of publication planning. In particular, it boldly states that the point of the activity is to position medical science to help market drugs. The science becomes part of the marketing efforts: publication planning creates a 'scientific platform' to 'support market positioning' of a product. If a drug is a molecule surrounded by information, publication planning helps to create and position that information.

How much of the literature is ghost-managed? From the limited number of cases where we have hard data, it appears that roughly 40% of medical journal articles mentioning in-patent drugs are parts of individual publication plans on the drugs.[4] A legal action gave psychiatrist David Healy access to a document listing eighty-five articles on the drug sertraline (Zoloft or Lustral), many of them written by medical writers and then authored by academics, all of them handled for Pfizer by a public relations firm, Current Medical Directions.[5] Lawsuits about rofecoxib (Vioxx) led to a systematic study identifying ninety-six published articles (twenty-four on clinical trials and seventy-two review articles) on which Merck had worked prior to their publication, and which were later published mostly under the names of academic first authors. The company

67

Scientific Therapeutics Information wrote a number of articles for Merck, and one document lists eight review articles for which they had intended authors and journals, and estimated delivery dates of first or second drafts. Interestingly, ghost-managed review articles were likely to be single-authored by academics who were especially likely not to declare any support for the work.[6] Forty percent is a very substantial amount, certainly allowing a company to attract interest in a drug and shape the perception of it, under the names of apparently independent authors.

Various facts make it reasonable to believe that thousands of articles per year are ghost-managed. First, pharma companies sponsor some 70% of all clinical trials, and 70-75% of these are run by CROs that have no interest in publishing the results under their own names – they produce data that is wholly owned by their sponsors. As a result, pharma companies have complete control over an enormous trove of clinical trial data. Second, more than fifty agencies advertise publication planning on the internet. Some boast of having hundreds of employees and handling many hundreds of manuscripts per year. Planners handle dozens of manuscripts per year, and one told me that she was in charge of a campaign involving more than a hundred manuscripts and conference presentations. The industry is large enough that there are *two* international associations of publication planners that run meetings and seminars. One of these associations, the International Society of Medical Planning Professionals (ISMPP), has over 1000 members. Both ISMPP and its competing association, The International Publication Planning Association (TIPPA) hold annual conferences, and the latter hosts regional conferences. This is a major activity.

PUBLICATION PLANNING 101/201: AN INSIDER VIEW OF THE FIELD

To learn more about publication planning, I wanted to hear what planners themselves had to say. My first step was to join ISMPP and register for a workshop, 'Publication Planning 101/201', intended for people new to the profession. As a new member of ISMPP, the workshop seemed perfect for me. Immediately following that, I also attended the 2007 annual meetings of ISMPP; over the next decade, I and/or some research associates attended two meetings of TIPPA, and then a European meeting of ISMPP in 2017. The rest of this chapter is an account that draws mostly from presentations at these five events, but also from written sources, to show publication planners' roles and the structure of pharma's attempts to shape medical science.

Both ISMPP and TIPPA hold annual conferences, and there are overlaps in their programmes and lists of speakers. ISMPP runs broader educational and accreditation activities, and creates guidelines for ethical and best practices. It is a larger organization than TIPPA, though the latter also holds regional meetings. Almost all attendees of these meetings are publication planners, some working for independent agencies and some directly for pharmaceutical companies; ISMPP is the more agency-dominated of the two. The non-planners are mostly invited speakers, including journal editors, ethicists, and consultants to the industry. Slightly more women than men attend, and at one meeting I estimated the average age of participants at approximately 40 or a little higher; this is a new field, and has few senior figures. Attire is roughly what you might expect in a group of medical writers and scientists working for industry: a range from business suits to business casual, but mostly of the ordinary and slightly rumpled variety. That said, some of the attendees are more 'corporate' types – at one small meeting a participant noted the arrival of a contingent from Pfizer, a group of young women who moved as a pack and looked, with their pencil skirt suits and stiletto heels, as though they had walked in directly from Wall Street. Four of the five events reported on in this chapter were in the US, and the fifth in the UK, billed as a European meeting. The US appears to dominate the publication planning world, but the UK is an important second centre.

Publication Planning 101/201 was supposed to provide 'an interactive and instructive introduction to the world of strategic publication planning', for those either new to it, working as support to planning, or working in connected areas. Most of the thirty women and thirteen men taking the course were new publication planners, though there were also medical writers, publishing company employees, and more experienced publication planners. Day-long seminars were held simultaneously in adjacent rooms: 'Publication Planning 301, Developing a Strategic Publication Plan'; 'The Life of a Manuscript: From Initial Concept to Publication (and Beyond)'; and 'Statistics for the Non-Statistician, and Publishing Pharmacoeconomics and Outcomes Research'.

The programme for Publication Planning 101/201 began with a history of the field, given by Mr Phillips, a senior member of the field and the CEO of a medium-sized agency. Somewhat artificially, Phillips pointed to 1984 as the origin of publication planning, when three employees of Pfizer realized that the company had extensive data on the drug amlodipine (Norvasc), and wondered where they should publish it. To do this rationally, they had to gather information about all of the trials to which Pfizer had access, harvest information from other publications, sort it all, and decide how to publish it in credible journals for non-overlapping global audiences. The company had to improve internal communication to achieve this. Even by 1988, publication planning was not well established within Pfizer, as demonstrated by an internal memo Phillips quoted: 'Please … return details of any new trials, new plans for publication of existing trials, or missing details.' He and some members of the 101/201 audience chuckled, because this sounds quaint today. Close tracking of all trials from their conception onward and top-down guidance of their publication means that '[t]oday, if you go to a meeting, you know pretty much what is going to be presented'.

The bare publication plan is a dynamic document that 'outlines the recommended medical communications and their timings'. However, the activity of publication planning includes the work to implement the plan, to produce the deliverables. Publication planning can and should start even before the research does, contributing to research design, mapping out key messages, charting out articles for different audiences and journals, and finding potential authors for those articles. The focus is communication, and the research is created with this in view. Once the research is available, publication planners hire writers for those articles, deal with potential authors and various interests within the pharma companies, and shepherd the articles through journals' submission and revision procedures. Publication planning is typically done by heterogeneous teams, and increasingly those teams include one or more professional planners who understand the process of turning data into articles and presentations and guide it. Most of these planners work for dedicated agencies, though pharma companies employ a substantial number directly.

New publication planners are told to pay attention to marketing. Publication planning is a key part of the process of surrounding a molecule with information. In the 101/201 course, Dr Parker explained that a publication plan begins with a SWOT (Strengths, Weaknesses, Opportunities, and Threats) analysis, which 'paints a complete picture of the market situation for a new product'. In case it isn't obvious, a SWOT analysis for scientific publications only makes sense if those publications are supposed to serve marketing goals. Shortly afterwards, Dr Price said that publication plans should identify 'target audiences', should lay out key 'scientific & clinical communication points', should do 'competitor publication & gap analyses', and need to outline 'top-line tactics' and 'critical timing'. Clearly, these analyses are parts of the apparatus of interest-driven persuasion, not the disinterested diffusion of results. Similarly, after an exercise in the 101/201 seminar, Parker asked, 'How are we going to create publications that have the right message, and a memorable message, for prescribers?' At a later meeting, speaking about his company's innovative model for evaluating the effects of publications, planner Mr Powers concluded: 'If you really want to make an impact and leave a footprint with your communication plans, you need to engage your scientific communication plan with activities that engage emotional and social intelligence.' Former publication planner Alastair Matheson describes the messages as 'narratives' that establish consistent profiles for drugs.[7]

In the opening speech at one publication planning conference, the speaker took it as one of her tasks to cheer on the profession. Holding an imaginary document in her hand and waving it around in the air, she chided an imaginary colleague: 'What is this? They're promoting the competitor! Well, you left it to the investigators.' Another planner agreed shortly afterwards, saying: 'The approach of an industry-authored first draft is a good one.'

As we've seen, there have been substantial changes in the structure of research in the industry since the 1980s, as industry funding moved from supporting academic research to purchasing research from CROs. The simultaneous rise of the publication planning and CRO industries is almost certainly not coincidental, because CROs, unlike academic researchers, make no claims on the data. If scientific data are to be systematically used for marketing, then pharma companies need to have as much control over it as possible. CROs may even do publication planning, which allows them to fully guide research from inception to communication. For example, the website of the CRO Quintiles (which has since merged with IMS Health to form IQVIA) notes that

> Effective communications require scientific and commercial specialists who can craft and convey messages backed by evidence and an acute awareness of market and regulatory environments.

And the CRO is in a good position to provide that effective communication:

> As the world's largest provider of biopharmaceutical services, Quintiles offers capabilities that surpass the typical healthcare communications agency. Our singular objective is to increase your probability of success by connecting deep insights with superior delivery for better outcomes.[8]

A SAMPLE MANUSCRIPT (1)

Before turning to more publication planners' descriptions of what they do, I want to follow a single manuscript that made its way through the publication planning process. The case comes from legal documents that were made public.[9]

The drug company Wyeth has faced thousands of lawsuits to do with over-promotion of hormone replacement therapy (HRT); it has lost most of the first handful of cases to be decided. Because of these suits, a number of documents have become available for public scrutiny.[10] We know, for example, that in the late 1990s and early 2000s, Wyeth turned to the medical education and communication companies (MECCs) DesignWrite, Parthenon Publishing, and Oxford Clinical Communications to work on publication plans and publications for HRT. These agencies created suites of articles and conference presentations that were intended to maintain and expand the market for HRT. Over the course of six years, DesignWrite produced for Wyeth 'over 50 peer reviewed publications, more than 50 scientific abstracts and posters, journal supplements, internal white papers, slide kits, and symposia'.

Hormone replacement therapy has been part of a somewhat speculative, though largely successful, attempt to label menopause a condition of deficiency. Reassuring doctors and patients would turn out to be particularly important commercially, because in 2002 the routine acceptance of HRT for women was shattered. The results of the Women's Health Initiative study indicated that women who used oestrogen plus progestin HRT faced an increased risk of breast and ovarian cancer. What is more, while it had been expected that HRT would decrease the risk of cardiovascular disease, the study suggested that the risk actually increased. After the Women's Health Initiative definitively showed problems with hormone therapies, Wyeth's new publication plan was called 'Achieving Clarity, Renewing Confidence'. That effort continued previous efforts to establish confidence in the face of cancer worries: on an earlier note about breast cancer risks, a Wyeth employee had written 'Dismiss/distract'.[11]

Here I will follow one of these ghostly articles, labelled PC(2) in Wyeth's plan, on a hormone treatment with the feminine-inflected brand 'Totelle'. The first draft of manuscript PC(2) was ready on 16 August 2002. Jean Wright, a member of the Totelle team working for the British MECC and publisher Parthenon Publishing, contacted a group of Wyeth employees. 'Please find attached the first draft of PC(2)', she wrote. This manuscript, based on data coming from a clinical trial of Totelle performed for Wyeth, had the unwieldy title 'A 2-Year Comparison of the Effects of Continuous Combined Regimens of 1 mg 17β-Estradiol and Trimegestone with Regimens Containing Estradiol and Norethisterone Acetate upon Endometrial Bleeding and Safety in Postmenopausal Women'.

Just under the title of that draft was written: 'Author: to be determined'.

Six months later, on 4 March 2003, a tracking report – we should remember that we are dealing with large corporations, so there are things like tracking reports – on articles and conference submissions to do with Totelle showed that PC(2) was making steady progress. At that point, this high-priority manuscript had been revised once by Parthenon in response to comments made on 7 December by Wyeth employee Daniele Spielmann (revision done on 3 January), a second time in response to 5 February comments by Wyeth's Sophie Olivier (revision done on 28 February), and had yet to be revised in light of the comments of another Wyeth employee, Richie Lu, on 28 February. It was moving toward its final shape. And it was making progress, especially good progress for a manuscript that was still without an author.

By 2 April, three authors had finally appeared on the tracking report: two medical professors and Wyeth's Daniele Spielmann. A note on the author list read 'Need to contact', perhaps suggesting that the first two had not yet been consulted. The fourth draft was sent to the publication team on 12 March, and the fifth on 2 July. By 6 June 2003, the manuscript had clear authors: 'Bouchard P, Addo S, Spielmann D, and the Trimegestone 301 Study Group', the last of those being a label for a long list of doctors who had provided patients for the Wyeth trial.

But that was not quite the end of the road for manuscript PC(2). A 27 October 2003 report revealed that in July Parthenon updated the manuscript before it was sent out to external authors for their final review, quite possibly their first opportunity to review it. An 18 August note showed that submission had been delayed during Wyeth's signoff process. A note followed on 29 August indicating that 'sign-off' was nearly complete, with another on 22 September confirming that it was in the 'final stages of sign-off at Wyeth'. But by this time the authors had changed. They had become 'Bouchard P, De Cicco-Nardone F, Spielmann D, Garcea N, and the Trimegestone 301 Study Group'. What had happened in the meantime, and what had happened to Dr Addo? When I was trying to follow this paperwork through all of the documents, I became concerned that I might be making a mistake.

However, an email by Spielmann explained: 'The 2 Italian authors agree with the paper and replace ADDO [who] went to our competitors'. In an earlier email, Jean Wright of Parthenon had written: 'Please note that S. Addo has been deleted from the author list for PC(2). Daniele was doubtful whether she should be included because she now has connections with Organon', another drug company.

In all of this, there is no indication that the external authors had any input, in contrast to the obvious and documented input from various internal actors. On

26 August 2003, for example, Wright had completed the draft on which Wyeth eventually signed off, and mentioned only that she had dealt with queries by yet another Wyeth employee.

Authors, it seems, were largely interchangeable. They were all 'to be determined' until the publication team thought that the manuscript was nearly ready to be sent out to a journal. At that point, Wyeth appears to have determined who the authors would be, and contacting them was added to its 'to do' list. Perhaps there was not much consultation even then. When Addo established ties with Organon, Wyeth no longer wanted to work with her, and simply replaced her with two other authors. It isn't clear that she was ever notified that she had been either put on or taken off the author list.

Although a 2004 tracking report listed the manuscript as accepted in the journal *Menopause*, it eventually appeared in the journal *Gynecological Endocrinology* – perhaps that had to do with the fact that the latter journal was then published by Parthenon. On its publication, article PC(2) took its place in the marketing effort for the new formulation Totelle. Not surprisingly, it found Totelle to be an improvement over earlier hormone treatment.

ALIGNMENT ON A PLAN

> This is what utopia looks like from an industry perspective. We have agreement and alignment on a plan, not even just a publication, a full plan, investigators on board, agencies lined up, everybody ready to play and we're going to get this done in a timely way, in an orderly fashion, and things work like clockwork. (Ms Perez, a planner working within a pharmaceutical company)

Publication plans set out goals: an imagined orderly performance of research and rolling out of presentations and publications; then appendices give the relevant data for each of the meetings and journals to which abstracts and papers will be submitted, the audiences they reach, their impact factors, their rejection rates, and publication lead times.[12] Tactical recommendations are for specific submissions, based on strategic considerations, parcelling out data for different target audiences, time and resource considerations, and the sequence in which one wants the data to roll out. Dates of submission are laid out, and dates of publication are supposed to quickly follow.

A plan may also describe other communication opportunities, such as symposia and roundtables, journal supplements, advisory board meetings, books, speaker bureau programmes and more. Though the publication plan should be a dynamic document, changeable if circumstances change, one gets the impression of a world without uncertainty, of articles written and published on schedule. And planners take pride in their efficiency: according to one presenter, the pharma company GlaxoSmithKline did a survey of sponsored publications, and compared to investigator-led publications and publications developed by people in the company's Clinical Research department, those developed by a planning team were submitted and published much more rapidly.

Ideally, the publication planning team should be put in place early, says seminar leader Ms Peterson, 'before too much data has gone unpublished'. The publication planning team might be formed upon proof of concept, or two years before the expected launch of the product, or at the start of Phase III trials (trials to establish efficacy and safety before the drug is approved), or when the company begins making expenditures on commercial plans. The planning team rationalizes expenditures by integrating the company's research, scientific communication, and marketing communication strategies. It also manages knowledge flow: planner Mr Perry advises that articles from Phase I (pilot trials typically on healthy subjects) should be written early, so that Phase II (small clinical trials to guide Phase III ones) articles can refer to them; Dr Price says that the number of articles should peak at about the time that the product launches, for maximum effect. The right knowledge flow should lead to increased presence in medical understanding and in the commercial market.

Yet much planning is more ad hoc. Articles can be delayed as they are multiply revised, authors change depending on the circumstances, and where an article is published can change at the last minute – all of these happened in the case of the sample manuscript I described earlier. In addition, publication planning has to react to changing circumstances and to the demands of marketers. Here, for example, is pharma company planner Mr Powell, speaking about how marketing messages come from the top:

At the beginning of the year, we kind of have a scientific strategy for every product, saying, y'know, these are the key messages that we're hoping to get out, depending on what clinical data we have available. We'll look at all the points that the upper management folks would like us to try and see if we have the data to address, and then we'll go through it point by point and try to see.[13]

GENERATING BULK RESEARCH

A common complaint in scientific publishing is the division of research into 'least publishable units', and the publication of overlapping or redundant analyses. Chopping findings into least publishable units fills journals with articles that have the advantage and disadvantage of making only one point each. Academic authors are well accustomed to multiplying papers, and also to complaining about it. However, in the pharmaceutical industry each publication is part of a marketing campaign and has an expected return. The professionalization and commercialization of publishing makes a science out of the multiplication of papers.

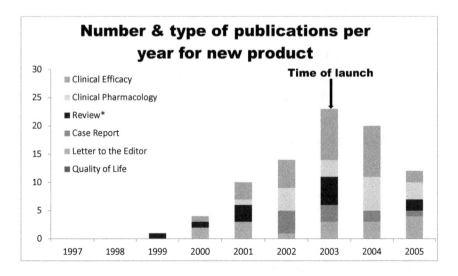

FIG. 3.1 A hypothetical trajectory of publications

There is no question that publication programmes can involve many articles. The chart in Figure 3.1, redrawn from a presentation, shows a trajectory of publications for a single fictional Product X, with approximately ninety articles in total.

I was astonished when, at an ISMPP meeting, Mr Edwards, the director of medical publishing for one of the world's largest academic publishing companies, chided his audience: 'You don't help when you take your research and you do your primary publication and then you follow it with twenty, thirty, forty secondary analyses. This is alarming publication and it is actually contributing to the whole peer review process grinding to a halt.' I am sure that he was exaggerating for effect. However, the salami slicing to which he pointed was promptly corroborated by Ms Perez, a pharma company employee who explained how to multiply articles:

> There are more publication ideas coming from my medical team than we can handle even if we had fifteen agencies and twenty people focused solely on publication for this one area. That's one of the bigger challenges, 'cause it adds more analyses. And now I need more statisticians, I need more investigators, I need more authors. I need more writers, whether they're agency writers or external physicians doing the writing.

Perez's eventual point was that it is important to winnow ideas early, to optimize production. She didn't object to multiple publications, but wanted to make sure that they are all merited. There comes a point when another article isn't cost-effective. Indeed, as another pharma-based planner observed, the bulk can become difficult to track if the manuscripts shift:

> Right now our team thinks some days that we're being a contract manager more than a publication strategist. So trying to figure out if we agreed with the author on fifteen different publications for a particular study, are we on number five, are we on number fourteen or are we approaching number sixteen and have to update the agreements? (Ms Pearson)

MARKETING

Publication planners explain that their work should, though isn't always, be independent of marketing. It should be in the service of scientific knowledge about results: 'We really do like to stress that the publication planning company is not an advertising agency, is not a PR [public relations] agency, even though it might look like one', says Parker. Planners understand that they are in a sensitive position. On a number of occasions, conference audience members were reminded to watch what was written down or entered into databases, because their documents and databases could become public through lawsuits or otherwise. Seminar leader Dr Price suggested, for example, that planners talk about 'communication points' rather than 'messages', because critics see the latter as driven by marketers. The *Wall Street Journal* in particular, with its readership in the world of finance, was mentioned fearfully several times over the course of the conference: planners want the results of their work to be reported on its pages, but not their work itself, especially work that is associated with any one drug company. Price said, 'A publication plan might be made public, might appear on the front page of the *Wall Street Journal*. So you don't want to make it appear that you don't have authors. This is verboten today.'

In their interactions with each other and with the industry, planners recognize that their work has marketing value. Websites of publication planning firms promote their ability to market products. Envision Pharma's website claims that 'data generated from clinical trials programmes are the most powerful marketing tools available to a pharmaceutical company'. Watermeadow Medical advertises its mission thus: 'Our highly qualified and insightful medical writing teams will work with you to understand your specific needs, to develop an effective and customized multichannel publication plan. Operating from principles of trust and transparency we liaise with authors, journals and internal stakeholders to translate complex scientific data into clear, clinically relevant publications'. 'Adis Communications works in partnership with clients to position their products at the right place, at the right time' through 'hundreds of well-respected, and high-impact factor journals'.[14]

Mr Edwards, the publishing company director, explains just how crucial journals are for pharmaceutical companies. Medical journals provide registration of ideas, vehicles for dissemination, an archive of results, and certification: 'the air of impartiality that you wouldn't be able to get if you publish elsewhere'.

Ultimately, publication planning needs to generate revenue by providing information that increases sales. It is difficult to measure return on investment directly, says Parker, because publications typically go hand-in-hand with many other activities that affect markets and sales, as well as constantly changing markets.[15] Nonetheless, one presentation by two junior planners, Ms Pham and Ms Potter, did a more direct study of return on investment for publications, by studying prescriptions of a hormone replacement therapy (HRT) by cardiologists before and after a group of published reports on HRT for hypertension, as well as patient use of HRT for the same use. After three major publications in *Circulation*, *Menopause*, and *Hypertension*, all showing that not only did HRT reduce the symptoms of menopause but also reduced hypertension, there was an increase in prescriptions by cardiologists, though not by gynaecologists. There were several advantages to this particular focus, including the fact that hypertension is an off-label (unapproved) indication of HRT: consequently, unless it was acting illegally, the sales force should not have been a complicating factor. Indeed, a questioner from the audience asked if the speakers themselves were doing illegal off-label promotion, an accusation they forcefully denied.

Though they appear inconsistent, planners are not merely being duplicitous when they distance themselves from marketers. They understand that their work has marketing value and is supported because of that value, but they see a clear distinction between what they do and what marketing departments do. Marketers, as planners portray them, would consistently ride roughshod over scientific standards, and would be relatively unconcerned with what the scientific data can support. To be compliant with 'Good Publication Practice', says Price, a publication plan is a basis for disseminating scientific and clinical data, and is 'not a marketing communications plan'. The marketing department, Parker said, is considered lucky to have one place on a publication team – it does typically retain that one place, because 'they're probably paying the bill'.

Publication planning negotiates between marketing and science, implies Ms Peterson. Without it, 'bottlenecks will inevitably occur' and 'vast delays are likely', but also 'marketing may drive the process' and 'the resulting publications might be "cherry picked"'. Especially in the context of scrutiny around publication of results, cherry-picking is a worry. A journal editor, Dr Ellis, corroborated the antagonism between marketing and science, exhorting her audience of publication planners to prevent marketers from writing manuscripts. She can tell, she said, when articles are written in the marketing department, and she typically rejects them; they are peppered with certain adjectives and adverbs that a scientist wouldn't write.

Because marketers would go too far, publication planners see part of their job as constraining their influence. Yet publication plans exist to serve the marketers, and therefore the planners have to convince the marketers that their more subtle approach, with a limited range of tools, is the right one. As we've seen, to 'sell without selling' is a marketing ideal, too.[16] Nonetheless, publication planning does its work almost entirely through scientific meetings and journals, without any contact with doctors.

Scientific standards are doubly important. Meeting them constitutes part of what is considered ethical behaviour, and so underpins the entire business and the distinction between doing publication planning and public relations. How, after all, could publishing high quality science be unethical? After planners persuade their sponsors that their work will provide a good return on investment, they want to obey ethical guidelines in the hands-on work they do, and to adopt high scientific standards for the writing of each article. Second, publication planners can only succeed if their work displays high standards, so that their articles will be published to best advantage. Medical journals have high rejection rates, as high as 95% in the case of such journals as the *Journal of the American Medical Association* and the *British Medical Journal*. Meanwhile, publication planners claim to have very high acceptance rates; for example, an 'acceptance rate on first submission of 94% for abstracts and 78% for manuscripts'.[17] It is only by stifling the marketing department's efforts to hype the product that publication planners can do effective marketing to scientific audiences. At least some of the time, marketing is best done if it is invisible.

CREATING KNOWLEDGE THROUGH MEDIATION

Publication planners are both outsiders and insiders to the clinical research world. They are outsiders because they aren't physicians or statisticians, and don't play a visible role in knowledge production. They are insiders because they often have detailed knowledge about clinical research, pharmacology, and medicine – in conversations I have had with planners, they have appeared fluent in the areas in which they are working. More importantly, they contribute to an enormous amount of research: a typical active planner is involved with many more research publications than are most medical researchers. Planners can, then, demonstrate expertise, though they wouldn't normally be seen as legitimate bearers of it.

Clinical research and publication is unusual, in that acceptable methods have been very precisely spelled out, and these have been widely accepted. Reports of clinical trials are relatively formulaic and constrained, as journals demand tightly structured articles, and are increasingly demanding structured abstracts.[18] Though there are many choices behind any article reporting a clinical trial, there are fewer choices about its format or language.

It may appear, then, that at least for clinical trials, the work of planners and writers is relatively mechanical, or that the work consists in balancing sponsors' and editors' demands, or the respective interests of marketing and science. However, designing, analysing and writing up results from clinical trials involves extensive decision-making. Planners also handle other kinds of research and manuscripts. And planners do not represent their own work as mechanical. Speaking without apparent humour, Mr Porter tries to present agency concerns to those working in pharmaceutical companies:

> My plea here is to think again about attempting to commoditize something [publication planning and medical writing] that is actually a highly tailored service, a professional skill. I believe that commoditization undermines the value of medical writing. You're not buying widgets.

Despite appearances, one cannot buy manuscripts by the gross – by the dozen perhaps, but even then they are individually crafted.

Manuscripts, and the drafts and analyses that precede them, pass through the hands of many skilled contributors and reviewers. In addition to making their own contributions, planners facilitate their teams' work, keeping in contact with medical writers, making sure that all documents produced are consistent with the plan, managing information, and reconciling divergent demands and suggestions. The work of the planner is creative mediation, using the insights of the many people who come into contact with data and drafts to develop manuscripts that will fare better in peer review and will have an impact.

Manuscripts run a gauntlet, being subject to scrutiny by many actors. Figure 3.2 is a composite image of the people and departments involved in a publication programme, pulled together from different presentations. The number of people potentially involved is enormous, and most of them are working with or checking manuscripts to make sure that they serve the company's interests.

The overall publication planning team, says Peterson, 'ensures buy-in from all stakeholders' because those stakeholders have input into the process and

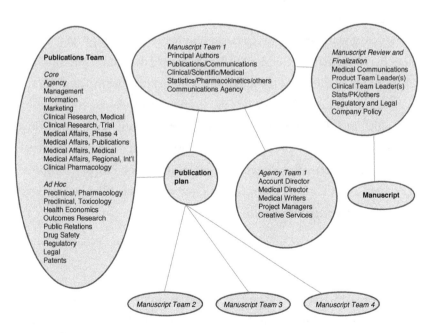

FIG. 3.2 Contributors to the publication plan and manuscripts

result. The multiplication of contributors multiplies the knowledge. Pharma company planner Ms Perez says:

> Involving folks early works. The sooner you involve them before you have data available the easier it is. Much, much easier. You go from having one manuscript to having eight from a pivotal programme. Which is phenomenal. And it's not data-mining, it's just things that are relevant to the clinical practice in that area.

Of course, many actors may give the manuscript only a cursory review, and may have little or no positive input into it. Dr Price notes, 'All the people on the [manuscript development] team have input. But if three or four can get together and work things out' it will be a lot more efficient. Similarly, Mr Palmer, an efficiency expert, claims that the internal review process is the most time-consuming part of producing a final manuscript, and so there are advantages in consolidating it.

Planners and the people who work with them have considerable expertise, often knowing something about their subject matter, but also having the experience of working on a much larger number of manuscripts than do most researchers, and therefore understanding the world of medical publishing very well. In addition, they sit in the middle of a number of other experts who are all interested in producing high-quality publications, and who are contributing to them, albeit in different and possibly contradictory ways. Major articles in any field involve careful rhetorical work, but ghost-managed articles are prepared by a distributed network with access to substantial resources. In the context of regimented demands from journals, and a suppression of individualized voices, science by committee works well.

A SAMPLE MANUSCRIPT (II)

To see more concretely how the publication planning process affects publications, it is worth looking at another sample manuscript. Here, I am mostly following the careful research and analysis conducted by psychiatrists Jon Jureidini

Multiple Stakeholders

FIG. 3.3 Multiple stakeholders in publication planning, redrawn from a 2017 presentation

and Jay Amsterdam and philosopher Leemon McHenry, who examined a trial of an antidepressant: the CIT-MD-18 paediatric trial of the antidepressant citalopram (Celexa and other trade names) by the company Forest Laboratories. One of the most controversial topics in medicine over the past few decades has been whether doctors should prescribe antidepressants to children and adolescents. A number of drug companies have targeted this potentially huge market, identifying anti-depressants as a possible response to the difficulties that many children, and especially adolescents, routinely face. Jureidini and colleagues were working from a trove of documents available as a result of a legal case on which they served as expert witnesses.[19]

The CIT-MD18 trial had 174 subjects, split between the citalopram arm and the placebo arm. They were also to be split between a group aged 7-11 and one aged 12-17, to allow for comparison between these two age groups. The trial protocol was the responsibility of Forest Laboratories' Associate Medical Director, Paul Tiseo. Therefore, Tiseo was a potential author on the eventual publication of results; as it turned out, he made a brief appearance as an author on the second draft of the manuscript, only to be dropped before it was published.

Many other people were involved. A professional writer, Natasha Mitchner, working for the agency Weber Shandwick Communications, wrote the various drafts of the manuscript. Jeffrey Lawrence, who worked in Forest's Marketing Department, was the liaison between the company and the agency. Various other people within Forest appear to have had the power to sign off on the manuscript, or to comment on it. Again, none of them ended up as authors on the publication.

The lead author on the publication was a prominent child psychiatrist, Dr Karen Wagner, chosen because of 'corporate objectives'. Her clinic had run one site of the trial, and Wagner advised Forest Laboratories about marketing strategy. However, Jureidini and his colleagues, who examined all of the Forest documents related to CIT-MD18 and the publication, report that they 'could find no evidence in the extensive documents … that Dr Wagner contributed to the study design, analysis of data, or preparation of the first draft of the manuscript'. In fact, Wagner almost certainly did not contribute to the first draft of the manuscript, because at one point Lawrence asked Mitchner, the writer:

> Could you do me a favour and finish up the paediatric manuscript? I know you said you only had a bit more to do. … I took a quick look at it and it looked good so I'd like to get it circulated around here before we send if off to Karen [Wagner].[20]

Three days later, Mitchner turned the draft in to Lawrence, referring to it as 'the Wagner manuscript'.

The marketing department's control was not incidental to the shaping and placing of the manuscript. In an email to Mitchner and the others, Lawrence wrote:

> As you know, we don't want to compromise the publication but we would like to wrap some PR [public relations] and CME [continuing medical education] around this data.[21]

Later in the same chain of emails, Christina Goetjen, one of Lawrence's colleagues at Forest and the product manager for the drug, suggested that they change the target journal. She wanted to take quick commercial advantage of this and other studies:

> I think it no longer makes sense for us to be looking at JAMA [Journal of the American Medical Association] as our publication of choice for PED [paediatric] data as the timing and policies restrict us from 'making hay while the sun shines'.[22]

During the trial there was a packaging problem, and nine of the subjects were able to see that they were taking citalopram, rather than the placebo. Jureidini and colleagues, examining the document trail, argue that, according to the study protocol, the nine subjects who received unblinded versions of the drugs should have been excluded from the analysis. Indeed, Forest ran the numbers without those nine, and the result fell just short of statistical significance, at which point eight of the subjects were added back into the analysis, improving the statistics enough to make the results significant – the problem was later hidden in the submission to the FDA, in a 'masterful stroke of euphemism'.[23] The company and its communications agency made various other small late decisions to ensure that the results would look favourable. In particular, they decided not to publish the secondary outcomes. Here is Mary Prescott at Weber Shandwick Communications:

> I've heard through the grapevine that not all the data look as great as the primary outcome data. For these reasons (speed and greater control) I think it makes sense to prepare a draft in-house that can then be provided to Karen Wagner (or whomever) for review and comments.

A number of months later, Forest's Dr Heydorn wrote:

> The publications committee discussed target journals, and recommended that the paper be submitted to the American Journal of Psychiatry as a Brief Report. The rationale for this was the following: ... As a Brief Report, we feel

we can avoid mentioning the lack of statistically significant positive effects at week 8 or study termination for secondary endpoints.[24]

And, of course, the eventual published article in the *American Journal of Psychiatry* did not draw attention to the serious adverse events suffered by participants in the trial.[25] The decisions were crafted so as to make the resulting article as straightforwardly positive as possible, with at least most of them being justifiable in terms of one or another opportunistically chosen norm. The courts will decide whether Forest's amount of spin in this trial exceeded the limits of ordinary scientific reporting.

CONCLUSIONS

Why should we care about the pharmaceutical industry's ghost management of medical publications? The most common answer focuses on the possibility of fraud – or at least untruths – and that people might be harmed as a result. Philosopher Leemon McHenry argues that '[i]f the results of industry-sponsored clinical trials were reported honestly, then aside from the question of deception and plagiarism, ghostwriting would not present a serious concern for advancing knowledge.'[26]

Pharmaceutical companies and others defending themselves against accusations of ghostwriting often also try to make the issue about honesty and truth. In a statement for a news story about Wyeth's ghost-managed hormone therapy work, Pfizer (which bought Wyeth) wrote of industry critic Adriane Fugh-Berman, 'Even with her critical perspective, she could not establish that there were inaccuracies in any of the peer-reviewed articles'. Defending two researchers accused of serving as authors on a ghostwritten editorial, a University of Pennsylvania spokeswoman insisted that the editorial 'notes conclusions that remain widely accepted today'. Trying to stake out the very highest ground, a founder of one MECC writes of a ghostwritten textbook in psychiatry:

the effort to produce this handbook led to a good quality project and everybody wins. The psychiatrists assure the quality, and they enhance their visibility and reputations. The writers improve clarity. The readers get good information. ... For all we know, the book could have saved thousands of lives.[27]

While I don't want to dismiss concerns about fraud and truth, I think that a singular focus on these concerns is the wrong approach.

Scientific knowledge is the result of much hard work: work in the lab or the field, analytic and conceptual work, work to get attention, work to convince other scientists, and much more. There is no easy and direct path from nature to knowledge of nature; if there were, then we could bypass the work. No method identifies truths with certainty; if it did, there would be a lot less disagreement in science.

We can assume that the same types of factors are at play in the production of truth as in the production of falsity. Since ideology, idiosyncrasy, interests and the like are routinely invoked to explain beliefs thought to be false, they should also be invoked to explain beliefs thought true. This is a kind of symmetry.[28] Symmetry suggests that good and bad science are alike in the fact of being shaped by interests, or that good and bad science are alike in the fact of being laden with choices.

However, commercially driven science is different from academic science in the *kinds* of interests that drive it, and the *kinds* of choices it contains. Commercial funding and control affect a myriad of legitimate choices in the design, implementation, analysis, description, and publication of clinical trials. We can reasonably expect, and there is abundant evidence, that the industry makes those choices to support its interests. The good science, and not just the bad science, supports pharma's interests.

Ghost-managed work succeeds by being of apparent high quality. Publication planning firms claim high acceptance rates for the articles they submit to medical journals; high acceptance rates are very credible, though we should suspect that all individual claims are exaggerated. Industry-funded trials – most of which I would claim are ghost-managed to some extent – score as well as or better than independent trials on standardized methodological tests.[29] Moreover, when I observed publication planners, they appeared to be trying to be honest and to be striving for sound science, while serving the interests of drug companies' marketing departments. So, pharma's ghost-managed science looks like its counterparts, and even looks particularly clean and successful in comparison. The industry does not have a monopoly on fraud and misrepresentation – as can be seen by taking a quick look at the website *Retraction Watch*, which reports daily on problems in published scientific articles.[30] The industry sometimes gleefully latches onto instances of misconduct in which it isn't involved, or in which it isn't the perpetrator. At times, pharma even assumes the role of victim, as when it was revealed that Dr Scott Reuben faked the results of twenty-one trials, many of them funded by the drug company Pfizer.[31]

From the cases of pharmaceutical industry misrepresentation, we know that at least some of the time publication planners and the others with whom they work fail in or set aside their goals of honesty and sound science. But we should also be concerned about what happens the rest of the time.

Ghost management produces a publication bias that covertly advertises particular drugs, supports them scientifically, and sets agendas for diagnosis and treatment. All of this affects prescriptions. Agenda setting is particularly important, as it can dramatically increase the number of patients seen to have a given disorder, and can dramatically increase the number of patients seen to need treatment; as drug-taking populations increase, so will rates of side effects. To the extent that all the above are different effects from those of a non-commercial scientific literature, they probably harm patients – without requiring any misrepresentation of data.

In the ghost management of medical research by pharmaceutical companies, we have a novel model of science. This is corporate science, done by many unseen workers, performed for marketing purposes, and drawing its authority from traditional academic science. The high commercial stakes mean that all of the parties connected with this new science can find reasons or be induced to participate, support, and steadily normalize it. It is likely to be around for a while.

We might then ask the widely circulating joke, 'is medical science for sale?' 'No, its current owners are perfectly happy with it.'

4

HOSTS AND GUESTS
IN THE HAUNTED HOUSE

AT THE FIRST CONFERENCE OF PUBLICATION PLANNERS I ATTENDED, THERE was a debate about whether authors on articles should be allowed to see the data reported in those articles. Yes, a debate, with people arguing on both sides! The conference organizers had decided to create a panel that would help foster a discussion about publishing ethics. The panel included Dr Aubrey Blumsohn, a medical researcher who had become a whistle-blower, and the discussion ended up focusing on the issue of author access to data.

How did things get to this point?

MEDICAL JOURNALS OPEN THE DOOR

Where are medical journals in the process of ghost-managing articles? Surely, for their own credibility, the journals are doing what they can to keep ghosts out of the process?

Almost every conference for publication planners invites a few medical journal editors to sit on a panel, and occasionally invites a representative from a publisher of journals. At these meetings, the editors don't show any hostility toward publication planners. On the contrary, they claim to value the work done by planners and the manuscripts they provide. Dr Eaton, editor of a very highly regarded journal, insists, 'We love publishing pharma papers – if they're good.'

These editors have extensive dealings with planners, though usually through author intermediaries. Dr Edge, editor of a general medical journal, starts his presentation with a sales job. 'The journal has a circulation of 87,000, plus reaching millions through the web. ... We have an impact factor of 13.25, which places us fifth among all medical journals.'

Other editors make very similar statements. At a different publication planning meeting, editor Dr Eklund promotes his highly specialized journal:

> Some statistics. We got more publications [sic] than any other journal in the respiratory field, we get about 3,400 new submissions each year. ... It's hard to tell about circulation today because a lot of things is electronic so it was easy when it was just a print version. When it wasn't a print version we had the highest circulation of any respiratory, sleep or critical care journal in the world. ... The impact factor ... is one way that you can get some idea of the quality of what's published in the journal and the 43 journals that are listed in the ISI with the impact factor we were third last year we still don't know what the results are for this year. ... When you now look at something called the eigenvalue, which takes into account the self-citations of those journals that self-cite themselves a lot, when you adjust for that we are very close to being number one.

And here again is Dr Eaton, shortly afterwards:

> To say a little about [journal name]: It's a flagship journal in [the field]. Our closest competitors, well there is another one with a fairly high impact factor but not with nearly the circulation we have. ... We have a circulation about 24,000 and we were also one of the top 100 journals named by the special library association last year. And our impact factor is over 8 and that is very good.

There are obvious reasons why editors would want to tout their journals' statistics at publication planning conferences, and why they would jockey for position with their competitors and encourage submissions of pharma articles. Some of those articles report on well-funded clinical trials. Given that clinical trials are the most valued sources of medical information, we shouldn't be surprised when editor Edge announces that his journal is interested in attracting companies' clinical trial reports, and has instituted a new streaming system to allow his team to make quick decisions on whether to fast-track clinical trial articles. Articles reporting on clinical trials are likely to be highly read and cited, and of the most highly cited clinical trial articles published recently, the majority are funded by the pharmaceutical industry.[1]

A portion of these high levels of citation may stem from an interesting version of self-citation, characteristic of ghost-managed work.[2] A publication plan that involves fifty or a hundred articles provides many potential entries in its reference list. Later articles will almost certainly cite earlier ones, and all articles can cite ones from earlier publication plans. Describing an episode in her work as a medical writer, Marilynn Larkin writes:

> I agreed to do two reviews for a supplement to appear under the names of respected 'authors'. I was given an outline, references, and a list of drug-company approved phrases. I was asked to sign an agreement stating that I would not disclose anything about the project. I was pressured to rework my drafts to position the product more favourably.[3]

Presumably, the list of references Larkin was given was just as drug-company-approved as was the list of phrases – medical writers and publication planners describe the literature review as a key step in the development of an article. It would be curious if reference lists were *not* skewed toward the company's previous articles, because those articles support the company's commercial interests and because those would be the articles or references to hand.

But the reasons why journals welcome ghost-managed submissions go beyond high numbers of citations. Some journals allow companies to sponsor supplements on special topics, at prices that help to subsidize the journal as a whole. Individual articles can become a significant source of revenue for journals, because sales representatives take reprints to physicians' offices to back up their claims, and reprints can be distributed at conferences and in other ways. As I mentioned in Chapter 2, Merck bought 900,000 copies of an article reporting a large trial of Vioxx.[4] That number is an extreme outlier. However, when I asked the *New England Journal of Medicine* to quote a price on an order of 10,000 reprints of an eight-page article in black and white, they responded within hours (US$15,974 at the time). Clearly this kind of business represents a conflict of interest, but it's one that journals willingly accept.[5]

The editors at publication planning conferences make remarkably uniform statements. They want to protect scientific integrity, and their approach is to insist on performing clinical trials well, reporting those trials honestly, and following rules for writing and disclosing support. Theirs is a formal view of scientific publishing that doesn't distinguish between pharma-sponsored trials and other trials. As long as companies follow the 'rules' of science and of medical publishing, they are valued contributors.

When talking at planning conferences, many journal editors give a basic course in trial design and reporting – far too basic, considering that most of the audience members are experts in medical publications. Dr East, a senior editor at one of the very best known of all medical journals, gives a very simple overview of issues of integrity in publishing, in the context of providing a history of the journal's conflict of interest policy. Dr Ellis, an associate editor of a major journal, but here wearing her hat as a member of the Council of Science Editors, emphasizes procedural matters to do with disclosure and authorship. In a long presentation, Dr Eaton does the same, emphasizing the steps that she and some of her colleagues have taken to improve full disclosure of funding and assistance. Dr Edge advises, 'The way to get an article published easily, which is what our goal is and yours, is to avoid practices that are going to slow things up and slow the period of time before you can start enjoying the acclaim and the revenue that comes with successful publication in a big journal' – Edge clearly recognizes the monetary value of articles to drug companies.

If medical journals are hosts in the haunted house of pharmaceutical research, they are inviting the ghosts to the table, recognizing that they have valuable offerings. All that journals ask is that the ghosts follow rules of good conduct, so that they don't create too many disruptions.

PUBLISHERS SEE EYE TO EYE

If journals are willing to work with the industry, publishers are even more so. Mr Porter, the head of a publication planning firm, complains about mixed messages:

'From publishers we often get quite a strong sell, engagement and willingness to work with. And from editors we often get very much a hands-off and keep your distance'. Porter wishes that journals could iron out this difference, but he understands its origins: 'We understand and recognize that tension. To me it actually mirrors very closely the relationship between medical and marketing within the pharmaceutical industry. ... And it's about the relationship between commercial needs and the integrity of the science.' As we saw in the last chapter, publication planners handle this relationship to their satisfaction; perhaps they hope that journals can, too.

Mr Edwards, who is at this publication planning conference representing a publishing company that owns many journals, explains that if the journal 'clearly has affiliations with the industry then you may get a more lenient ride'. But independent journals – such as ones run by medical associations – tend to have higher circulation, prestige, and impact factors, and their editors tend to have more independence, which 'impacts their attitudes to the industry'. Here, and at a number of other points, Edwards aligned the publishing industry with the pharmaceutical industry, against the scientific editors who generally sit between the two.

In his talk, Edwards also stands up for editors; the diverse members of his panel were asked to list complaints, and he performs well, chiding his audience and eliciting laughter. Edwards is a young and articulate British executive, exuding London cool while talking to a somewhat more homespun, mostly US-based audience. He emphasizes that most editors are hard-working volunteers, and that they need to be treated well:

Stan at [major medical journal] had an industry author submit a couple of papers a few years ago now, to the journal. The journal put them out for peer review and the answer was, yeah, OK, it's in need of minor revisions but essentially it's publishable. So the comments went back to the author. No response. Never. Same author submitted a paper a month ago, and Stan said, 'So what's going on, then? What happened to those other papers we bothered to peer-review and sent back to you?' 'Oh those, yeah, well the company's downgraded the efforts on that product so we didn't bother continuing with the publication of those articles.' Well again, think. It's not exactly going to put you in a very good light when you want to continue to publish in that journal if you're taking all of that expertise in peer-review and just throwing it down the toilet.

Yet throughout Edwards's barrage, there is no doubt that he is on the side of the industry. He wants the business:

If you have a deadline, it's a really good idea to tell us about it, and tell us nice and early. If you have special requirements, like you need an ad or a logo, you need information about prescribing, information whatever it might be, again, tell us. Don't leave it until one day before we go to press before you start dropping this stuff on us.

In a promotional moment, Edwards mentions a new journal, an online, open-access, peer-reviewed journal, financed by payments from sponsors, that will publish negative or inconclusive data; its main criterion is that the study be well performed. 'This is a service to the pharmaceutical industry. You may have large quantities of data .... This is peer-review – light.' The journal is a medical version of the dead letters office, where unwanted results go so as not to be read.

Publishers are willing to think much bigger than individual articles. The publishing giant Elsevier produced an entire line of made-to-order medical journals in order to place articles marketing drugs.[6] The planning firm Excerpta Medica, at that time an arm of Elsevier, brokered the deals and provided the imprint for the journals; these included *The Australasian Journal of Bone and Joint Medicine* (*AJBJM*), produced to market two of Merck's drugs. Presumably, the articles placed in *AJBJM* were chosen for their commercially valuable messages. They were probably written with those messages in mind. The studies on which they are based were probably designed to maximize the chance of Merck-friendly results. Some of those studies may even have been performed only for their public relations value. This isn't an isolated event: Wiley, known best for publishing in the sciences, advertises on its website that it can produce 'custom books and journals' for the healthcare industry.[7] A bespoke journal can offer pharma companies an extremely efficient marketing vehicle.

LAYING DOWN THE RULES: WHO CAN BE AN AUTHOR?

Medical journals try to govern their relationship with pharma mostly by making authors responsible for the content of articles. In effect, that means trying to restrict authorship to those people who can be accountable.

There are different sets of criteria for authorship of medical papers, but the most important is that of the International Committee of Medical Journal Editors' (ICMJE), adopted by most journals. For the ICMJE, authors have to claim all of the following:

- Substantial contributions to the conception or design of the work; or the acquisition, analysis, or interpretation of data for the work; AND
- Drafting the work or revising it critically for important intellectual content; AND
- Final approval of the version to be published; AND
- Agreement to be accountable for all aspects of the work in ensuring that questions related to the accuracy or integrity of any part of the work are appropriately investigated and resolved.[8]

Versions of the first three requirements have long been in place. The ICMJE added the fourth in 2013, in direct response to concerns about ghostwriters and guest authors, though also about misconduct more generally.

The ICMJE definition tends to restrict authorship. The only people who qualify will have been involved in multiple stages of the research and writing of the article. The ICMJE recognizes fewer and more important authors, which probably reflects medicine's cultural preferences for how to assign credit. Restricting authorship poses some problems when it comes to large-scale medical research, however.

Clinical research is increasingly decentralized and complex, with teams distributing tasks widely. A large clinical trial, for example, may involve more than a hundred doctors who recruit and deal with subjects in sites around the globe. It may involve experts in statistics, pharmacology, multiple medical specializations and other fields. Even in fully independent research, the authors don't necessarily write the articles, because the task of mere writing may be left to more junior colleagues. So, there may be *nobody* who meets the criteria for authorship of articles stemming from a significant project. The ICMJE definition is an attempt to enforce traditional ideas of authorship, tying credit to intellectual and moral responsibility, but often there simply are no authors in any traditional sense.[9]

In response to some of these problems, though, some medical editors have tried to move in a very different direction. In the 1990s, there was a serious proposal to replace the notion of 'author' with that of 'contributor', whose precise contributions would be listed in something like film credits.[10] Rather than restricting authorship to a few, the proposal expands contributorship to many. This idea hasn't been taken up, though a few medical journals, such as *Neurology*, have defined authorship in an expansive way, requiring that everybody who makes substantial contributions to a manuscript be listed as an author.

Medical journals have difficulties addressing ghost-managed science. First, as I've already noted, the journals are conflicted because they want pharma's manuscripts, which they find valuable. Second, at the practical level, ghost management is by definition hidden. Efforts to ban it have to start by exposing it, perhaps by designing and implementing procedures that trace histories of manuscripts – all difficult tasks.[11]

While most editors speaking at publication planning meetings explicitly condemned ghostwriting, there was also some recognition of the medical writers' role in improving manuscripts. Here is Dr Ellis: 'We appreciate [professional writers] as editors because we have to read a lot of papers and we can tell which ones have had expert writers participate in their development.' She goes on to describe what *authors* need to do to make sure that medical writers don't become ghostwriters:

> An academic researcher needs to insist on early active involvement in the
> research project. They should decline any offers to sign off on already-written
> manuscripts, particularly in review articles. They should insist that the article

reflects their own interpretation of the evidence. They have to be adamant about full disclosure.

The burden, then, is placed on academic authors who, by implication, sometimes fail at one or more junctures. True, sometimes the authors are egregiously at fault: one editor, in a private conversation, told me that a major difficulty he was dealing with would have been prevented had the lead author even *read* the manuscript he had submitted.

Ideally, the journals want to apply their rules evenly. Editor Dr Eaton, whom I quoted above as saying that she loves publishing pharma papers, repeated the statement several months later: '[W]e really love to publish really nice clinical trials, we like that, we really want to. We just want to make sure that everything is as transparent as possible, full disclosure: we want to know who did it, who did what.' Similarly, Ellis is keen to keep the playing field even for pharma: 'All these comments about authors and sponsors apply regardless of the affiliation of the author or the sponsors. So the sponsor can be the NIH, it can be a private foundation, it can be a university, or it can be a pharma company.'

Despite her comments expressing her love of pharma papers, Eaton was the most critical of all the editors I heard, and she was even more critical when I interviewed her. She was also somewhat resigned. Until economic structures of medicine and medical research change, she thought, pharma will have a major presence in medical journals. To a publication planners' meeting at which she spoke she brought some clear cases of fraud, and she was quick to emphasize that they were recent – she was ready for the common industry response that ethical lapses were a thing of the past! In addition, Eaton recounted her own and her fellow editors' efforts to try to improve authorship criteria, to try to enforce them, and to try to establish full disclosure of the industry's involvement in publications – efforts such as the added ICMJE criterion. This last criterion, that authors agree 'to be accountable for all aspects of the work', is supposed to convince authors not to sign on if they haven't seen enough of the study and the data, to try to ensure that the people agreeing to be authors will have had access to the data. But this depends on the honour system, which is almost impossible to enforce.

CONJURING AUTHORS

The most prominent ethical concerns voiced in publication planners' conferences involve authorship. Publication planners have difficulties dealing with criteria for authorship, because their position involves coordinating work by people who they typically do not want to become authors, such as company statisticians, company and agency researchers, and medical writers. Perhaps a few company employees could meet authorship criteria, though it's more likely that no single person would, given the ICMJE's traditionalist concept of authorship. For example, publication planners and pharma companies do not give writers the authority to approve final manuscripts, so they fail to reach author status.[12] Research as managed by planners is therefore hard to fit into the ICMJE's criteria. Worse, it directly opposes the ethical stance implicit in those criteria.

Most authors on ghost-managed articles play limited roles. A flowchart drawn by a publication planner working in a major drug company puts decisions about authorship at the fourth step in the preparation of an article, after company employees have presented and discussed the data and its implications, established 'tactical plans' and identified the target journal.[13] However, planners want much or all of the important work behind an article to appear to have been done by its authors – or more precisely by key opinion leaders (KOLs) who happen to be authors.

As explained by Mr Edwards, a KOL is a well-known specialist, highly regarded by peers, who 'can influence other physicians' and who has experience with the product. In this way, a KOL is defined by being able to act as a mediator between companies and physicians. In practice, the term is only applied to people who are already enmeshed in relationships with pharmaceutical companies, not to fully independent specialists. KOLs are essential to the credibility of the manuscript, and so to the whole project of publication planning.

KOLs may have multiple reasons for agreeing to serve as authors on pharma manuscripts. On the basis of very little work, they add articles to their CVs, and those articles are likely to be more prominent and better cited than average. Although pharma companies don't pay for authorship, they often ask authors to give generously-paid presentations of, or related to, the research. (Payment to a KOL author contravenes guidelines of good publication practice, and a lawyer at one publication planning conference strongly cautioned against it, because it might be seen as a kickback, and as part of an attempt to manipulate prescribers.) Finally, it can be flattering to be considered an expert, and the manuscripts themselves may even contain more flattery, as this short excerpt from a legal deposition of a publication planner, discussing a ghost-managed review article, shows:

> Q. All right. So before Dr M. Brincat [the eventual author] saw the outline, Designwrite [the publication planning firm involved] had done the medical research, the literature research, to determine whether there was sufficient scientific evidence to support a scientific platform for this article. An outline was drafted and then [Designwrite] approached Brincat and Brincat agreed to be an author; is that correct?
>
> A. That is correct, because it mostly cited Dr Brincat's research.[14]

Planners often portray KOL authors as lazy and greedy. According to planners, they typically make few substantial contributions to the manuscripts they author, are slow to respond, and miss deadlines. They expect prominence in authorship order and sometimes demand money for their contribution. Authors even try to violate ethical practices, for example by trying to remove acknowledgement of medical writers.

Planners would like authors to make some contribution to manuscripts, for the sake of legitimacy, and to gesture toward good publication practice guidelines. However, authors need to be coaxed and coached. When an audience member asked, probably tongue-in-cheek, about deadbeat authors, planner Ms Pace recommended very specific questions as a way of eliciting a contribution:

> You can actually guide them to where you want feedback. So don't just say, 'Here's a first draft, and can I have your comment.' Say, 'Here's a first draft, and I've tried to figure out the methodology, to fit within the word requirement. However, I feel, could you pay some attention to this, and have I picked up the right point?'

Pace tries to create authors in the ICMJE sense (though adopting a broad inter-pretation of the criteria), by giving KOLs very specific writing responsibilities. In the extreme case, the author's complete non-contribution becomes a kind of contribution, agreement with and endorsement of the manuscript.

While planners complain about deadbeat authors, they create the conditions for those deadbeats. According to Mr Palmer's estimate, 50% of companies show only the penultimate manuscript to authors, to solicit their input. It's likely that authors have little to add to a well-crafted penultimate manuscript. Having nothing to add is especially likely if authors are given tight deadlines. They may see abstracts for conferences only after they have been submitted (and accepted) for meetings, and receive manuscripts only days before the planners' deadlines for journal submission. The orderly and efficient rollout of presentations and articles means that authors are likely to contribute little, and are a potential source of disorder.

Publication planners bristle at the term 'ghostwriter', and are quick to assert that medical writers are not ghostwriters.

> Now we often hear this term 'ghostwriting'. … My point is that we use this term sometimes indiscriminately, without understanding necessarily how it will be picked up by those other channels, particularly journalists and the media … In fact, ghostwriting and medical writing could not be more different. And that is the heart of my concern. So my plea is the very careful use of this term, since it has negative connotations, which really damage all of us involved in the process. (Mr Porter, the head of a large [220-person] publication planning firm)

Increasingly, to forestall potential criticism, medical writers are acknowledged on the final articles, credited with providing 'writing assistance'. To try to limit accusations of ghostwriting, publication planning associations have adopted codes of ethics. Although most planners think that this is a step in the right direction, not everybody is happy with the attention to ethical codes. At one conference, Dr Klein, a professor of medicine, opened his remarks by saying, 'My message to you is … stop with the integrity crap, OK, and *let's fight back.*

So I'm never coming back here if we have any more trust and integrity trust-athon events again.' What's wrong with integrity? It gets in the way of profitable interactions between physicians and industry.

Codes of ethics often serve to promote a kind of quasi-transparency. Here, for example, is a typical detailed acknowledgement section from a recent article, the first five authors on which are university faculty and the last three employees of the pharma company GSK:

> The authors thank all study participants and their families, all clinical study site personnel who contributed to the conduct of this trial, and the following coordinators/contributors: Dominique Descamps, Karin Schulze, and Pam Kalodimos. The authors also thank Monique Dodet for her precious input during the revision of the manuscript and Benedicte Brasseur for the management of the HPV serology testing. Authors would like to thank Business & Decision Life Sciences platform for writing, editorial assistance, and manuscript coordination, on behalf of GSK. Jonathan Ghesquière coordinated manuscript development and editorial support. The authors would also like to thank Sasi Taneja (GSK, India) and Carole Nadin (Fleetwith Ltd on behalf of GSK) for providing medical writing support.[15]

Descamps, Kalodimos, Dodet and Brasseur all work for GSK, in different offices around the world; Schulze works for the Swiss MECC Solutions for Life Sciences and Ghesquière for the Belgian CRO Business & Decision Life Sciences. Quasi-transparency here means that we don't know how much or how little input the academic authors had on the research and writing behind this article; but we *do* know that many people working directly or indirectly for GSK made substantial contributions.

The concept of ghostwriting often presumes the violation of old-fashioned norms of authorship. In the prototypical case, a single author's writing would be done by a single ghostwriter. However, medical writing is part of a larger process of the corporate production of knowledge. A vice-president of a large pharma company, addressing publication planners, reminded his audience: 'I am going to have my chance to say one final word to you, and that is, please remember [that] in the industry we work in a system which is like conveyor belt. Everybody has a section to do.' Articles are produced by teams, perhaps no one member of which meets requirements for authorship. In this largely unseen process, pharma companies initiate and fund the planning, research, analysis, writing and placing of articles, and typically maintain control of data throughout. In the corporate production of knowledge, medical writers perform their functions, just as planners, company scientists and statisticians do. Authors are there to give a sheen of legitimacy and independence to articles.

SHOULD AUTHORS HAVE ACCESS TO THE DATA?

Let's return to Dr Aubrey Blumsohn and the debate about access to data. Blumsohn, originally from South Africa but long ago relocated to the UK, is a bone metabolism expert with a broad smile, a slightly scruffy beard and an intense commitment to scientific ideals. The company Procter & Gamble (P&G) had asked Blumsohn's research unit to do new tests on some old samples, to determine whether, though trial evidence had suggested that its osteoporosis drug was less effective than competing drugs, the drugs might be equally effective in practice. The samples were blinded, so Blumsohn had no way of knowing which were from subjects on the drug at issue, or for how long those subjects had been on that drug.[16] He submitted his results to the company, and was shortly afterwards, along with his immediate superior, made an author on several conference presentations and three journal articles. The articles were put together by a writer, Mary, who had been hired by the company. Mary was introduced to Blumsohn and his superior, Dr Richard Eastell, in an email:

> Mary is based in New York and is very familiar with both the risedronate
> data and our key messages, in addition to being well clued up on competitor
> and general osteoporosis publications.[17]

Incidentally, the same email included information on other articles:

Mary and I have just finished writing a publication with [another researcher] (Richard you will be contacted as you're a co-author!) and Mary was involved at the very beginning and wrote from scratch.

Perhaps this was included to reassure the recipients that they wouldn't have to do much work on the publications.

Blumsohn, though, focused on the data, which looked odd: 'A key conclusion of all three papers was that there was [a] plateau at a commercially convenient point in the response relationship for the drug – a matter of practical clinical relevance.' When he asked to see the unblinded data, he was stonewalled:

They claimed that 'we don't need to ask an independent person to analyse the data just to make a few people happy'.[18]

The 'independent person' being referred to was Blumsohn, the primary researcher on the work and the intended first author on articles stemming from it. One article was published before his suspicions hardened. On the next article, he refused to sign the medical journal's author declaration forms; he would have had to attest that he had had full access to the data and took responsibility for the results. The result is that two more articles were not published. Meanwhile, P&G continued to deny him access to the data.

Unfortunately, Blumsohn lost his job for speaking publicly about his conflict with P&G and for accusing his immediate boss of fraud on behalf of the company. When he eventually saw the data, Blumsohn's suspicions were vindicated, as it turned out that the company had misleadingly focused on the most supportive portion of his results, truncating the analysis where it showed the drug to be ineffective.

Dr McGrath, a medical director at a pharma company (*not* P&G), was given the unenviable task of presenting the 'industry perspective' on the case. He worked for a direct competitor to P&G, but he nonetheless defended the company's position. Reading stiffly and religiously from the bullet points on his slides, McGrath drew this contrast:

In an ideal world, the data from the research studies would be available freely to everyone, and everyone would have the time and ability to analyse and write up the results accurately and effectively. No one would have a bias or an agenda, and everyone would agree on the results.

But in the real world almost everyone has an agenda, sometimes hidden. And not everyone is skilled at analysing or reporting the results of studies. Differences in interpretation can and do occur, and there are grey areas around such important things as authorship decisions, access to data, and accountability. We all enjoy scientific controversy from an intellectual standpoint. In particular, journals, academic authors and lay press benefit greatly. ... Anything that's newsworthy is considered a win by these participants, especially because it not only attracts attention but an opportunity for additional publications in the future.

Departing from his slides but still speaking carefully, McGrath then reminded the audience of how complicated the analysis of data is, and how individuals might misinterpret it:

I'm aware of cases where amateurs have tried to analyse databases and failed to match up IDs, for example, when they are merging variables from different places and you end up with complete garbage. You wouldn't be able to identify that if you weren't already familiar with the database. It puts the sponsor in a position where they have to go back and verify any analysis that is done outside, which is time-consuming and can result in disputes that are very very hard to resolve.

Finally, in a lovely piece of sceptical argumentation, McGrath pointed out that it's never clear what the data are. Are they the paper records of individual research subjects? Are they the computerized version of those records? Are they the spreadsheets? Or are they the cleaned and analysed spreadsheets? There is no one set of objects that must be 'the data'. Therefore, the request for investigators to have access to data is incoherent.[19]

At the time of this debate, the US lobbying group PhRMA had a clear policy that applied to its member companies, and McGrath drew attention to it: 'As the owners of the study database, the sponsors will decide who will have access to the database. ... PhRMA companies commit to making a summary of the results available to the investigators.' Revisions to that code published in 2009 state that '[i]nvestigators who are authors of study-related manuscripts will be given all study data needed to support the publication'.[20] However, the companies themselves can decide what data are – whether they are hand-written patient records, electronic versions of those records, already-analysed reports, or statistics based on them – and what access authors need to support the publication.

CONCLUSIONS

Medical researchers have normalized their relations to the industry to the extent that most prominent experts have substantial ties to it.[21] Publication planning takes this process several steps further. The *visible* experts who serve as the prominent authors on ghost-managed research stand in front of a number of other people who have likely done the bulk of the intellectual and organizational work to pro-duce the published knowledge. Visible experts are needed for their authority and independence, not for their actual expertise. In the commercialized science I've been describing, published research is valued for its marketing potential. Ghost-managed research does not merely shape academic cultures and the knowledge they produce but makes them unnecessary except to provide authority.

So, in the ghost management of articles, what are authors? They are shown well-crafted manuscripts that have been reviewed by many scientists, writers, and marketers. They are given only limited access to the data. They are asked for their views on very specific points. They are given short deadlines. For these and other reasons, authors on industry manuscripts are largely sidelined from the process of analysing, writing and publishing research. In these circumstances, authors are unlikely to make major contributions to the analysis or writing of an article.

In the ghost management of medical research, authors are valued for their authority and to obscure the work of others. The more hidden contributors to the research, analysis and written material are entirely capable of producing texts on their own, but without KOLs their work has much less value.

Just as medical research in general has normalized ties to the pharmaceutical industry, so has medical publishing. Journal editors can address an audience of 400 or more publication planners, warn them against ghostwriting and the inappropriate manipulation of data, and then solicit their business. At the same time, the planners are keenly attentive to scientific norms, because it is only by meeting these norms that they can distinguish themselves from marketers, and in so doing achieve their marketing goals. Theirs is the job of persuading without appearing to persuade, selling without appearing to sell.

Almost everybody systematically connected with publication planning wants to work with formal rules of conduct. As sub-contractors, publication planners would like to reduce uncertainty, so that they can produce exactly the papers that will satisfy all of the different parties with whom they interact. Both publication planners and pharmaceutical companies want formal rules to guide and cover their work, to legitimize it so that its exposure doesn't automatically become a scandal. When planners invoke ethics, it is as a defensible code within which work can go on, not as a substantive goal. Meanwhile, editors express the hope that a combination of authorship guidelines, standardized procedures for the performance and analysis of clinical trials, and standard formats for journal articles will control problems of bias; this is even though publication planning generally runs directly opposed to the goals behind those guidelines and standards. Regulatory agencies look to rules to govern the use of medical journal articles because there is an intrinsic conflict of interest in this arena, and these agencies are either not powerful enough to eliminate it or don't care to; the conflict of interest can only be managed.

Everybody recognizes that there is plenty of interpretive flexibility in any of the rules guiding good scientific publication or marketing conduct.[22] That may not matter – indeed, it may be attractive to some of the parties – because the rules are largely designed to insulate institutions and people from charges of unethical behaviour, rather to achieve objectively valuable science or ethical behaviour. Rules to govern good publication practices may enable trust by creating a kind of formal objectivity,[23] but the primary purpose of the rules is to enable plausible deniability.

When pharma companies, publication planners and others are confronted by cases of apparent ghostwriting, one of their standard refrains is to insist that ghostwriting is a thing of the past. For example, when one pharma company was contacted in 2010 for a news story about ghostwritten articles from the early 2000s, it declared that it had instituted policies that require authors to be involved throughout their writing. For the same news story, Dr Thomas Stossel of Harvard University, who frequently writes and presents pro-industry commentaries, claimed: 'This behaviour has happened, but arguably not often, and probably not recently.'[24]

After I published my first article on publication planning in 2007, the then-President of ISMPP penned a response, saying that my overall claims were out-of-date. He suggested that if I attended an ISMPP meeting I would have a completely different perspective. He did not know that I had taken him up in advance, and that what I took from the meeting, including some of the information I report here, perfectly confirmed what I had written earlier.[25]

My research associates and I attended publication planning meetings spanning 2007 and 2017. In terms of how publication planners present their activities, I didn't see any substantial difference during that time in terms of the practices being discussed. Yes, later presenters emphasized new codes of ethics, guidelines and operating procedures, but the core of their work has not changed over the course of this decade.

Even though standards are changing, the central conflict has never gone away. Companies want to maintain as much control as possible over the shape and content of publications, so that they can best market products. They also want the names of independent authors at the tops of those publications, to increase their credibility, again so that they can best market products. Industry control, however, is incompatible with independent authorship.

5

POSSESSION: MAKING AND MANAGING KEY OPINION LEADERS

THE QUINTESSENTIAL KOL

DR KESSEL, A SMILING, CLEAN-CUT PHYSICIAN AND PROFESSOR IN HIS FIFTIES, steps up to the podium. He is wearing what looks like a seersucker suit with a striped white and blue shirt and a yellow tie, a good outfit for very hot weather, as it is in Philadelphia on this summer day. Kessel, who was introduced as having authored over five hundred publications and being 'one of the brightest stars in neuroscience', gives his talk without PowerPoint, the first time he has done so in years, he says. A mishap that morning involving his cat and his laptop led him to scramble to assemble notes for this talk and one he will give later that afternoon to the same conference. Nonetheless, he is a confident speaker, comfortable providing his perspective to this audience, which is mostly made up of drug company managers. He is the representative key opinion leader (KOL) at a drug industry conference on how to manage relationships with people like himself.

After explaining how the cat lost his presentation, Dr Kessel discloses his conflicts of interest. This is a practiced move. With apparent pride, he announces: 'In the past decade, I have been a consultant to the manufacturer of every compound that has been developed for the treatment of depression or the treatment of bipolar disorder, and some number of other compounds that haven't made it through the multi phases stages of development.' Normally, he presents this as two slides. He adds a list of six drug companies that have paid him to give talks in the past three years, and lists another four that have recently funded research projects.

Dr Kessel is the quintessential high-level researcher KOL, a nationally recognized expert who is personable and a good public speaker. Kessel started his connection with the industry in the 1980s, doing dinner speaker programmes, and later giving promotional talks, serving on various advisory boards, and helping to run speaker training programmes. There are different kinds of KOLs, corresponding to the many uses drug companies have for them. Kessel's path to this point took him through all of the most common KOL roles.

In their efforts to capture the minds of doctors, drug companies often turn to KOLs. The abbreviation is standard within the industry, though they are also sometimes more modestly referred to as 'opinion leaders' or 'thought leaders'.

The idea of a KOL has a sociological pedigree, stemming most directly from the work of Columbia University sociologist Paul Lazarsfeld. After his study of political views and voting behaviour during the United States Presidential election of 1940, Lazarsfeld coined the term 'opinion leader' for somebody who was particularly influential in their networks and among their peers.[1] The concept and term were extended beyond politics and public affairs to other walks of life, including fashion, movies, and marketing more generally.[2]

Its application to medicine began in the early 1950s, when, funded by a grant from Pfizer, Lazarsfeld's student Elihu Katz and his co-workers studied the expansion of the prescribing of tetracycline. A decade later, the research was published as a well-regarded book, *Medical Innovation*,[3] which became important to social network theory. On the basis of the data they saw, Katz and his colleagues recommended that Pfizer make systematic use of opinion leaders, explained how the company should do it, and provided details of their recommendations in the researchers' report to Pfizer. Pfizer found the concept of opinion leaders so valuable that it paid the Columbia researchers to not publish the results in any medical journals, so that the company could get a small jump on its competitors. It wasn't long, though, before others in the industry picked up the idea and put it to work.[4] Although growth in the use of the idea was intermittent, KOLs are now a crucial part of pharma companies' marketing efforts. They are key parts of the process of placing information around a molecule to create a successful drug.

THE PHYSICIAN KOL

One industry analysis defines KOLs as

> Highly respected medical experts within their domain, by which their
> thoughts and actions have a greater (asymmetric) effect on their peers with
> regards to adopting a new idea, product or service. In other words, KOLs
> have a large impact on the diffusion of innovation.[5]

This definition reflects a relatively academic approach that descends from
the 1940s and 1950s sociological work on opinion leaders. Its author and his
company do different kinds of analyses, echoing Lazarsfeld's work, to identify
established and new KOLs who inhabit the centres of social networks.

But there also is a less academic approach. In an article on the importance
of engaging KOLs on their own terms, the medical education and communications company (MECC) Watermeadow Medical writes that the term is usually

> a convenient shorthand for those people – usually eminent, usually physi-
> cians – who we co-opt into our development and marketing strategies.[6]

KOLs are agents sent out by companies to convince doctors to prescribe particular products. This blunt definition is linked to a set of activities that not
only identify potential KOLs, but also plan and implement campaigns to use
them – to capture doctors' minds and change their behaviours.

I divide KOLs into two groups: those who are identified primarily as physicians and those who are identified primarily as researchers. Drug companies
and the agencies that work with them all have their own classifications of KOLs,
for their own purposes; mine captures one of the important divisions in almost
all of those classifications.

Today, drug companies generally hire physician KOLs only to give pre-
prepared talks to other doctors, usually in their own regions. Researcher KOLs,
in contrast, may be hired to give talks at conferences or continuing medical
education courses, to serve as consultants on clinical trials or advisory boards

for marketing or research, or to interact with companies by performing research and serving as authors on company manuscripts for publication in medical journals. In practice, these two groups are not fully distinct, and people move from one to another.

Speaker Bureaus

While the word 'key' before 'opinion leaders' might suggest that researcher KOLs are the model ones, there are many more physician KOLs and they are part of much larger industry programmes. The scale of the drug industry's use of physician KOLs is sometimes staggering. Companies typically run thousands of talks per year for each of the drugs they are heavily promoting. For example, in Australia, with its small population, disclosures from forty-two pharmaceutical companies showed that between 2011 and 2015 they were running a weekly average of over 600 events for more than 10,000 attendees. Food was provided at 90% of those events.[7]

Because of their scale, the conversation among people who plan speaker bureaus (or speaker's bureaus or speakers bureaus) is often about logistics: How can attendance be better recorded? How do competitors standardize speaker reimbursement? How can speakers be more efficiently reimbursed? Can paper records be eliminated in favour of electronic ones? For speaker bureau managers, volume is a problem, and for that reason they are interested in the software and hardware that can streamline their work.

Drug company manager Mr Mah, presenting at a KOL management conference, raises the spectre of a government investigation of a speaker programme: 'When you say "I need 700 to 1000 speakers in this activity", the questions [that are] going to get pushed back to you in investigations are, "Why do you need so many? How many is each speaker going to do? Why did you need a thousand?"' With so many speakers, Mr Mah muses, government investigators might conclude that speakers' fees are bribes to prescribe.

Of course, the core goal of speaker programmes is to help companies reach doctors. The companies send KOLs to get messages into doctors' brains and prescribing habits into their hands. Mr McDonald, a KOL management agency executive, makes this clear: 'What's really important there [in speaker programmes, medical symposia, etc.] is promotional effectiveness. It's the ability to say, "How have we engaged that audience, are they better prepared?"'

But prepared for what? Kimberly Elliott, a former drug company sales representative, says, 'Key opinion leaders were salespeople for us, and we would routinely measure the return on our investment, by tracking prescriptions before and after their presentations. ... If that speaker didn't make the impact the company was looking for, then you wouldn't invite them back.'[8] Measuring sales before and after KOL talks and other events is common enough that industry insiders recognize that it may be risky since it may reveal the monetary stakes behind KOLs. Concerned about government scrutiny, pharma manager Mr Matthias warns: 'This thought that you have a key opinion leader engagement with a group of doctors, and you measure sales before and after the engagement, that's perhaps not the appropriate way to proceed.' KOL speaking events have to appear to serve an educational purpose.

Typically, physician KOLs are nominated by sales representatives, who have a sense of their abilities. Sales reps will know what 'their stage presence' is, suggests Ms Legrand, a legal and regulatory compliance expert, or that 'he looks good in a tie' – though this latter is not an acceptable recommendation, she quickly interjects, because good looks aren't connected to educational potential.

In an essay in the *New York Times*, psychiatrist Dr Daniel Carlat describes his invitation into the ranks of KOLs:

> On a blustery fall New England day in 2001, a friendly representative from Wyeth Pharmaceuticals came into my office in Newburyport, Mass., and made me an offer I found hard to refuse. He asked me if I'd like to give talks to other doctors about using Effexor XR for treating depression. He told me that I would go around to doctors' offices during lunchtime and talk about some of the features of Effexor. It would be pretty easy. Wyeth would provide a set of slides and even pay for me to attend a speaker's training session, and he quickly floated some numbers. I would be paid $500 for one-hour 'Lunch and Learn' talks at local doctors' offices, or $750 if I had to drive an hour. I would be flown to New York for a 'faculty-development program', where I

would be pampered in a Midtown hotel for two nights and would be paid an additional 'honorarium'.[9]

When sales reps make KOL nominations, companies are hiring their customers, creating the potential for conflicts of interest. Sales reps might be trying to reward good customers by giving them speaking contracts, regardless of how convincing those speakers are to other doctors. For this reason, most companies vet nominated KOLs through their marketing and their medical departments – with no input from sales, insists legal expert Ms Legrand. Despite the professed checks, the companies still seem to see value in having customers who are speakers.

As Carlat tells us, a KOL programme begins with a training session, to ensure that the speaker is well versed in the positive aspects of the product, and able to speak about it effectively. The training allows KOLs to speak with conviction and to answer questions from their audiences. Dr Koch, a psychiatrist earning more than $100,000 per year giving talks for the drug industry, explains in an interview,

> Usually, [speaker training sessions] are two- to three-day meetings where you're sort of in meetings from about 8 o'clock in the morning to about 5 o'clock at night for a few days where you're learning about the clinical research, the FDA approval process for the medicine, get a chance to speak with some of the people that were involved in the original research, and sort of try to become more educated about the details.

After physician KOLs have been trained, they become part of a speaker bureau for a company, and wait to be offered opportunities. They may give talks in a variety of settings, but the most common are to doctors in clinics or at dinner events; more occasionally they will be asked to give a talk to a community group. In most of these cases, the talks are arranged by sales representatives. Transportation is booked, the time and place are set, invitations are sent and resent, and the equipment is set up and the food laid out. All the KOL has to do is deliver the presentation.

Not much training is needed to make the presentations themselves, because physician KOLs aren't permitted to adjust the pre-packaged PowerPoint slides, or to deviate from their scripts. As Dr King reports, 'So if I am doing a promotional programme for a company, I have to use the slide deck that they provide me – I am not allowed to alter it in any way and every word in that slide deck is basically reviewed by their own internal counsel.'

In addition to the slides and the scripts, answers to standard questions are also scripted, and speakers are trained not to answer questions in ways that might either be illegal or run against company interests. Dr Khan warns, 'When you're out there actually doing a talk, you really have to follow those rules to a T. If you don't follow those rules then … you're at risk of, you know, breaking procedure and I mean arguably I guess you're at risk of breaking the law.' The presentations are fully ghost-managed.

Talking about her experience as a sales representative working with KOLs, Elliott says, 'I would give them all the information that I wanted them to talk about. I would give them the slides. They would go through specific training programmes on what to say, what not to say, how to answer to specific questions, so that it would be beneficial to my company'.[10] These KOLs really are possessed, inhabited by the spirits of the companies they're speaking for, like the original zombies of Haitian folklore.

Firms that identify and work with KOLs might even create training sessions to make those KOLs more effective. For example, Wave Healthcare claims on its website:

> It's vital that advocates are able to communicate and influence colleagues
> with clarity and conviction. To ensure speakers are at the top of their game,
> we have developed a communication skills programme for clinicians.[11]

Another firm, KnowledgePoint360, which owns Physicians World Speaker Bureau, offers programmes for training speakers, and its promotional material appears to treat KOLs and employees in the same terms: 'Whether it is for external resources, such as speakers, or internal staff, including sales representatives and medical science liaisons, a robust training programme is critical to the long-term success of any pharmaceutical, biotech, or medical device company.'[12]

KOLs can be very effective salespeople. According to a Merck study, the return on investment from KOL-led meetings with physicians was almost double the return on meetings led by sales reps.[13] Physician KOLs make excellent mediators between drug companies and physicians.

One of the reasons that KOLs are so effective, even given the striking extent to which they are constrained, is that they serve as models for others to emulate, in addition to sharing information. When they speak, they generally not only communicate trial results, but also that they are acting on those results. Their audiences don't have to translate the data into action, because the KOLs have already implicitly shown how to do that.[14] As long as the KOLs can be presumed to be good and responsible physicians, they model the behaviour that pharma companies want to encourage.

Pushing the Boundaries

Some doctors who attend training sessions may not only be budding KOLs, but also targets, convinced to prescribe because of the excellent advertising provided in the training.[15] This fits with claims made by sales representatives that one of the goals of a speaker programme is increased prescriptions *by the speaker*. Former sales representative Shahram Ahari writes that,

> [a]s a rep, I was always in pursuit of friendly 'thought leaders' to groom for the speaking circuit. Once selected, a physician would give lectures around the district. ... The main target of these gatherings is the speaker, whose appreciation may be reflected in increase prescribing of a company's products.[16]

Sometimes, interactions with KOLs and their audiences cross the line into illegality. The US Department of Justice has accused the company Novartis of running 'sham' speaker sessions for some hypertension and diabetes drugs, where the goal was more to wine and dine doctors, perhaps including the speakers, than to educate them. In 2017, the company was ordered to turn over records for 79,200 events, including for dinners costing many hundreds of dollars per person – and in a few cases thousands of dollars, as in a $9750 dinner for three at the famous restaurant Nobu in Dallas in 2005.[17] The events included dinners and drinks at restaurants unlikely to be among the best venues for standard medical education, like Hooters, known for its revealingly dressed young female servers. The lawsuit claims that at many occasions it was 'virtually impossible for any presentation to be made, such as on fishing trips off the Florida coast'.[18] The events even included multiple dinners where the same group of doctors would meet repeatedly to hear the same speaker give the same presentation!

A few companies may have hired speakers in direct trade for prescriptions. In a legal case against Insys Therapeutics, maker of the fentanyl product Subsys, former sales rep Tracy Krane describes an early 'ride-along' training session with the company's director of sales, Alec Burlakoff. Burlakoff told Krane

> that the real target was not the audience but the speaker himself, who would keep getting paid to do programs if and only if he showed loyalty to Subsys. It was a quid pro quo or, as the Department of Justice later called it, a kickback. 'He boiled it right down', Krane recalled: We pay doctors to write scripts. That's what the speaker program is.[19]

Although speaker bureau events are sometimes shams, and are sometimes held over good dinners in fine restaurants, 'gone are the days of all-expenses-paid trips to the Dead Sea, complete with sumptuous banquets, luxurious Bedouin tents and belly dancers'.[20] Just to be clear, the banquets, Bedouin tents and belly dancers are not embellishments, but were features of actual educational events. There was a period, peaking in the late 1990s, when no extravagance – and no level of crassness – was unthinkable where blockbuster drugs were concerned.

KOLs today draw contrasts to those bad old days: 'In the past there was so much excess spending on doctors that it was repugnant – people thought it was unethical', says Dr Kramer. But for some doctors, like Dr Koren, the pendulum may now have swung back too far:

So I do agree that in the past it was a little excessive and there was probably too much influence in a negative way but now I think it's the other way around – it's stifling innovations and when I meet, you know, I'll be honest, when I meet doctors who refuse to attend any promotional events they honestly are usually the ones that are the least educated about products in our field.

Younger KOLs manage to both regret and respect the changes:

I've never had the opportunity to go to a Chicago Bulls game or you know being taken on a trip or anything of that sort. ... I know that's happened in the past where um ... they would come up with these kind of bogus reasons then pay for entertainment or whatever. ... I think there's really no place for that in our profession. (Dr Khan)

Since new regulations have reined in pharmaceutical companies' efforts to influence practitioners and researchers through generous and frequent gifts, lavish travel and more, those companies' current efforts through more transparent or more subtle mechanisms seem relatively innocent.

THE RESEARCHER KOL
Establishing Relationships

Drug companies identify most of their researcher KOLs quite differently. Because the companies want larger and larger numbers of KOLs, independent firms have arisen that specialize in identifying and managing relationships with them. There are dozens of companies that identify, map the influence of, recruit, and manage KOLs internationally; many more focus on national or regional markets. A major example of such a firm is Thought Leader Select, which advertises multiple services for identifying, mapping, and planning engagement with KOLs, including 'Thought Leader ID, Thought Leader Impact, Thought Leader Engage'.[21] Other companies describe overlapping services and skills. Some tout their sophisticated use of social network analytics, citation analysis and other scientometric tools.[22] Others focus on KOL relationship management, and have proprietary software systems for planning and tracking interactions. KOLs are key to successful pharmaceutical marketing, so all of the work of engaging and engaging with them makes for a sizeable amount of business.

Research is highly valued in medicine. Therefore, many doctors enjoy and seek elevated status by participating in research. Being a physician KOL can develop into becoming a researcher KOL: 'Anything that, you know, puts you in front of people gives you the opportunity to enhance your professional status' says Dr Kourakis, a physician KOL with a research profile. Some research KOLs are developed through years of interactions. For example, Dr Kessel, with whom I introduced this chapter, spent many years giving promotional talks, speaking from company slide sets. As he became established as a researcher, he continued to give talks for drug companies, but they were generally scientific talks. He gradually changed from a well-connected and thoughtful physician presenting other people's data, to a research scientist presenting his own. Physician KOLs can graduate. All along the way, they are helped along in their increasing influence by the platforms, networks, and resources their sponsors offer them. But by the time they are researcher KOLs, they have also established their own reputations. They have attained a certain amount of independence from individual drug companies, because their own status is in demand.

Medical presentations in universities usually begin with speakers making statements about their conflicts of interest. Sometimes, those conflicts number into the dozens. A medical researcher told me that while people outside medicine – like me – would look askance at a presenter with a large number of conflicts, a standard thought inside medicine is: 'I wish I were like him.'[23] Drug company connections represent money, status, perks and upward-looking careers. Through these connections, physicians and medical researchers can become 'players' in their areas. Conflicts of interest, for many in medicine, can be disclosed, handled and used.

So, for researcher KOLs, relationships with drug companies offer more than payments for advising and speaking. Most prominently, the companies offer research support to their more valuable contacts. Sometimes this comes from companies proposing trials that they want done, and offering research roles and expected authorship. As we saw in the previous chapters, KOLs may even be offered authorship on ghost-managed company manuscripts, another relationship that serves both sides handsomely. Because of the commercial importance of having the right sort of author, publication planners find KOLs willing to put their names at the top of articles. This allows planners to make it seem as if the articles are by independent researchers, instead of by coordinated corporate teams. KOL authorship increases the perceived credibility of an article and also functions to hide features of the research process.

Relationships are built over time, beginning with the early stages of development of a new product. As their names suggest, advisory boards and consultancies allow companies to benefit from outside expertise: consultants and advisory boards help develop R&D plans as well as marketing plans. But they also allow companies to pay physicians, and to develop relationships with them. According to John Mack of *Pharma Marketing News*, 'Pharmaceutical companies view KOL advisory boards as the first and most influential activity in thought leader development' in the context of a plan for a new product, and 'Companies that assemble KOL advisory boards early in the product development phase stand to benefit by forging long-term ties with these experts'.[24]

Overall, enrolling allies is a more important function of advisory boards than is collecting advice. A pharma industry consultant, Mr Lange, explains the function of advisory boards through a story:

> One of the things with a couple of investigations and ad [advisory] boards in particular is they have the ad board, it's got a great agenda, the minutes are taken, and nothing happens. They ask, what did you do with the minutes of the meeting? Around here somewhere. We looked in the file cabinet, found them later on, blew the dust off, nothing is ever done. Then they run the same ad board again, [pause] and again. And they run it on a quarterly basis and then they run it on both a regional and national level and same results happen with the results. They're in the file cabinet.

Or they may not even be in the file cabinet. A former sales representative describes how she would promote drugs by hiring physicians to serve as consultants, asking them to provide expert advice on marketing presentations:

> At times, attendees were paid an 'honorarium' to act as marketing consultants and just 'listen, give feedback and fill out a piece of paper'. This information was thrown away when the checks were handed out.[25]

We can see another hint of advisory boards' role in developing allies in a warning from the European industry compliance expert Ms Linder, explaining the risk that payments to sit on advisory boards might be seen as payments to prescribe:

> There's got to be a legitimate [need] for the services. Where we have issues, it may well be that there are too many advisory boards. You don't need 30 advisory boards when you're looking at a particular part of a new product, perhaps. Or perhaps there might be reasons as to why you need that many, but you need to be able to justify it. It's always useful to prepare your defence before you go down this path, I think. And certainly if you're involved with key opinion leaders.

We saw the danger Linder is concerned about earlier in this chapter, in the form of criminal charges against Insys Therapeutics and Novartis.

Spreading the Word

Like their physician counterparts, researcher KOLs are used to influence physicians and researchers. They are paid to speak. They are paid to deliver continuing medical education courses, to give talks to specialists and other important physician groups, and to present at workshops and conferences – and even sessions for other KOLs. For these important talks, the honoraria are $2500 or more,[26] as opposed to the $500 to $1000 paid to most physician KOLs for their presentations. According to industry analysts, drug companies spend 15-25% of their marketing budget on speaking events.[27] 'Sunshine' laws in the US and Europe require drug companies to publicly reveal how much they pay to physicians.[28] Earlier reports, on the basis of legal settlements and earlier versions of these laws, show that some physicians can make huge sums of money: they can earn amounts up to several hundred thousand dollars in speaking fees in a single year.

A number of governments are in the process of regulating payments to physicians, lowering payments to the level of 'fair market value', however difficult that is to assess. Fair market value is a constant topic of discussion at industry conferences on KOLs, and there are entire industry reports devoted to it.[29] The topic is important not because companies want to pay less – quite the opposite – but because they want to avoid legally dubious payments that might be seen as inappropriate influence or even bribes.

Although researcher KOLs do not engage in the direct sales/promotion activities of their local counterparts, they influence prescribing both directly and indirectly. According to InsiteResearch, 70% of the US specialists writing the most prescriptions were 'directly or indirectly related' to the top five opinion leaders in that specialty.[30] Promotional and educational material may also be built on research or studies executed or authored by KOLs. And, of course, KOLs can influence physicians with whom they are not already related, both by speaking to them directly, and also by affecting the medical knowledge landscape in their areas.

Continuing Medical Education

Although many physicians treat all talks by KOLs – whether explicitly promotional or not – as educational, in most places a formal level of continuing medical education (CME) exists in the form of small courses that physicians must take to maintain their accreditation. CME is supposed to be independent of corporate interests – so industry sponsors are not allowed to control the course content. For pharmaceutical companies, this is the best kind of marketing: directed at receptive audiences that need to educate themselves, and provided by sources the audiences have reasons to trust.

The independent agencies that run most of these courses are typically allowed to provide administrative support, pay for speakers, help speakers prepare their talks, and provide entertainment for participants. In 2012, commercial support for CME (including advertising and related income) in the US accounted for roughly 40% of income for accredited CME providers (a considerable reduction from a few years earlier).[31]

Accredited CME providers are subject to regulation, the most important aspect of which is that sponsors such as pharma companies may not control the content of courses. In the US and Canada, though, pharma companies can provide funding for CME, help organize the courses, pay for KOL speakers, help them prepare their talks, and provide entertainment for participants. In some cases, even fully independent bodies may invite pharma companies to influence content: for example, one letter by a Canadian medical association soliciting funds for a CME conference stated that 'major sponsors will be given the opportunity to nominate participants to represent the industry's interest and to participate actively in the conference'.[32] In theory, though, the company must allow speakers complete freedom when it comes to the actual content.

For pharmaceutical companies, it is only a modest challenge to align KOLs with their own interests when it comes to CME. If providing logistical, scientific and financial support is not enough, companies have further methods of orchestrating CMEs indirectly. If the sponsors have chosen their speakers well, supported the research of these speakers, and given them templates and slides for their talks, the courses will convey the preferred messages.

The companies attempt to carefully manage their KOLs, their promotional talks, and their contributions to CME. At the very least, those talks tend to strongly endorse the sponsors' products. As one medical education and communication company advertised: 'Medical education is a powerful tool that can deliver your message to key audiences, and get those audiences to take action that benefits your product'.[33] Both promotional and CME talks, then, are part of pharmaceutical companies' promotional campaigns. Any education their talks provide and any health benefits that result from them have to be understood as shaped by the sponsoring companies' interests. According to an industry education specialist, the ideal for CME is 'control – leaving nothing to chance'.[34]

Facilitating Regulation

KOLs can smooth the path to acceptance of diseases and drugs. Jennifer Fishman describes how researchers on female sexual dysfunction acted as mediators between pharmaceutical companies, the US Food and Drug Administration (FDA), physicians, and potential consumers. For example, in 2001, researchers ran a consensus conference on 'Androgen Deficiency in Women', designed to establish the definition of and diagnostic criteria for this developing disorder. The conference was paired with a CME course, to communicate the issues more broadly.[35]

The 'Androgen Deficiency in Women' conference was supported by grants from several companies that were developing testosterone products for women, and was important to the prospects for success of these products, because the FDA only approves drugs that treat established medical disorders. The conference's consensus document, then, was a key step in establishing the regulatory legitimacy of female sexual dysfunction in the form of 'female androgen insufficiency syndrome'. In addition to looking at documents, the FDA turns to researchers like the conference organizers and participants in order to judge the documents: these KOLs have the expertise to contribute to the agency's decisions.

Generalizing the above points, the firm InsiteResearch claims:

> Interacting with qualified investigators, physicians experienced in regulatory reviews, well-known and respected speakers, and highly published authors will help to efficiently manage tasks within the critical path of the product and disseminate the message of the product to the end prescribing audience.[36]

The companies draw on KOLs' influence in a broad variety of contexts, and also put them in better positions to have that influence, making them better KOLs. A director of medical science liaisons for a small drug company, Ms. Mandel, lists the functions and 'touch points' for high-level KOLs in her company: 'advisory boards and scientific summits, internal training, consultants, publications, media activities, speaking at local and national meetings, congresses, peer-to-peer communications, patient communications and education, and policy, advocacy and social media activity'. In this company, KOLs are asked to serve in a wide range of important outreach roles.

MANAGING KOLS

Ms Monroe, a senior manager of medical science liaisons (MSLs) at a mid-sized drug company, emphasizes that MSLs must have goals in all of their interactions with KOLs:

> When you go in, that might be your goal, your objective, is to just continue to develop that relationship. And that's OK. It's just that at some point you need to expand on that goal. … At the end of the day we do want something from them. … We have needs that need to be met by KOLs, on the medical affairs side.

Ideally, interactions between MSLs and a KOL should be part of a general 'KOL management' plan. That said, those people in charge of KOL management recognize that that term suggests a one-sided relationship and might suggest that the primary use of KOLs is to market products. Even though the goal of managing KOLs is to make scientific knowledge about products and diseases more widespread, and thereby to market products, the people who engage with KOLs tend to be committed – in their public statements – to an ideal on which KOLs are independent. KOLs are typically portrayed as communicating scientific information. For example, Ms Mathis, who works for a large company, explains:

> Particular [sic] as you start to enter Phase I, Phase II, and you know these molecules are moving along, it looks to have some promise, okay there are unique aspects perhaps about the mechanism of action, it's going to be very important to help start to educate the community, the physician community, the patient community, the professional societies on this mechanism of action on the disease state itself.

Let's return to Dr Kessel. In one of his talks as a representative KOL, he described how he once saw, inadvertently, an 'individual management plan' tailored for him, which was normally kept under lock and key within the company. It included such entries as 'so-and-so will meet with him on such-and-such a date with this expected result, and then we'll invite him to do this'. Needless to say, Kessel found this somewhat offensive. He objected to being managed, saying that he and his colleagues wanted to be treated as partners in the drug companies' work rather than as mere tools.

After Kessel told this story, the response from the audience was to look for another *term*, avoiding 'management'. A director of MSLs suggested 'opinion leader engagement'. Ms Laird, a consultant who had formerly worked for a large drug company, suggested that they talk not about managing KOLs, but about 'managing relationships with KOLs'. (At a similar juncture one year later, Ms Laird dropped the 'KOLs' in favour of 'stakeholders', wanting to incorporate KOL relations into larger company plans for stakeholder relations, including patient groups and others. However, Laird's model of stakeholder relations remained very similar to standard models of KOL relations.)

Mr Chaudhary, a senior marketing director for another major company, suggested that they think in terms of 'managing experiences'. Mr Maxwell, the head of Medical Affairs at a small company, sees KOLs as part of a broad 'coalition around a drug', a coalition that can also involve advocacy groups, non-profits, and other companies. Coalitions involve genuine collaboration, and Maxwell is right in this, because the relationships aren't merely unidirectional or unidimensional. The companies want to influence these influence leaders, but they also provide incentives to them and sometimes want to learn from them.

If the coalition metaphor works, then relationships with KOLs extend the company beyond its formal boundaries. This theme was echoed by other commentators on KOLs: Mr Marchese argued that building a KOL network is 'building an armamentarium of expertise' outside the company. Mr Chaudhary spoke of KOLs as part of companies' 'activation networks' for particular products. In this way of seeing them, KOLs are agents whose interests have been aligned with those of the companies, enabling an extension of action to new domains.[37]

Most of these people quickly fell back on the familiar, older term, as developing and implementing KOL management systems was a central topic of the meeting. And they never suggested that any *activities* needed changing.[38]

Though there may be efforts to move away from the instrumentalism of terms like 'KOL management', influential physicians and researchers are enough of a resource that, as I pointed out above, there are firms that provide lists of KOLs for drug company projects, design KOL management plans, integrate those plans with publication plans, and will even train KOLs in public speaking, so they will deliver more effective lectures. The term 'management' is exactly right, suggests InsiteResearch in an article for the magazine *Next Generation Pharmaceutical*. Drawing on a dictionary definition, the firm argues that management should involve 'handling, direction and control' – precisely what is needed to make KOLs effective.[39] It goes further, claiming that a holistic programme is one that 'incorporates the total spectrum of experts including advocates, non-advocates, or those which are neutral. It is best to engage as many experts as possible with various programme activities even if those activities are to neutralize a non-advocate.'

The distinction between non-advocates and advocates is a telling one. Mr Magyar, a director at a major medical device company, speaking to an audience of mostly pharmaceutical industry MSLs and managers, says:

> How often do you have an *anti*-opinion leader of clinical trials that get released, and you have an anti-opinion leader outfit that undermines the validity of the trial or its meaning or its relevance. You don't have any control really on the anti-opinion leader, you only control the opinion leader and it's a critical role.

He goes on to say that it's an enormous challenge to 'really cut off those anti-opinion leaders that are out there'. The term 'anti-opinion leaders' firmly shows that, for Magyar, the only real opinion leaders are the ones who can be in companies' control.

Magyar doesn't explain concretely how to 'cut off' non-advocates, but there are well-known cases; for example, Dr David Healy describes systematic efforts to challenge and silence critics of anti-depressants.[40] A company's control of opinion leaders can neutralize opponents and make sure that clinical trial results receive the company's preferred interpretation. John Virapen, a director of a large company's operations in Sweden in the 1980s, describes a quid pro quo arrangement with one opinion leader:

He was only activated if there was bad press about us and our products. Unexpected side effects, impure substances, ailing patients; that was bad press. He promptly wrote positive articles about us in medical journals – the medical fraternity was pacified and could continue to receive our reps unreservedly.[41]

The opinion leader was paid with a substantial cheque, hand-delivered to him when he was on a trip outside Sweden, so that no connections could be made between payments and his articles.

When done correctly, KOL management should spread knowledge and change opinions and prescribing habits. It should produce a good return on investment, although this is impossible to measure – a point much lamented by people who put together and work in MSL programmes.

To take a different look at the preceding two chapters, publication planning engages in another form of KOL management, though it is focused more on scientific content than relationships. It presents itself as being in the service of developing and disseminating scientific knowledge. Tongue in cheek, industry consultant Ms Lane asks her audience of publication planners: 'By the way, is anything you do ever used in a promotional context? Oh yeah!' On its website, Watermeadow Medical says that 'We'll ensure your products and markets are thoroughly prepared, supported by persuasive and professional communications.' Their services include 'developing all types of manuscripts, such as primary manuscripts, secondary manuscripts, review articles, letters, editorials and proceedings supplements, as well as abstracts and posters'.[42] All of these different marketing vehicles need KOLs.

Unlike their physician counterparts, independence is key for the status and effectiveness of researcher KOLs. Mr Leone, a consultant to the industry, asks a conference on KOL management, 'With key opinion leaders and thought leaders, what is the single most important asset you work with? Credibility.' These researchers are useful to the companies largely because they are not company employees. Presumably, a KOL who appears to be just an arm of the sales force will quickly lose status, and hence effectiveness, among his or her peers. Both the possessors and the possessed value the appearance of independence.

For this reason, part of KOL management is somewhat ghostly. The KOLs themselves probably do not see all of the ways in which they are managed by drug companies, because this management often happens through more subtle tools than money. They are engaged in ways that further their careers while also furthering company interests. Most of the time, that involves scientific research: performing it, communicating it, or taking credit for it.

When they give talks, KOLs contribute to the enormous influence that the pharmaceutical industry has on medical knowledge. The promotional talks and CME courses in which KOLs participate are thoroughly shaped by the interests of the companies that sponsor them. What is communicated will often be sound medical science, which is why KOLs are willing to communicate it; nevertheless, it will be science chosen to help sell a product.

JUSTIFICATION SCHEMES

As a whole, medicine is conflicted about its interactions with the pharmaceutical industry, and many individual physicians are also conflicted.[43] This conflict, though, doesn't deter KOLs from interacting with the industry in a range of ways, most of which involve presenting pharmaceutical companies' data, arguments, claims and views. What do they say about their interactions with industry? How do they rationalize those interactions? What makes exchanges with companies acceptable or unacceptable to KOLs? Do they understand the extent to which they are being controlled? Do they care?

With questions like these in mind, I arranged for interviews with fourteen KOLs, all of whom had been paid more than $100,000 by different pharmaceutical companies in a single year. A research assistant, Zdenka Chloubova, who is much better at this than I am, did the interviews. Here, I focus on the most prominent things these KOLs said to justify and explain their positions.[44]

As it turned out, we didn't need to directly ask these KOLs how they justify their work with the industry. Once they started speaking, they all answered our questions without our having to ask them. In a similar study, the anthropologist Emily Martin interviewed sales representatives and marketers. Martin was interested in how her interview subjects reconcile their sense of their own personal integrity with an industry vilified as 'rapacious and profit hungry'. Exactly matching the experience with KOLs, she writes that '[n]early every person I interviewed spent considerable time, without much prompting, telling me what makes their work meaningful to them and why'.[45] Clearly, the problem looms large in the minds of many people working for or with the pharmaceutical industry.

Money

There is no question that money is a central reason why physicians give talks for pharmaceutical companies. However, Dr Kramer is one of the very few interviewed KOLs who openly admits it: 'Well, I enjoy doing promotional talks and I actually try to do education, but when it comes down to it it's really about earning extra money.'

One of the ways that highly paid KOLs downplay the role of the money is to acknowledge the income, but to emphasize how reasonable it is or how it fits into their lives. 'You know, my kids are grown up ... I use a lot of the income to support my parents', says Dr Kourakis. When payments come up, so do fairness and appropriateness; these KOLs want to deny that payments are anything other than what they seem. 'We're paid well. But we're paid I think fairly', suggests Dr King. Time spent giving talks replaces time in the clinic, and they all give the impression of being successful practitioners, so they expect to be appropriately reimbursed. Dr Khan spells out the fairness more fully:

> It would be ridiculous to say that the money was not relevant, of course the money was relevant. You know, I got paid very well to give these talks. But on the other hand, I think what I was paid for giving talks was absolutely fair market value when it comes to you know transportation to the talks, giving, transportation from the talks, taking time out of things that I was doing, you know like potentially seeing patients during the time, etcetera.

KOLs also sideline the role of the money they receive by mentioning the other rewards of giving talks. These include increased recognition or status, networking with other physicians, the possibility of gaining referrals to their practices, future opportunities for benefits from the companies for which they speak, learning about new products, being at the vanguard of their practices, and simply the enjoyment they get from speaking and teaching: 'The main reason was just, I really enjoyed [giving talks]', insists Dr Khan. For example, many note with pride their abilities as teachers or speakers, in the way that Dr Kramer remarks how flattering it is to have that recognized:

> So I got picked up as … a disease state educator and then everyone became so interested in my teaching ability that I became a promotional speaker and you might imagine, since you're doing this research, [the] promotional speaking thing really took off and now I have, every company that I know of is texting me to be a promotional speaker.

Being a KOL puts physicians in private practice at the apparent leading edge of medicine. Dr King communicates the excitement of this:

> So here I am in a room with you know maybe fifteen people where thirteen of them are all the guys whose papers I read or people who are doing cutting edge research in sleep and then me … who's in private practice. So that kind of opportunity to sit there with these really smart guys and learn from them and help me know more about sleep and help me be a better doctor to my patients which is one of the things that I really get a charge out of.

KOLs understand, though, that their work for pharmaceutical companies also creates a potential threat to their reputation and self-esteem. As a result of a sales rep asking an industry KOL to speak with a particular physician after a lunch talk, he found himself 'literally standing in the drug rep spot begging for a minute of this doctor's time, like a cocker spaniel begging for a leftover piece of meat from the table'. He promptly quit speaking for the industry.[46]

It's likely that most outsiders and many physicians would have a negative view of speaking for drug companies, at least when they think about it in the abstract. For Dr Kirk, 'the number one reason not to do a promotional talk is that it could possibly tarnish one's reputation ... if there's an appearance that my interest in earning money or in promoting a drug and being a sales person outweighs my clinical expertise'. Sunshine acts in Europe and the US are premised on questions about integrity. Dr Kane: 'So now my name ... is able to be published on the front page of the paper with how much money I made, you know, doing this many talks etcetera, etcetera. So it's a matter of public record ... making out the clinicians to be sort of selling their souls.'

As one might expect, KOLs are concerned about defending their integrity. They take affront at any suggestion that they might be less than independent, failing to present the truth as they see it, or doing anything else questionable. 'You're not just a paid monkey reading slides', insists Dr Kane. '[I won't] be a paid stooge for somebody', avows Dr Koren. Giving talks for companies 'doesn't mean you're a paid shill of the company', says Dr Kourakis. 'I'm not for sale', Dr King bluntly claims. And because of their concerns about integrity, they provide some public-spirited reasons for giving paid talks for the industry, mostly to do with educating other physicians and helping patients.

Providing Education and Promoting Health

The KOLs we interviewed take pride in their teaching, and teaching is how they frame even promotional talks. 'I am educating fellow physicians. I spend my day educating patients, I spend some of my evenings educating fellow physicians', explains Dr Kourakis. These KOLs all invoke education as a reason for speaking on behalf of companies, even when they are doing purely promotional speaking. They are divided about the value of promotional versus formal CME talks, but they always see themselves personally as engaged in important teaching.

With public institutions not providing much continuing education for doctors, Dr Kirk looks to pharma: 'I believe that the majority of funding [of] professional education is promotional which I think is not very helpful and really truly the thing that I think is the biggest flaw in promotional education is not that it's promotional, it's that you are limited to what's in the label.'

Dr Koch, though, finds promotional talks more educationally valuable precisely because they are more tightly regulated and focused:

> Based on my very direct experience, quite frankly, the CME lectures which
> everybody espouses as being appropriate interaction[s] ..., can be the most
> biased presentations of any you'll ever see given – and you don't ever trace
> back the funding for the CME group to the couple of companies giving the
> vast majority of the money to one of those speakers bureaus. So while CMEs
> are given a veneer of legitimacy they actually can be very dangerous to the
> public educational experience.

Dr Keith is much more critical of the industry, and especially of its role in promotional talks, though he gives them regularly. 'The reason for giving the promotional talks is to help the company sell its drug – I mean that's basically – that's
what a promotional talk is.' Dr Kramer echoes this point, but manages to find
educational value despite the problems. 'The honest answer is that promotional
talks are not really for educating so – and I give plenty of promotional talks – ...
but some speakers are better than others at bending it into an educational talk.'
Kramer is, as I mentioned above, the most forthright about speaking to earn
money. So, he is not exactly a cynic, though he is mercenary.

Very closely related to education is the presumed goal of improving health
outcomes for patients. Discussing his KOL work, Kourakis enthuses, 'Oh, it helps
other patients elsewhere, it's spreading the word – it's spreading the gospel.' It
is a particularly effective way to help patients, as King observes:

> It also gives you the ability to sort of extend your impact. I mean in the office,
> I may see 20 patients a day. But if I'm out at a talk and if I'm talking to 20 or
> 30 primary care docs and if I help them be better at treating a certain disease
> state then I've sort of extended my potential impact that way.

Integrity

The ability to portray their work in terms of education and helping patients
depends in part on KOLs' ability to counter charges that they are merely paid
company stooges. Almost every one of the KOLs interviewed said forcefully and
without prompting that they believe in the products they promote, proclaiming

their integrity and their independence from the companies and the payments they receive:

> If I don't believe the data, I won't do it. If I don't think the agent ... has a real role or a real niche, if it's not one I'm supportive of, then I don't do it. If I feel the drug company is pushing a sales pitch more than a proper therapeutic use, I won't do it.

For evidence, they point to their own prescribing patterns and habits:

> I believe in the product that I recommend and won't say anything that is untrue. Drug talks are a simple way to increase my visibility with my peers as well as earn a few extra dollars recommending a product that I routinely recommend to my patients multiple times a day.[47]

In extreme cases, evidence is even closer to home, as when Dr Kourakis says: 'My mother and father are on a lot of the drugs I speak for. I think they're terrific. So, I am not putting my parents on it because I am speaking for the company – it's the best drug'. And believing in the product can go as far as feeling strongly about its value. Dr King claims: 'I'd have to feel sort of passionately about it in order to do a good job as a speaker, and I don't want to be a speaker if I don't feel like I can do a good job for them.'

It should be said that a number of these physicians mentioned how at least a few *other* KOLs tied their own prescriptions to company perks, including speaking. In our interviews there were some half-dozen mentions of other physicians who demanded speaking engagements in exchange for prescribing a company's product, or sales representatives who offered speaking engagements in trade for those prescriptions.[48] But Dr Knapp speaks for all of his fellow interviewees when he says, 'the vast majority of doctors and pharmaceutical reps that I know are very ethical and really never did anything like that and certainly I was never party to anything like that.'

However, there are at least three ways in which KOLs' sense of their own integrity fails to address important political and epistemic issues to do with their work for pharmaceutical companies. First, the companies go to some lengths to gain control over the actions, habits, beliefs and loyalties of KOLs with whom they engage. KOLs are fully managed, and so is their sense of integrity. Indeed, KOLs' appearance of independence and integrity even helps the companies to achieve their goals. Second, even if those companies did almost nothing to co-opt KOLs, there would be lingering issues about conflict of interest: KOLs are often very well paid, and it's difficult to imagine that that wouldn't affect them. Third, pharmaceutical companies pay KOLs to be conduits of information. The companies' preferred KOLs are doing the circulation and the companies' preferred information is being circulated. The companies' enormous resources can disproportionately influence medicine.

CONCLUSIONS: CREATING KOLS

KOLs are recruited, trained, developed, engaged, and deployed by drug companies and their agents. Those companies' interests are almost always close by, at stake in every interaction. To their audiences, companies' interests are either partially obscured (in promotional talks) or entirely hidden (in ghost-managed CME and conference presentations, journal articles, and other kinds of actions) by the KOLs' mediations.

Successful physician KOLs don't need to be opinion leaders before beginning to work for drug companies. At this level, KOLs only need the ability to become good speakers, and the ability to maintain their status as insiders to physician communities while delivering presentations prepared by the companies. The idea of the opinion leader articulated by Paul Lazarsfeld and his students in the 1940s and 1950s is not actually very similar to the one enacted in drug companies' current practices. Whereas Lazarsfeld found opinion leaders in existing social networks, the drug industry creates KOLs for target audiences.

This difference is interesting, and to explore it further it's worth going back to the original Columbia University work on opinion leaders. Christophe Van den Bulte and Gary Lilien revisited the data set for the research that Pfizer paid for in the mid-1950s, research that introduced the idea of opinion leaders to the industry. Van den Bulte and Lilien argue that the study never actually provided strong support for the 'social contagion' model centred on opinion leaders.[49] Moreover, it failed to consider the effects of advertising. The Columbia researchers were already focused on opinion leadership, leading them to ignore the advertising and sales representatives who were promoting tetracycline. While Pfizer itself was not heavily advertising tetracycline, its competitor Lederle, which had been the first into the US market with the drug, was. Van den Bulte and Lilien introduce 'advertising volume' as a variable, and find that it had a significant effect. And once this variable is introduced, there is no significant social contagion effect in the data. It appears that US physicians started prescribing tetracycline in the early 1950s more because of advertising than because influential members of their social networks were prescribing it.

This reanalysis suggests something interesting. Drug marketers picked up the work's central term, 'opinion leaders', and perhaps more. The industry's development of a whole set of practices around opinion leaders, then, starts from a piece of research that showed only weak influence of medical opinion leaders at best, and may have been more seriously flawed. So, how can we understand the industry's investment in this model, and its apparent success?

The drug industry has the resources to facilitate career advancement. It offers opportunities for ghost-managed presentations and publications, and audiences for both. Physician KOLs speak to audiences of colleagues assembled by sales representatives, and are paid handsomely to do so.

Before their deployment, most physician KOLs aren't pre-existing opinion leaders, at least not for all of the audiences to which they speak. They aren't physicians who are already influential or who have a place in a social network that would allow them to be influential. But drug companies' hiring of them makes physician KOLs influential. They are networked with other physicians, turning them into important social nodes. In an important sense, then, drug companies turn people into KOLs by providing the right training, resources, and venues to make these physicians influential. Even if local opinion leaders didn't have much of an effect in 1950s medical practice, they do now. With the industry's support, the opinion leader research was a self-fulfilling prophecy.[50]

Similar patterns apply to researcher KOLs. First, the companies hold valuable resources for boosting researchers' reputations and status. Over the past fifty years, the pharmaceutical industry has become the largest funder of medical research in dollar terms. Although most of that industry funding goes to contract research organizations and biotechnology firms, the total volume of industry funding is still very attractive to academic medical researchers. Second, even without research funding, publication planners make KOLs their authors on articles, and their speakers at conferences, workshops and other events. In so doing, they build reputations, turning people into ever more influential opinion leaders. As long as they maintain the appearance of independence from their sponsors – and perhaps even when they don't – their talks increase their prominence. Repeatedly being billed as a leading expert can give a person the status of leading expert. Dr Katz realizes this when he wonders why he agrees to give talks: 'When you're being asked to be the thought leader, that's a bull's-eye exactly where academics live. They want to be thought leaders.'

A model of the social world can have effects, when participants align their behaviour with the model and then change the world to fit the model's description. Belief in the truth or value of the model leads people and institutions to invest in it, and to reshape the world around it.[51]

Turning people into opinion leaders has allowed the industry to change the social landscape of communication in medicine. In the same moves as the industry provides audiences and builds the careers of physicians and researchers, it contributes to hierarchies of influence. Scientific presentations in clinics and at dinner events have become ordinary, and are common ways of communicating information, presumably contributing to the formation of opinions. Conference and CME presentations by research stars and rising stars are equally ordinary. Reprinted journal articles by those same stars are given to physicians in large numbers. All of this communicated science represents the most highly valued information, information that forms the basis of many opinions. Whatever the structure of opinion leadership among 1950s US physicians, the drug industry has now firmly established the social contagion model wherever it works with KOLs.

6

DRAINING AND CONSTRAINING AGENCY

I: CHANGING HABITS

ALTHOUGH PHYSICIANS CAN FOOL THEMSELVES — AND THEY DO SO SURPRIS-ingly often – the sales reps who visit their offices are pretty transparently engaged in sales. Tactics vary widely, and some don't look much like high-pressure selling, such as the precise 'detailing' of the drugs in their portfolios, which involves providing key physiological, pharmacological and prescribing information. But in the end the sales reps are clear that they're sales reps, making them some of the more visible hands of the pharma world, and some of the less ghostly marketers in this book.

In the first half of this chapter I show some of the work sales reps do to try to shape physicians' actions, making those actions less independent than they appear. Sales reps have a range of tools to influence doctors, meaning that they can respond differently to different doctors and situations, gaining advantage no matter what their target doctors do. Almost invariably, the result is more prescriptions. In the second half of the chapter, I show the work of a specialized follow-up group of invisible hands, experts in increasing patient adherence to doctors' prescriptions – increasing rates of filled and refilled prescriptions. Like sales reps, patient adherence specialists have a range of tools, and can respond differently to different patients and situations. Both sales reps and adherence specialists, then, can effectively drain and constrain the agency of their targets.

In almost every detailed account of the work of pharmaceutical sales reps, their overarching goal is stated in terms of 'changing prescribing habits', or some close variation of that phrase. Sales reps want to increase the number of prescriptions, or 'scripts', for their products, 'changing physicians' prescribing behaviour' in favour of those products. In these phrases, we can see a behaviourist model of the physician. At issue are behaviours and habits, not decisions.

Jamie Reidy, the affable author of the book *Hard Sell* (which led to a loosely inspired movie, *Love and Other Drugs*), puts this bluntly:

> An official job description for a pharmaceutical sales rep would read: Provide health-care professionals with product information, answer their questions on the use of products, and deliver product samples. An unofficial, and more accurate, description would have been: Change the prescribing habits of physicians.[1]

In sales reps' accounts of their tactics, the physician is implicitly a creature whose pen is hovering over the prescription pad as they consider the patient in front of them. What will they write when the pen touches the pad? The sales rep's job is to induce a specific prescription, a specific 'script' for the doctor and patient to follow. Michael Oldani, a sales rep turned anthropologist, writes, 'Once doctors form these habits, it takes either a new and improved class of medications or a lot of resources (expert speakers, money, and more gifts) to change that habit.'[2] We've already seen the expert speakers, so I'll turn to the gifts and money.

Gifts and Money

Oldani argues that strategic gift-giving is the most important element of the relationship between sales reps and physicians. There is a long history of anthropological studies of gifts, and from those studies Oldani emphasizes two elements: the 'spirit' of the things given, and the importance of a 'third party' in the gift-giving. In pharma, I interpret these two elements in terms of relationships and a reference – however subtle – to the care of patients.

Gifts from one person to another almost always either establish or express relationships. Ideally, they are well chosen for the recipient, or communicate something about the giver. This is why cash – the most neutral of goods – is an inappropriate gift in most situations, unless perhaps it is wrapped nicely and comes with a personalized card. Precisely because interpersonal gifts convey relationships, they demand reciprocity. There is a paradox here, because, unlike an economic exchange, a gift appears not to, but in fact does, demand repayment.

When pharma's sales reps give gifts to physicians and their clinics – the most standard gifts come in the form of free lunches for staff – there is also some gesture toward patient care, or perhaps toward medical education or research that will affect patient care. This lends gifts legitimacy, making them distinct from bribes.

When Oldani was trying to make his quota for an antibiotic in his portfolio, he focused on a hospital and designed a nearly-perfect generic gift: a card worth ten free cups of gourmet coffee from the hospital's coffee cart, with the antibiotic's name on the reverse of the card. The cards were quickly in high demand among residents, staff doctors and the hospital pharmacists. Free coffee communicated that Oldani understood the sleep-deprived culture of the hospital, and that he was caring for the people who worked there. '[S]ales far exceeded my expectations and I achieved my quota.'[3]

Kimberly Cheryl is the author of a bitter book, *Escape from the Pharma Drug Cartel*, about her former life as a sales rep and her eventual sense of betrayal by the industry. For Cheryl, '[w]hatever obligation doctors felt to write scripts for my products usually came from the general sense of reciprocity implied by the ritual of gift-giving'.[4] This could sometimes get out of hand:

> My career as a caterer began. I arranged to buy lunch for the staff of certain private practices every day for a year. I often invited a group of physicians and their guests to high-end restaurants, bought drinks and lavish meals. I scored sports tickets for my favorite physicians.[5]

She reports that she distributed 'unrestricted educational grants', a tool mentioned by another former sales rep.

> The highest prescribers receive better presents. Some reps said their 10's [the very highest prescribers] might receive unrestricted 'educational' grants so loosely restricted that they were the equivalent of a cash gift, although I did not personally provide any grants.[6]

Even research and educational grants that aren't convertible to cash can easily be gifts, if they are awarded in the right way. At one point my research brought me into contact with a former sales rep (technically a 'medical science liaison', but acting as a sales rep) who spent several years working on only a single expensive product, with a beat of slightly more than a dozen specialist physicians. He also had a sizeable budget for research grants, which he used strategically. Every time the prescriptions of one of his physicians fell below the level he wanted to see, he would visit them and offer them a $10,000 or $20,000 unrestricted research grant. Prescriptions would follow.

Small gifts are much more ubiquitous. Two kinds of small gifts stand out: food, and drug samples. The food part is obvious, because food is the most common tool for building relationships in all walks of life. Reidy jokes that 'the way to a man's heart may be through his stomach, but the way to a doctor's heart went straight through his office staff's collective stomach'.[7] Sales reps try to figure out what offices want, and to be just creative enough to stand out from their competitors. Cultivating a rapport with the receptionists and nurses translates into time with physicians. Imagines Reidy: 'I can hear it now: Ban the pharmaceutical salespeople! Without drug reps, though, who would bring free lunch to the receptionists and nurses every day?'[8]

Drug samples serve multiple purposes. They are gifts to physicians that can be re-gifted to patients – perhaps saving the patients money and time on the first few doses of a drug. This makes samples exemplary gifts, since they directly contribute to medical care. But they also encourage the physician to start a prescription with the samples at hand, rather than some other drug.[9] Cheryl observes:

> Sampling may be the single most important factor in a pharmaceutical rep's success. Once a patient is started on a sample medication and is doing well on it, physicians are usually very reluctant to change. Therefore, it is essential and vital to have a significant and prominent presence in the sample cabinet of a medical office.[10]

John Virapen, writing about his work as a sales rep travelling from town to town in rural Sweden in the 1980s, tells the story of how he filled his physicians' cabinets with his samples. At the onset of flu season, he explained to physicians that he wouldn't be back for a few months. He wasn't allowed to leave large stocks of samples, but,

> 'We can solve that. It's only in the best interest of your patients. Look here, I've brought you a few extra receipts, one for this month – and these are for the next months.' …
>
> With a shrug, [the doctor] went ahead and signed the predated receipts.[11]

The result was a cabinet crammed with his company's drugs, rather than those of the competitors. Oldani, working in a context in which providing samples was more routinized, explains the art:

> [T]he actual placement of samples within a 'sample closet' could influence prescription-writing practices of doctors. In many cases, you needed to place your samples at 'eye level', especially if your product was one of other medications in a similar class of drugs. Reps would engage in 'sample wars', that is, moving competitors' samples to the back of the closet or out of sight in order to have the doctor or nurse focus their gaze only on our product. … A classic technique was to get your samples placed on the doctor's desk as a reminder of his or her commitment to using (writing for) your product.[12]

Samples promote specific prescriptions, tell the physician how much the sales rep cares about patients, and are valuable because they can be re-gifted. In the end, however, all gifts are important, if they are the right ones. One website reminds sales reps, 'Always remember the fastest way to convince any doctors is by giving them gifts according to their personality.'[13] Perhaps this is why a 2010 ruling in a discrimination suit against Novartis found that the company expected its female sales representatives to be 'available and amenable to sexual advances from the doctors they call on'.[14]

The Playbook

Sales reps typically enter a physician's office already knowing many things about that physician and their practice. They often have access to prescription records, sold to their companies by firms that collect data from pharmacy chains. They already know which drugs the physician prescribes, and have a good idea of what the practice looks like. As one training guide puts it, an 'individual market share report for each physician ... pinpoints a prescriber's current habits'.[15] Sales reps also enter with playbooks: however their targets act or react, they have ready responses. If the sales reps have enough information, good instincts and detailed enough playbooks, they effectively trap their targets, denying them meaningful agency in the situation.

The playbooks divide physicians into categories, with a variety of 'profiles' or 'personality types'. A humorous article on a website for sales reps lists six personality types of doctors that the reps meet: Techie, Curmudgeon, BFF, Pupil, Super Ego, and Lost Cause.[16] To the extent that this list works as humour, it's because of all the more serious lists based on prescriptions of the drug at issue or tactics for the sales rep to use. Cheryl's personal playbook was based on the immediate context. 'If the doctor was busy or was in the middle of a crisis, the smart representative would discreetly leave samples, get the signature and leave. ... If their body language indicated that they only had a few seconds, I would go directly into my sixty-second presentation with product, features, benefits and closing.'[17]

Even when sales reps don't have formal playbooks, they keep detailed records on their physicians. Writing about Sweden in the 1980s, Virapen explains the practice of profiling that he and his colleagues undertook, which included information about the practices' patients, and the drugs prescribed. To get that information might have required first developing a relationship, and finding out about a physician's 'age, marital status, number of children and all their birthdays. You need good ties to them, the more the better. Which hobbies, favourite cars, favourite wine, favourite music? ... You create a psychological profile.'[18] Anything can be put to use. Tracy Krane, a novice sales rep at the time, describes a dinner with her director of sales, Alec Burlakoff, and Steven Chun, a potentially very high-prescribing physician for an expensive drug. Krane marveled at the way [Burlakoff] drew on a wealth of information about the doctor – intelligence gathered over the course of years – without letting on just how much he knew. Before he worked for Insys, Burlakoff worked for Cephalon, Insys's chief competitor, and he knew a bit about Chun's romantic history. ... He also knew that Chun liked to visit the casinos up in Tampa, so Burlakoff made a point of talking about his own penchant for gambling. ... She had no idea if he was telling the truth.[19]

We can see a tactics-based list in a useful and insightful short article by Adriane Fugh-Berman and Shahram Ahari.[20] Fugh-Berman is a physician who studies the industry, and Ahari is a former sales rep who served as an expert witness in a court case in the US. In the case and the article that followed, Ahari provided a rich description of the ordinary tactics that sales reps employ. His short classification of physicians breaks them down into categories: 'Friendly and outgoing, Aloof and sceptical, Mercenary, High-prescribers, Prefers a competing drug, Acquiescent docs, No-see/No-time, and Thought leaders'. In a clean chart next to each of these categories Ahari provides his approaches and explains how they work. I'll elaborate on a couple of his categories as examples.

Aloof and Sceptical Physicians

One of Ahari's categories is the 'aloof and sceptical' physician. This is the kind of target who asserts superiority over the sales rep, claiming to prescribe purely on the basis of hard evidence. Dr Krueger, a KOL interviewed for this book, might serve as an example of the aloof physician:

> If a drug company tries to promote things that are not correct the doctor is going to figure that out ... Well, you know, being a doctor I guess I am a little biased but my thought is that well it's not like the guy's gone to medical school for four years, done a residency, and whatever his or her specialty is – they probably have a pretty good insight into what's true and what isn't.

Since their prescribing is science-based, sceptical physicians probably see them-selves as the least susceptible to sales reps' influence. In fact, though, pharma has more resources to throw at these prescribers than at any others.

Pharma sales reps distribute the companies' preferred knowledge directly to physicians, for example by providing reprints of ghost-managed articles. The fact that they provide knowledge actually legitimizes their presence in physician's offices. Addressing an audience of publication planners at a large conference, Ms Lane, a former sales rep and now a fiery industry consultant, gives a bit of a pep talk about the importance of journal articles: 'Folks, they're dying for your work, by the way. Field reps are dying every day for more of your work. You know that, right? Because that's what doctors are going to see.'

Ultimately, it is the fact that sales reps provide information, whether in the form of scientific reprints or product information sheets, that legitimizes their presence in physicians' offices. The transmission of medical knowledge is what allows sales reps to make their pitches, offer their friendship, and convince physicians to prescribe specific drugs.

Oldani writes that 'these tremendous R and D budgets and the entire flow of knowledge and information used to discover new products rests on the ability of the industry to convince those who can write a prescription ... to write that script for their particular product'.[21] For the sceptical physician, the relationship also runs in another direction. The 'entire flow of knowledge and information' is there to be *used* to convince prescribers 'to write that script for their particular product'.

Ahari describes how, in dealing with the sceptical physician, he would 'play dumb and have the doc explain the significance of my article'. Then, the 'only thing that remains is for me to be just aggressive enough to ask the doc to try my drug in situations that wouldn't have been considered before, based on the physician's own explanation'.[22] It's an ingenious move, because the journal article allows the physician to verbally provide the evidence for the new prescriptions. The sales rep only has to ask the physician to try writing prescriptions for the drug in, say, the next five patients who present appropriate symptoms. That may be enough to establish a new prescribing habit.

Though they may sometimes choose to play dumb, sales reps have extensive knowledge about the drugs they're representing, the competing drugs, and the conditions for which all those drugs might be prescribed. All this information has been drilled into them in training events, and they've continued to study it since. Cheryl recalls her initial training session: 'Training was four weeks of living hell.'

> I will never forget days of constant grinders. We stood in two straight lines. One group played that of a physician, one the representative. We finished one detail and rotated our way down the line. We detailed until the corporate message came to us flawlessly. We knew the key messages for each product. We knew the data on the graphs and how to use them to sell and make our drugs look better than our competitors.[23]

She proudly claims, however,

> I can still detail every bit of information of every product I sold, including the drug's molecular weight. We [could] go toe to toe in any discussion on just about any medical issue with a physician and we weren't uncomfortable with our knowledge.[24]

Reidy also reports weeks of learning about the drugs he would promote, their pharmacological properties, and sales pitches. 'I began dreaming at night about detailing trainers playing the role of doctor. … Again and again, we detailed each other; people rehearsed over lunch, in the hallways, even in the bathrooms.'[25] Against this kind of drilled-in expertise, the sceptical doctor will give way. But many doctors, like Dr Koren, are firm in their beliefs about their ability to do their own thinking:

> I mean, to me it's an insult to physicians that we can't recognize bias and we can't sift through it. I mean, we're more trained than any professionals who make life and death decisions so by saying we need to restrict access to information that's provided by pharmaceutical companies is basically to

say that we're not smart enough to make our own conclusions – but if we are smart enough then it's an invaluable source of information that many of the companies are paying for.

Friendly and Outgoing

Sales reps establish relationships with all their physician targets, using whatever common interests they can find, and what Ahari calls 'finely titrated doses of friendship'. Most reps don't need much training to be friendly. Reidy describes the boot camp he attended to kick off his sales rep job at Pfizer: 'With few exceptions, every one of my 149 classmates was impossibly friendly. I had never spent time with so many people who were as chatty as me, and it was fairly annoying. When would I get to talk?'[26]

Ahari recounts: 'During training, I was told, when you're out to dinner with a doctor, "The physician is eating with a friend. You are eating with a client."' Physicians do sometimes see sales reps as their friends: 'Sometimes we don't even talk about drugs, we just chat about the kids and it's good to have a relaxed and friendly lunch', explains one physician.[27] And they can have good reasons to see their friendships with sales reps as genuine, as Dr King does:

> A good number of my very close friends are sales representatives. … I like to think that those are real relationships just because they're relationships – and even when people have moved on to other companies or don't sell a product in my disease state. … Like last weekend I had two other couples who are both representatives – neither of them call on me anymore – over for dinner and a swim party.[28]

Although friendship is a tool across the board, it becomes the overarching tool for those targets who are friendly and outgoing. 'I frame everything as a gesture of friendship', explains Ahari.

> I give them free samples not because it's my job, but because I like them so much. I provide office lunches because visiting them is such a pleasant

relief from all the other docs. My drugs rarely get mentioned by me during our dinners. … When the time is ripe, I lean on my 'friendship' to leverage more patients to my drugs … say, because it'll help me meet quota or it will impress my manager, or it's crucial for my career.

These physicians, meanwhile, genuinely appreciate the interactions. One tells a story in which

they stopped allowing reps in my office, and this one had information for me, so I told her she could join me for a run. She went not only the extra mile, but an extra 2 miles and talked to me about the product the whole way. That was really helpful. You bet I still see her any time she wants to see me.[29]

Again, the 'friendly and outgoing' physician who wants to go running or swimming with reps is just one among many. But there are other approaches that work for the 'Mercenaries' (trade gifts for prescriptions), 'High-prescribers' (establish strong personal connections), 'Prefers a competing drug' (wear them down), 'Acquiescent docs' (pair commitments with gifts), 'No-see/no-times' (focus on the staff), and 'Thought leaders' (provide speaking opportunities).

Influence

Most of pharma's customers want drugs to be part of a rational world centred on health: drug decisions should be based entirely on solid evidence about their health benefits and costs, not on advertising, hearsay, or fashion. Though prescribing habits may be one of the best studied and precisely understood of markets, physicians routinely claim not to be personally influenced by all the things pharma throws at them. Pharma companies are happy to maintain this fiction, as they never want obvious marketing to overshadow science in importance. Sales reps know this. Cheryl describes a subtle dance in which physicians pretend – often to themselves – that they aren't affected by sales reps' actions:

> When the encounters between a physician and drug rep went well, there
> was a delicate ritual of pretence and self-deception. I began to pretend that
> I was still giving the physicians impartial information and the physicians
> pretended to take me seriously. My job was to influence the physician in
> any way that I could while the physicians told themselves that they weren't
> being influenced.[30]

The result is changed prescription habits that allow the prescriber to maintain
a sense and appearance of integrity. The reps laugh amongst themselves:

> The most comical thing is doctors' attitudes. You will never hear a physician
> say, 'This is influencing me.' They are just so arrogant and naive.[31]

Not only do physicians tend to believe that they are immune to pharmaceutical
company influence, but their confidence about their immunity increases with
the amount of contact they have with industry representatives.[32] This is a finding
that resonates with the theory of cognitive dissonance: the greater the internal
conflict, the greater the likelihood and volume of denial.

All of the tools that a playbook might hold are tools of influence, designed
to change physicians' behaviour. In addition, the playbook as a whole works to
constrain and drain physicians' agency. Whichever way physicians turn, however
much they feel they are making decisions, sales reps have a response that pushes
them in the direction of specific scripts.

II: THE ADHERENCE PROBLEM

As we've seen, pharma companies invest enormous amounts of money into
producing and shaping medical information, transporting that information
to physicians, guiding those physicians to act on the information in particular
ways, and prodding patients to go into their doctors' offices with well-articulated
complaints. The result is prescriptions.

Then, a significant percentage of patients simply do not fill their prescriptions. A significant percentage of the rest do not *refill* their prescriptions. And

the drop-off continues. For the companies selling the drugs, these unfilled prescriptions look like lost sales. They are lost opportunities, and reduce the return on investment of all of the other interventions made to get prescriptions into the hands of patients. An ad for a podcast reads: 'As regulatory hurdles mount and product pipelines shrivel, pharma companies must seek new revenue drivers to maintain growth. Addressing patient adherence, and thereby improving health outcomes and increasing potential revenue, is a popular answer to the problem.'[33]

The pharmaceutical industry is not alone in seeing 'patient adherence' (or 'patient compliance', though this term is falling out of favour because of its more obvious paternalism) as a huge problem. Drug distributors and pharmacies also see this problem in terms of lost sales: real customers are brought very close to their businesses, but then turn away at the last moment. And for many in the medical profession, non-adherence is dangerous and is contributing to the ill health of populations. If a physician writes a prescription, filling it should be in the patient's best interests, all else being equal.

As a result, on display at industry conferences on patient adherence is a fascinating mix of idealism about patient outcomes, scientific interest in what leads people to take and not take medications, and cold calculation about returns on investment. For example, a single slide at a 2010 presentation displayed widely cited and widely repeated estimates that non-adherence is responsible for 125,000 deaths each year in the US and 11% of hospitalizations,[34] a recognition of the complexity of the issue, and the claim that the US industry loses $30 billion annually to non-adherence. In the end, return on investment dominates, because in bold on the same slide is 'Opportunity: A 3% increase in adherence translates to $1.0 billion in revenue for the pharmaceutical industry'.

Given the sales opportunities involved, many of the presenters at industry conferences on adherence are peddling something, usually in transparent ways. They represent firms offering products, services and expertise, and they want the pharmaceutical industry to pay for their programmes. Increased sales, they chime, will provide a healthy return on investment in these programmes.[35]

A Paradox?

For the pharmaceutical industry, one of the worst features of the patient non-adherence problem is that it seems intractable. Although measurements vary considerably – among researchers, among disease groups, among kinds of treatments – overall patient non-adherence is consistently and stubbornly high.

At industry conferences on patient adherence, a typical presenter might lead with some figures on the number of prescriptions filled and refilled. For example, Mr Allen, working for a firm that helps large organizations manage their health benefits, provides these numbers: 88% of prescriptions are filled, 76% are taken and 48% are refilled. Dr Anderson, who works for a large pharmaceutical company, asserts that, across many diseases, roughly 15% of prescriptions aren't filled, and that of those that are, 28% are not refilled after thirty days, and 50% have stopped the treatment after six months. Mr Alvarez, an independent consultant, breaks down adherence rates by conditions. He reports that for treatment of type-2 diabetes, only 53% of patients are taking their medications after three months, 41% after six months, and 38% after twelve months. In Alvarez's presentation, rates for many other conditions are similar, though depression is an outlier with only 30% of patients taking their medication after three months.

These estimates vary somewhat, and vary in how they are measured and reported. But more striking is just how similar they are. Moreover, Dr Anderson insists that the general picture hasn't changed much during her long experience of working on the issue – though scientific understandings of the issue have changed considerably. Non-adherence seems to be a constant problem for the industry. Other research agrees: overviews and systematic reviews show reasonably consistent adherence levels over time.[36]

Yet many people at these conferences are presenting solutions to sell to pharma companies and other interested parties. Not only are they presenting solutions, but they appear to be presenting *proven* solutions, with data demonstrating that they really work. These solutions range widely. They include programmes in which pharmacists, nurses and others engage patients throughout the duration of their prescriptions; specialized agencies are happy to sell such services to pharmaceutical companies. There are phone apps that reward patients for checking in on their phones when they take their drugs. There are programmes to make refilling prescriptions easier – including having packages of drugs delivered directly to patients. There are devices to help patients and healthcare providers track whether and when drugs are being taken.

Ms Alexander, who works for a large pharma company, describes the analysis that led to a programme to focus on a particular group of patients prescribed a statin to reduce their cholesterol levels. To move the average number of 'days on therapy' for this group from 162 to 216, their costs for the drugs had to drop only slightly. The result was an increase in sales of $58 million, for a mere $3 million total wholesale price drop, or a return on investment of 18:1.

Another presenter, Mr Arnold, is transparently selling a product. His small device attaches to the top of a pill bottle, glows when it's time to take a pill, chimes an hour after a pill has been missed, and transmits information via Wi-Fi whenever the pill bottle is opened. This allows monitors – perhaps paid for by the drug company and working in a call centre – to spot a missed day and call the patient. The cap will even contact an online pharmacy to deliver a refill of the prescription, with a simple push of a large button. According to Arnold's company's study, the system increases adherence by 27%.

How can we reconcile the persistence of non-adherence with the development and deployment of so many creative and effective interventions?

Almost certainly, effective drug marketing up to the point of prescription increases the challenge of non-adherence. In assemblage marketing, eventual demand is a product of initial demand and marketing effort. Without careful work to address patients themselves, marketing efforts can increase the costs and decrease the benefits as felt by some patients.

To explain this, let me take a very slight detour. In a provocative article, bioethicist Howard Brody and sociologist Donald Light argue that pharmaceutical marketing itself makes drugs less effective and less safe. They call the result the 'inverse benefit law': 'The ratio of benefits to harms among patients taking new drugs tends to vary inversely with how extensively the drugs are marketed.'[37] Their central argument is straightforward. Imagine that there is some ideal population of patients for some new drug, for all of whom the benefit-to-risk ratio is at the right level or higher, whatever the 'right level' is. Pharmaceutical marketing is aimed at increasing the patient population for drugs. But the benefit-to-risk ratio for the additional patients will be at a lower level than it was for the original ideal population, and so won't be at the right level.

Brody and Light point out that many of the industry's technical strategies feed directly into the inverse benefit law. For example, the industry attempts to expand patient populations by supporting research and guidelines that reduce thresholds for diagnoses of particular illnesses. Industry research also promotes studies that focus on surrogate markers and risk factors, rather than on the diseases that presumably sit behind them; there are far more cases of elevated cholesterol levels than of heart attacks.

To the extent that patients perceive that the balance among costs, risks and benefits isn't worth it, they will tend to be non-adherent. There is no paradox, then. Programmes to reduce non-adherence work, but the industry's very success at increasing prescriptions tends to increase non-adherence. The result is that non-adherence is a recalcitrant problem. Adherence programmes then become an additional part of assemblage marketing, and work in concert with everything else.

Shaping Patients' Actions, Changing Patients' Behaviour

Other than its apparent cost to the industry, patient non-adherence is a poorly understood problem. I was struck by how almost everybody at adherence conferences has a different approach to understanding the causes of the issue, leading to some divides when it comes to addressing it.

One senior figure in the field, Dr Anderson, is a commanding presence at one adherence conference. Everybody else seems deferential, and she is mentioned many times. A friendly-looking social scientist in her mid-sixties, Anderson has spent most of her career studying non-adherence and related phenomena, working within a large pharma company. She gives a presentation summarizing a history of changing models of non-adherence and what she takes to be the key take-home messages of the past generation of qualitative research on the topic. In particular, she claims, patients' non-adherence is the result of a cost-benefit analysis involving concerns, benefits and needs; patients make active and reasoned decisions about filling prescriptions and taking their drugs. There is, then, no non-adherent personality (the focus of study of the phenomenon in the 1960s); nor are there non-adherent demographics.

Many of the speakers agree. They emphasize problems in communication, and how these can be remedied with the right interventions. Twenty-five percent of patients do not tell their physician if they stop taking a drug, reports Mr Armstrong, and physicians are poor at predicting which patients will become non-adherent. So, to pick just one of the facts that Armstrong lists, there are 33% more refills among patients who, when switched to a different cholesterol medication, are told why the new medication is the right one. Patients need to be given information in order to make a good decision.

Pharmacists can be particularly valuable, and many of the interventions are or involve programmes to pay pharmacists to spend more time with patients, both at the point of the original prescription, and again when the patients return for refills. Representatives of different pharmacy chains describe several nearly identical programmes. One speaker describes how pharmacists can be trained in 'motivational interviewing', which makes a two- to five-minute consultation session effective.

An article in an industry magazine touts new technologies as solving the problem of communication. It lists the following, almost all of them focused on communicating with patients to lead them to make more adherent decisions: 'Smart phone apps that remind patients to take medication at the correct time; Websites to present disease and product information; Emails focused on product, disease or condition; Automated reminder calls; Surveys to engage patients and improve program; Text messaging focused on compliance; Call centre to handle inbound calls compliantly; Emails focused on compliance; Apps that [educate] and inform patients, their families and caretakers; Desktop reminder tools focused on compliance; RSS feeds focused on compliance; Calendar stickers focused on compliance'.[38]

Despite Dr Anderson's emphasis on the rational patient, and notwithstanding the fact that she is treated as the most expert on the issue, a number of the other presenters at the same conference talk in terms of cause-and-effect models. They put forward remedies framed in terms of interventions that change patients' behaviour, not their reasoning. For these speakers, good programmes address patients at least partly in terms of triggering preferred behaviour, rather than in terms of making rational decisions. A patient engagement manager at a large pharmaceutical company insists that 'knowledge is *not* power', and that because of this, her company has moved to 'behavioural programmes'. Another speaker claims that there is no correlation between patient knowledge and adherence, and that 'over a hundred studies' prove it.

Although most of the presenters at these conferences work for pharma companies, pharma distributors, chains of pharmacies and specialized agencies, there are among them a few academic researchers. One group of university professors presents the results of a large quantitative meta-analysis of inter-ventions to improve adherence in seniors. Their take-home message is that behavioural modifications are most likely to be successful: special packaging, dose modification, stimuli to take medications, and self-monitoring of some outcome such as blood pressure. Patient education, they argue, is generally not effective, unless it is in the form of succinct written instructions used as a prompt. On this issue, academic medicine and the pharmaceutical industry are having the same discussion.

Mr Allen makes one of a number of direct pitches for behaviourist approaches: 'We have long used financial incentives … Now we're finding that tools that build upon the insights of behavioural economics and psychology can have powerful, positive effects.'[39] Allen builds a theoretical account of his programme, starting with three psychological bases: (1) 'loss aversion', the claim that in most situations people care more about losses than gains, (2) the 'social norms' principle that social comparisons drive consumer behaviour, and (3) the idea of 'hyperbolic discounting', that people value small, immediate rewards more than larger ones in the future. With this in the background, Allen claims that the messaging and other interventions in his programme were derived from these principles. It looks to me as though he is merely applying a gloss of science to his work, because the connections to the programme are somewhat opaque. Nonetheless, that gloss highlights the value of exploiting ways in which people don't make decisions that are conventionally seen as rational. I have no reason to doubt that value.

Segmentation and Integration

Most of the work addressing non-adherence combines different approaches, modelling patients as making rational decisions but as influenced by other factors. For example, Mr Agnelli, CEO of an adherence-focused company, sets up a pairing between 'behaviour modification' – involving 'classical conditioning, operant conditioning and social conditioning' – and 'pedagogical science' – with its 'integrative learning, experiential learning and timed learning'. The result, claims Agnelli, is a 'comprehensive behavioural system' on which the company builds a tailored programme with multiple, integrated channels. Again, I suspect that there is a certain amount of scientific gloss being applied to the programme, but it comes with good efficacy data from an RCT of patients with type-2 diabetes.

Since no one approach to addressing patient adherence is completely successful, programmes need to be focused on the right sub-segment. 'Why don't people adhere to their medicine regimens?', asks Agnelli. 'Each person has his or her own set of complex and interrelated reasons.'

To address these reasons, many people are mining databases. For one brand, a pair of presenters working for a big pharmaceutical company and a healthcare services company respectively set out an adherence goal of increasing 'days on therapy' by 10%. Their central pitch is about the importance of leveraging patient data to increase patient adherence. The key is to segment the patient population by building on surveys and databases. Some patients may respond better to a 'co-pay card' that gives them a discount on their portion of the drug costs. Some may respond better to an information campaign that reminds them about the benefits of staying on the drug and the risks of going off it. Some may respond well to face-to-face contact. Adherence experts develop playbooks for patients.

Even within communication approaches, segmentation of data is important. One speaker, Mr Adler, presents a European case study on 'driving profitable behaviour through engagement', where the drug in question is suboxone, a treatment for opioid addiction. For this drug, non-adherence rates are many times higher than for most other kinds of drugs. Adler divides the population into four categories, and then provides 'key insights' about the patient type,

	POSITIVE AND PROACTIVE	TRUSTING OPTIMISTS	ANXIOUS UNINFORMED	PASSIVE AND APATHETIC
KEY INSIGHTS	• Active info seekers • Feel they are in charge of treatment • See decision as partnership	• Moderate knowledge • Feel MD knows more about treatment	• Not active in seeking information • MD makes decisions	• Low knowledge of condition • Least active in seeking info • MD makes decision
COMMUNICATION STRATEGIES	• Put them in charge Provide a full array of resources	• Help them understand • Help communication with Dr	• Help them understand • Drive engagement with the brand	
CHANNEL STRATEGY	• Multiple contacts • Choice of channel • Push to web for more	• Multiple contacts • Choice of channel • Provide tools and resources	• Simple, efficient communications • Less frequency	

FIG. 6.1 Segmenting patient populations to improve adherence

and 'communication strategies' and a 'channel strategy' for each. Figure 6.1 is a simplified version of the table he presents.

Adler goes on to articulate these strategies in terms of media for communication, whether social media, SMS reminders, websites, or telephone contact. For each patient segment, the communication strategies are paired with differently timed cash payments, as incentives for engagement. But there remains the problem of how to measure the success of the programme. Patient adherence is tricky to measure, but in Adler's case study a control group of patients were taking the drug but opted not to join the communication programme. For a modest cost of €55 per patient, the number of patients in the communication group was five times higher than the number in the control group.

A presenter working for a firm specializing in adherence programmes offers a stunningly comprehensive approach. Working with a sizeable number of pharmacy chains, the firm has developed a database covering nearly 50% of US patients, their addresses, and their pharmacy transactions going back many years – and often current to the previous week. The firm's deluxe programme, presented through a case study of a blood pressure drug, includes five different components: (1) a letter-based campaign targeting patients at high risk of non-adherence, (2) an autofill programme by which patients will receive refills of their prescription delivered to their homes, (3) a face-to-face compliance programme involving initial counselling by pharmacists and follow-up phone monitoring, paid for by the drug company, (4) packaging that helps patients keep track of their medication consumption, and that advertises the compliance programme, and (5) a phone-based programme that follows up on prescriptions with direct-to-patient endorsement of the drug. The deluxe programme makes it very challenging for patients to casually stop taking the drug. The firm in question sponsored the wine and cheese reception at the conference.

Mr Alvarez presents several case studies on increasing 'patient-centricity', focusing most on a campaign to drive a particular statin use and adherence in Mexico. 'Lack of adherence is often an emotional and conscious decision on the part of the patient to stop taking the medication [and] in such situations the traditional pharma-sponsored programmes sending out messages to remind patients to take their pill are going to be of limited effectiveness.' He identifies opportunities for pharmaceutical companies to up their game, including 'improving customer service' and drawing on 'patient advocacy' and 'peer-to-peer communication'. These are areas in which Alvarez's company sees itself as particularly innovative, and he presents examples of magazines and websites owned by the company and used as vehicles to allow patient organizations to reach out to patients and help make them more adherent to treatments. In the Mexican campaign, his company built a database of patients, offering a 50% discount on the drugs for those who registered. This database became the infrastructure for establishing ongoing relationships with those patients. The campaign as a whole saw a 350% increase in sales of the drug.

Patient-centricity can bring together pharma companies and patient advocacy organizations (PAOs), the focus of the next chapter. In an interview, Mr Code, a very reflective marketing consultant in the UK, told me about a compliance project he had been involved in, to do with asthma patients not refilling or not renewing their prescriptions for inhalers. The company's view was, 'We don't need more patients, we just need the blooming patients to be compliant!' To that end, says Code, 'we either created or we seeded [an] idea with the UK's major patient advocacy group in asthma'. The idea was to fund trained nurses to 'go into doctors' surgeries ... and put this proposition on the table that there were patients who were dying who shouldn't be dying'. The nurses would then identify asthma patients who hadn't been seen for a long time, and arrange for the clinic to contact them to encourage them to come in for a fresh evaluation, or perhaps just a renewal of their prescription. The company paid for the nurses for the first few years, though it routed those payments through the asthma PAO.

We should not forget the appeals to idealism. Even the most revenue-focused actors in the adherence world justify what they are doing in terms of helping patients. They see marketing and increasing patients' welfare as entirely compatible. For this reason, across different adherence conferences, and in multiple talks, presenters quote former US Surgeon General C. Everett Koop: 'Drugs don't work in patients who don't take them.'

'Scripts' and Scripts

Sales reps often refer to prescriptions as 'scripts'. Although 'script' is merely an insider's shorthand, the prescription is a script and is surrounded by scripts, in the ordinary sense. Prescriptions contain directions for pharmacists (the name, strength, quantity and number of refills of a drug to be sold to the patient) and for patients (the quantity of drugs to be consumed, and the frequency, duration and circumstances of consumption). But prescription may also be a result of sales reps' many scripts for influencing doctors, and of doctors following the scripts that reps try to get them to adopt. Patients may then be following the scripts given to them by their doctors, among others, and may be helped to do so by the efforts of adherence specialists. All in all, pharma tries to shape the behaviours of physicians and patients, allowing them the appearance of agency while doing as much as possible to constrain it.

7

SIRENS OF HOPE, TROLLS OF FURY AND OTHER VOCAL CREATURES

A SATISFYING ENCOUNTER AT THE FDA

THE YEAR 2015 WITNESSED A NOTABLE VICTORY FOR PHARMA-CRAFTED patient advocacy. That year, Sprout Pharmaceuticals resubmitted flibanserin, with the commercial name Addyi, to the US Food and Drug Administration (FDA) for market approval. This was the third attempt through the process for flibanserin, intended to treat female sexual dysfunction. Despite the fact that the FDA's advisory committee had originally voted eleven to zero against the application, and despite the fact that the FDA had concerns about both the efficacy and safety data supporting the application, the agency approved the drug on this third try. Within two days, the larger company Valeant Pharmaceuticals snapped up little Sprout and the drug for one billion US dollars.

The submitted trials showed that women on flibanserin had only 0.5 more satisfying sexual events per month than women on the placebo. Because the trials excluded women with even mild depression and anxiety, the FDA wasn't convinced that the safety data was adequate. In fact, women on the drug had higher levels of sleepiness and sedation than had women on the placebo, and drinking alcohol while on flibanserin was connected to dangerous drops in blood pressure.[1]

The difference between the FDA's first and last decision on flibanserin was almost entirely due to Sprout's aggressive public relations campaign, 'Even the

Score'. Even the Score put the blame for the lack of female sexual dysfunction drugs on sexism, and put pressure on the FDA to approve flibanserin as a matter of women's equality. One of the central designers of the campaign knew her target: Audrey Sheppard had joined Sprout shortly after having served as the head of the Office of Women's Health at the FDA.[2] The campaign involved an extensive online presence on Twitter, Facebook and other platforms, involving such things as parodies of Viagra ads: 'What the fuck?', asks a woman in one such ad. 'Are we really so far behind we don't think women have the right to sexual desire? Yet again we come second.'[3] The campaign also gathered a number of important partners, including the National Organization for Women, the Black Women's Health Imperative, and many other national women's organizations in the US. For the National Consumers League, Addyi was 'the biggest break-through for women's sexual health since the pill', and other organizations made similarly expansive statements.[4]

When the FDA held public hearings on the drug, scores of women showed up to make the case for this 'pink Viagra'. Many were 'carrying gift bags, matching scarves, and large buttons with the "Even the Score" campaign slogan', a not-so-subtle sign of their having been been recruited and bussed in by the company.[5] Indeed, disclosures showed that the expenses of many of the women had been paid by Sprout, directly or through an intermediary, Veritas Meeting Solutions; a number of them also shared a urologist, Irwin Goldstein, a Sprout-connected KOL who had recruited them for the FDA meeting. As reported by Judy Segal, a scholar of the rhetoric of science who attended the meeting, some speakers appeared to be 'ventriloquized' by Sprout. Says one,

> I think the thing that makes me most angry and most disappointed is that if I went to my doctor and I was a man and I said these things they would be able to write me a prescription within a couple of minutes for a drug that is insurance covered and FDA approved.[6]

Moreover, 'most of the testimony the FDA would hear came from married women who had no interest in sex with their husbands and felt themselves to have a biological disease that was, moreover, threatening their marriages. Eight women testified; six of them told deeply personal stories that ended with an emotional call for drugs.'[7] The company had developed effective patient advocates.

Despite its eventual success at the FDA and for the owners of Sprout, Addyi has not been a sales success so far, with some insurers declining to cover it. This may be because it's an expensive pill taken daily, requires its users to abstain from drinking alcohol, and offers only modest rewards. 'Where', ask commentators from the organization PharmedOut, 'are the crowds of women with low libido clamouring for Addyi? They never existed, except in a PR firm's fantasy.' But that PR firm's fantasy was rich enough to get the drug past a key gatekeeper.[8]

LEVERAGING PATIENT ADVOCACY ORGANIZATIONS

For the pharmaceutical industry, patient advocates and patient advocacy organizations (PAOs) are excellent spokespeople and potential allies. They are and represent key stakeholders in markets for drugs. More importantly, they are *recognized* as stakeholders by government regulators and insurers, and are often seen as important *independent* voices in public spheres. PAOs are thus perfect candidates to be phantom hands for the industry.

The idea of stakeholders has gained some importance in the industry. 'Stakeholder relations' and 'stakeholder engagement' are recent industry catchphrases, ways of talking about the diverse work of assemblage marketing. Mat Phillips, co-founder of Engage Health Alliance – Europe, a 'multi-stakeholder engagement organization', insists that all stakeholders should be 'aligned' to 'ensure innovation delivers the fullest value possible to those who can benefit'.[9] In assemblage marketing, pharmaceutical companies often treat all the different actors as stakeholders, but patients and the PAOs that represent them are the most obvious stakeholders and carry the most legitimacy. Because of this, companies befriend existing advocates and organizations and try to build relationships that can be used whenever and wherever independent patient voices will have value.

Patient advocacy has become especially important over the past thirty years. Though effective PAOs already existed in the mid-twentieth century, it was the successes of AIDS activist groups at shaping research that charted the path for organizations focused on many other diseases and conditions.[10] PAOs can do many things, including raise public awareness, promote or oppose the medicalization of conditions, voice demand for particular treatments, advocate for research, shape or engage in research programmes, provide research and other funding, provide access to patients, advocate for relevant legislation, and more.[11] With only a little work, pharma can often align PAOs' interests and activities with its own.

The EveryLife Foundation for Rare Diseases runs an annual conference – the Rare Disease Legislative Advocates conference – in Washington, DC. The event provides patients and advocates with a day of training, where they learn how to make their organizations stronger, how to have successful meetings with politicians and others, and 'how to tell their stories'. After that, the participants go to the US Congress for a 'Lobby Day'. They meet with congressional staffers and legislators, to press cases for funding or for particular laws. Everything is organized by EveryLife. According to Dr Emil Kakkis, EveryLife's president, the foundation doesn't 'tell patients what to do on the Hill. They are given options.'[12]

EveryLife can provide travel grants for 100 of the 300 participants, thanks mostly to the generosity of pharmaceutical companies. In fact, the EveryLife Foundation itself is a creature of the pharmaceutical industry, receiving donations, some of them substantial, from two dozen companies. Kakkis himself is the founder of Ultragenyx Pharmaceutical, a small company that looks for treatments for rare diseases.[13]

I saw a more modest version of this approach at the Drug Information Association (DIA) meeting I went to in Vienna. The DIA is an association for contract research organizations, regulatory support and connected agencies involved in drug approvals. The DIA has a 'patient fellowship' programme that pays for a dozen or more patient advocates to attend its annual meetings each year. The programme's published goals include improving 'alliances between patient groups and other health care stakeholders'.[14] As the programme was explained to me, the patient advocates who win fellowships tend to be relatively new to advocacy and tend to represent people with relatively uncommon diseases. Like participants at the EveryLife conference, they are treated generously, being invited to speak about their work on panels and at specially created media events, encouraged to attend sessions at the DIA that can help them develop insights and skills for successful advocacy, and introduced to potentially valuable contacts in the private and public sectors. Representatives from the fellowship programme refer to past fellows as 'graduates', as if they had attended a course,[15] and one such graduate, describing her very positive experience, clearly portrays herself as a novice student.[16] 'Engaging and partnering with emerging stakeholders has become a crucial pharma priority', writes a columnist in the online magazine *eyeforpharma*.[17]

In a 2010 article in the DIA's member magazine *Global Forum*, Amber Spier and David Golub, both of whom work for a major consulting firm, provide an overview of ways in which PAOs can be 'leveraged' by the industry. They want to make a 'compelling case for engaging advocates well before a product comes to market'.[18]

Engaging PAOs does not mean simply supporting them with funding. In their short case study, Spier and Golub describe how their firm convened a working group of PAO representatives before Phase III trials, in much the same way that we saw companies convene advisory boards of key opinion leaders (KOLs). Working groups can gather important market and medical information, but they're also useful for 'forging durable links with these key customers'. Quoting Spier and Golub, the networked patient advocates can then:

- help with many details in the design, execution and communication of clinical trials
- provide input into relevant regulatory processes
- connect companies with valuable KOLs
- offer understandings of 'market dynamics'
- help design drug adherence and disease management programs
- influence policies, public decisions and treatment guidelines
- provide testimony to and share personal experience with regulators and other government bodies

Spier and Golub sum up the influence of PAOs in the following graphic (Fig. 7.1), which echoes several images presented in earlier chapters. Like

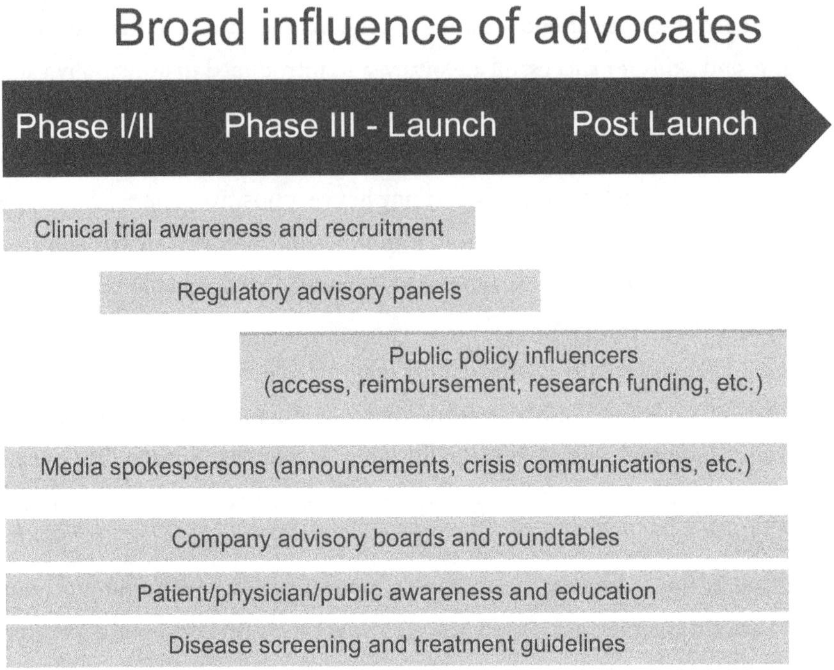

Broad influence of advocates

Phase I/II   Phase III - Launch   Post Launch

Clinical trial awareness and recruitment

Regulatory advisory panels

Public policy influencers
(access, reimbursement, research funding, etc.)

Media spokespersons (announcements, crisis communications, etc.)

Company advisory boards and roundtables

Patient/physician/public awareness and education

Disease screening and treatment guidelines

FIG. 7.1 The influence of advocates[19]

medical publications and like KOLs, patient advocates are co-opted into the marketing process.

Established PAOs themselves often welcome partnerships. In her book *Health Advocacy, Inc.*, Sharon Batt chronicles changes in Canadian breast cancer PAOs between the early 1990s and the late 2000s. Batt was a co-founder of one such organization in the 1990s, and uses her extensive knowledge of the terrain and the people involved to understand the changes over the following decades. At the beginning of that period, there was some Canadian government funding for PAOs, but little industry funding. The 1990s saw reductions in opportunities for public funding, followed by a vocal split within the community of cancer patient advocates about whether or not they should work with pharmaceutical companies. Those in favour of industry funding often had the rhetorical upper hand, arguing that relationships with companies 'foster the values of trust, collaboration, information sharing, horizontality, networking, negotiation, consensus and flexibility'. In addition, PAOs that accepted *government* funding could be seen as having the more important conflicts of interest, because they were in a poor position to criticize government policies. In the end, industry funding became the norm.[20]

In 2007 the Canadian Breast Cancer Network sponsored a survey about the risk of relapse, finding that only one in ten women were aware of their risk of relapse after five years of treatment with tamoxifen, a treatment for some specific breast cancers. The Network produced a press release, an information fact sheet, and a slick video on YouTube. Batt, who followed the Network's work for her study of breast cancer PAOs, recounts that the 'professionalism of the package was striking and had all the hallmarks of a help-seeking ad'. Seen as an advertisement, it would have been precisely targeted, because the package was circulated through the Network's members and contacts, who would have had reason to pay attention to a risk of relapse of breast cancer. The entire project was paid for by Novartis, which makes a drug specifically for follow-up therapy after five years of treatment with tamoxifen![21] This was the Network doing something within its mandate, by sharing useful information. At the same time, Novartis was spreading precisely the information it most cared about to its own target audience.

ALLIES TO TRANSMIT HOPE

As in the case of flibanserin, many clinical trial results are not, by themselves, strong evidence for a drug's value. Hope can transform weak or equivocal data into something more medically meaningful. Patient voices, often collected, articulated and amplified through patient advocacy organizations, are the most important conduits of hope, especially for regulators, but also for medical researchers. PAOs can challenge the 'cold guardians of the public purse', and in the process can change the meaning of data.[22]

Many PAOs are in the business of building on hope. They advocate in the hope of better treatments, both in terms of improved drugs and other interventions, and in terms of access. PAOs' public faces, especially in their advertisements, appeals and websites, often present hopes in terms of perfect cures and solutions, medical 'magic bullets'[23]: 'Your gift today will help us find a cure tomorrow', 'Change the future', 'End [disease X] now'. Other PAOs channel hope differently, trying to make existing treatments more widely available: 'When caught early, [disease Y] is highly curable'.

Government agencies listen to patients and PAOs – it is widely accepted that patients should have input into the processes of drug and other health regulation, and it is in the mandates of most regulatory agencies to listen.[24] By themselves, PAOs' pleas may not be enough to get regulators to act in one way or another. However, they can make the plight of patients more urgent and the hope contained in treatments more salient. They can make poor or equivocal data more adequate and may allow, or even convince, regulators to support the drugs at issue.

We can see some of the value to the industry of alliances with PAOs in a detailed story told by Ms Laird, who was promoting a 'stakeholder' approach to marketing at a pharmaceutical conference, as part of her consulting company's approach. After describing a client company's investment of £50 million in 'translational medicine' to engage with patient advocacy groups and other stakeholders operating in Scotland, Ms Laird told the following story to establish the importance of the investment, and the interactions it created:

> We had a negative decision on approval of a drug for the Scottish Medicines Consortium, which is the Scottish equivalent to NICE, and the negative decision there would impact on the NICE decision which was going to happen six months down the line.

NICE is the UK's National Institute for Health and Care Excellence, which, among other things, assesses the cost-effectiveness of drugs for the National Health Service. NICE decisions can make or break a drug in the UK.

> The data was robust, there is nothing more we could have done with the data. And no other studies, no more data was required. It was absolutely, the data couldn't have been stronger. ... It was rejected on cost.
>
> It didn't extend life, and when they look at QALYs [Quality Adjusted Life Years], life outcomes, does it tend to excel [sic] the patient's life? ...

And that is not what this product did. So the outcome of the decision was no reimbursement in Scotland. As you can imagine that wasn't a very good day in the office.

We had four weeks to overturn or to do something about the decision before it went live on their website. And this is why it is important that you think outside the box and you work with external stakeholders. We approached six key stakeholders. ... Now all the of [these] wrote to the SMC [Scottish Medicines Consortium] on their own behalf, but it was on patient choice and dignity to the patient.

Laird's firm had earlier supported and established good relations with all of the six chosen stakeholders, but in her presentation she insisted that they all lobbied primarily because they had seen the drug's effects, directly or indirectly.

They went way, way over and above what we asked them for, asked them to do. It was all about because they'd experienced it, they'd seen the effect that the drug had had for the patient.

And the SMC overturned the negative decision! Like I said, it wasn't to do with the science, the science got us so far. And if we had ignored everything else then it would have been the same negative decision. So just to show you that the right result was achieved for the patient. And the learning is obviously that ... this would not often have been achieved without this networking, without bringing all the organizations with us along the journey.

These guys were with us from before launch, pre-launch and they knew exactly what we were trying to achieve, they knew the outcome of the patients, they had seen it, the nurses had seen it but seeing the results they knew where we were. ... No matter how good your data, you need to plan and take other people with you. Because if we had approached them with four weeks to go we would not have got the result for the patient, because they wouldn't have been with us along the journey, they wouldn't have understood the science, the data, they wouldn't have seen the patient experience.

Of course, the SMC had seen data on the patient experience, but wasn't initially convinced that that data made a strong case for the drug. In Ms Laird's words, in terms of 'QALYs, life outcomes, does it tend to excel [sic] the patient's life? ... And that is not what this product did.' The drug's benefits were more intangible. But when prodded by the company, these patient organizations felt able to appreciate them, no doubt on the basis of their earlier good relations with the company. Focused hope is one of a drug's most valuable ingredients.

PUBLIC RELATIONS IN ECHO CHAMBERS

In the US, at least five-sixths of the hundred largest PAOs, and two-thirds of all PAOs, receive funding from the pharma or medical devices industry; 12% receive more than half of their funding from those industries.[25] At the same time, these organizations are very unlikely to report industry funding: one study compared the grant registry for Eli Lilly and the disclosures of all the PAOs on that registry; only a quarter of them acknowledged the funding.[26]

When the FDA invited select groups to hearings about new rules for evidence to speed up drug applications, thirty-nine of the forty-two PAOs had received funding from drug companies, and at least fifteen of those had pharmaceutical or biotech executives on their governing boards. A reporter remarked that the most eloquent speaker in these hearings was Marc Boutin, CEO of the National Health Council, 'a united voice for people with chronic disease and disabilities'. But not only does the Council receive 77% of its funding from pharmaceutical and biotech companies, but those companies are well represented on its board of directors and its key committees.[27]

When the European Medicines Agency (EMA) proposed in 2012 that all the clinical trial data submitted to it in drug applications should be made public, the pharmaceutical industry went into high gear. As we've seen, clinical trial results submitted to regulators often provide only weak evidence for drugs' effectiveness and safety. A 2013 leaked email from the European Federation of Pharmaceutical Industries and Associations to a long list of drug companies set out a four-pronged campaign to oppose the EMA's move. The first step was 'mobilising patient groups to express concern about the risk to public health by non-scientific re-use of data'. (The other three prongs of the campaign involved creating other alliances: convincing scientific associations of the dangers of data transparency, recruiting allies from other industries that might be concerned about trade secrets, and creating a network of KOLs ready to counter specific interpretations of data.) But why would PAOs be opposed to transparency? And why would they be opposed to transparency of results submitted in drug applications and not, for example, all the results published in medical journals?[28]

When Novartis challenged India's patent law over the decision not to grant a patent on the anti-cancer drug Glivec, the mobilization of PAOs was crucial on both sides. The company had been denied a patent on the grounds that the drug was a mere tweaking of an earlier one that wasn't protected in India. The case became symbolically important in fights around globalization, between competing pharmaceutical industries and over healthcare. As a result, the alliances on both sides involved PAOs. Through a programme that provided Glivec for free to some low-income patients, Novartis recruited patient voices in the political battle. Meanwhile, the central organizations in the anti-Novartis alliance included the Cancer Patients Aid Association and the Indian pharmaceutical industry, which manufactured generic versions of Glivec. Although Novartis lost its Indian court case, its programme to selectively give Glivec away won public relations wars elsewhere, and this was the company's prime concern.[29]

Conflicted PAOs and spokespeople talk to regulatory agencies that are themselves often rife with conflicts of interest. Employees of national regulators routinely move from government to industry and back again. People working at the highest levels of government, setting policy profoundly affecting pharma, also walk through those same revolving doors. In the UK, within six months of stepping down from his position as CEO of GlaxoSmithKline, Andrew Witty was asked to head the Accelerated Access Review programme, which is tasked with bringing 'innovative' treatments to patients more quickly – something that benefits pharma.[30] Two months *before* he left his position as Executive Director of the European Medicines Agency, Thomas Lönngren set up a consultancy within a company that helps pharma companies get drugs approved.[31] The former President of Eli Lilly, Alex Azar, is, at the time of writing, Secretary of the Department of Health and Human Services in the US.[32] Meanwhile, the Commissioner of the US Food and Drug Agency is Scott Gottlieb, a venture capitalist who has served on the boards of various pharma companies.

On 1 September 2017, the prominent health newsletter *STAT News* published an op-ed by Dr Robert Yapundich, entitled 'How Pharma Sales Reps Help Me Be a More Up-to-Date Doctor'.[33] Yapundich, a neurologist who has been in practice for more than twenty years, argued that sales reps should be allowed to discuss 'off-label' uses of drugs – uses for which the drugs aren't approved. This, he said, drawing on anecdotes about patients, would allow him to better help his patients. Yapundich's bio mentioned that he was a member of a US group called the Alliance for Patient Access. Another newsletter, *HealthNewsReview*, quickly pointed out that Yapundich had accepted a considerable amount – more than $300,000, as it turned out – from the drug industry in recent years, and hadn't noted the conflict of interest. Embarrassed by these and other revelations, *STAT News* withdrew the article.[34]

Although the name Alliance for Patient Access suggests a patient organization, it is officially an organization of physicians. The physicians who sit on its executive include some of the industry's most highly paid KOLs, including Dr Srinivas Nalamach, who received $800,000 from drug companies between 2013 and 2015, in connection with the promotion of opioids and drugs to treat the side effects of opioids.[35]

Yapundich had not reported his conflicts of interest, but more importantly, he had neglected to mention that the article was drafted for him by a public relations firm. Yapundich stood by the article, though he acknowledged that the ghostwriters had either fabricated or made mistakes about some details of the anecdotes.[36]

That's not all. The Alliance is supported primarily by membership dues paid by pharma companies and trade associations, and is operated by the public relations firm that commissioned the ghostwritten op-ed. So, what is apparently a patient organization is officially a physician organization that is actually a pharmaceutical industry organization – or a creature of the industry.

It is less of a paradox, then, that the Alliance for Patient Access opposes limits on drug costs, even though high costs clearly affect patients' access to drugs.[37]

Strong patents create monopolies that allow for very high prices. Nonetheless, there is no shortage of PAOs willing to advocate in favour of patent protections for pharmaceuticals in the name of increased innovation. In response to discussions on a United Nations panel that pointed the finger at drug patents as key culprits in maintaining high prices for much-needed drugs, thereby keeping them out of the hands of patients, fifty PAOs wrote to then-Secretary of State John Kerry, to support the US government's strong defence of the patent system. Some of those PAOs might have been acting out of hope for magic bullets, and some might have been acting purely as creatures of the pharmaceutical industry. The Global Alliance for Patient Access, a spin-off project of the US Alliance for Patient Access, was one of the signatories.[38]

Among all these PAOs with similar names, and which invoke similar high-minded principles, are some that genuinely advocate for public access and affordability.[39] But there are just as many that are deeply conflicted. The Centre for Medicine in the Public Interest, operating in the no-holds-barred arena of US politics, is one of the most blunt and troll-like of all the PAOs supporting the pharmaceutical industry's interests. It describes itself as a 'non-profit, non-partisan organization promoting innovative solutions that advance medical progress, reduce health disparities, extend life and make health care more affordable, preventive and patient-centred'. To illustrate just how aggressive the Centre can get, a column on its website awarded a 'Pharma Idiocy Award' to two Yale professors, Cary Gross and Abbe Gluck, for their editorial on the 'Soaring Cost of Cancer Treatment'. Robert Goldberg, writing for the Centre, alleged that the 'authors managed to synthesize every pedestrian and inchoate assault on drug companies into an editorial that took the genre to a new level'. Goldberg writes:

> The failing heart of the article ... can be obtained by reading one paragraph:
> (I am sparing you the painful waste of time required to slog through the
> entire article and endure the smell of decomposing bromides).

He then quotes what he takes to be the most offensive few sentences from the article in question. Here are Gross and Gluck, quoted by Goldberg:

We know that the cost of cancer drugs has increased dramatically, even though most drugs are brought into the market without compelling evidence that they prolong survival or improve quality of life. We know that these high costs render state-of-the-art cancer treatment unaffordable to patients without insurance and even to some patients with insurance. Furthermore, financial distress associated with paying for cancer treatment is common and is associated with stress, decreased adherence, bankruptcy, and worse outcomes. Finally, we know that the cost of new drugs is not well correlated with their effectiveness, nor with the presence of competing products.[40]

Gross and Gluck's words appear unexceptional. However, Goldberg takes aggressive exception to their view:

I won't take on every citation Gross and Gluck (Gross-Gluck sounds like a Borscht Belt act) use to assert perfect knowledge about the havoc price increases have had on society.

Goldberg concludes by calling the article a 'half-baked convoluted diatribe', and calls '[s]hame on the medical journals that continue to publish [such] anti-pharma crap'.[41]

Advocates and PAOs can do important work to distract attention from the costs of drugs – with more subtlety than the Centre can muster. Almost every time that PAOs call for more support of innovation, they echo pharma companies' refrain that high prices are necessary to bring new drugs to the market. Much of the time they point the finger at insurers (public and private) for not covering all drugs, in an attempt to deflect attention away from pharma.

PROMOTING DISEASES AND TREATMENTS

In 2016, a public relations company, CGI Group, sent out a press release inviting prominent Canadian newspapers and broadcasters to interview a well-known Canadian comedian, Cathy Jones, on the topic of 'vaginal atrophy'. The Toronto

Globe and Mail took Jones up on the interview, and ran the story. As a comedian, Jones was comfortable having a light-hearted discussion about what could have been an uncomfortable topic.[42]

There wasn't any mention that Jones was being paid to do these interviews. Nor was it made clear whether she had or didn't have vaginal atrophy – as she puts it, she was just trying to convince women to talk to their doctors, because she feels 'passionate about vaginal health'. There wasn't any mention of drugs, or of the drug company paying for the PR campaign. 'No parties including GCI want any mention of the drug or drug company', a contact for CGI told the Canadian Broadcasting Corporation in one of its pitches for an interview. 'It's an unbranded campaign.'[43]

'Vaginal atrophy' is a recently developed name for a loose collection of symptoms, including dryness, itching, burning and soreness. Most of the prominent medical science publications that mention vaginal atrophy are either sponsored by or are based on the direct research of one drug company, Novo Nordisk. These publications tend to prominently feature local oestrogen therapy, a treatment manufactured by, of course, Novo Nordisk. In 2007, The North American Menopause Society published a positive statement on local oestrogen treatment for vaginal atrophy. That statement, too, was supported by Novo Nordisk, and it was turned into a continuing medical education course for doctors.

For a condition like vaginal atrophy, it's valuable to have patients approach their doctors to seek treatment. Therefore, Novo Nordisk wants to get both patients and doctors using its preferred way of understanding symptoms, and even its preferred term. To that end, it does things like hire PR firms to have stories about the condition planted in the media, featuring 'patient advocates' like Cathy Jones. CGI is right that it's an 'unbranded campaign': unbranded in the sense that the official brand is lurking in the murky background. But the unofficial brand is the term 'vaginal atrophy' itself, and that is firmly front and centre.

The vaginal atrophy campaign was a broad one, intended to reach many readers of newspapers and viewers of television. Especially in countries like Canada, which partially restrict direct-to-consumer advertising of drugs, companies find it valuable to use both broad and narrow campaigns.

CONCLUSION: ARRANGING THE CHORUS OF PATIENT ADVOCATES

I began this chapter with the case of the approval of flibanserin, the drug for female sexual dysfunction. The company owning the drug worked with women who were diagnosed with the dysfunction, and developed individual advocates to help make the case that a treatment was urgently needed. This is just one of an increasing number of similar stories, especially for drugs for rare diseases – a growth area for the pharmaceutical industry. The advocates were acting in what they saw as the women's best interests, which was also in the company's best interests.

If companies can bring patient advocates onside, they can use those advocates in a variety of ways and for a variety of ends. They can articulate need, urgency and hope where it can make a difference. In addition to intervening with regulatory bodies, advocates can influence policy, serve as conduits of information, act as spokespeople for public relations campaigns, and promote treatments and diseases to other patients. When they need to, companies can create patient advocates and advocacy organizations out of thin air (and money), to give voice to their interests in a way that has or can be taken to have legitimacy.

Carefully engaging sirens of hope can make the difference between a molecule and a profitable drug. Ventriloquizing the occasional troll to beat the drum for companies' interests and to silence critics can make for a profitable environment more generally.

8

CONCLUSION:
THE HAUNTED PHARMAKON

ASSEMBLAGE MARKETING AND CORPORATE DISGUISES

TOGETHER, THE MANY ELEMENTS THAT PHARMACEUTICAL COMPANIES SHAPE, adjust and assemble constitute markets. These markets are new creations, but because they draw together medical science and health needs they take on an appearance of necessity. They look like entities that have emerged whole from just below the social surface.

The goal of pharma's assemblage marketing is to establish conditions that make specific diagnoses, prescriptions and purchases as obvious and frequent as possible. Ideally, all of the elements of a market can be directed towards the same issues, claims and facts, so that the drugs sell themselves. Pharma companies can then recede into the background, and apply only minimal pressure when needed. From the original image of assemblage marketing I presented in Chapter 1, pharma tries to achieve something more like Figure 8.1. Here, the drug is at the centre of the diagram, surrounded by actors, institutions and information that make it successful. In a sense, the assemblage makes not just the market but also the drug.

While a *perfectly* tight assemblage is only an ideal, sometimes pharma companies get close to that ideal. It should now be clear that these companies systematically influence the production, distribution and consumption of medical knowledge. Pharma companies and their agents make decisions in the running of clinical trials, in interpretations of data and established medical science, in the messages conveyed in articles and presentations, in the timing and location of publications, in the identities of authors and presenters, in what their

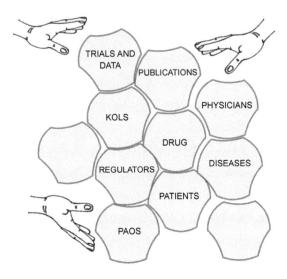

FIG. 8.1 The goal of assemblage marketing

representatives communicate, and in what their allies say. Companies sustain large and partly invisible networks to do all of this, creating and participating in shadowy knowledge economies.

In the ghost management of research, publication and dissemination, pharma companies see value in letting apparently independent academics and physicians serve as their conduits for scientific information. These key opinion leaders (KOLs) can be thought of as disguises for corporate faces, allowing companies to market their products through more neutral representations of medical science.

Sometimes, the disguise is nearly perfect. Many ghost-managed publications, talks and continuing medical education courses are presented as more or less independent research. Sometimes, not only is the sponsoring company unseen, but so is the product. When it comes to marketing to physicians and researchers, pharma companies can, if they choose, make themselves almost invisible.

Even when they are more visible, pharma's agents can use elements of disguise. Physicians can take advantage of something like plausible deniability when company influence is cloaked in science – in speaker bureau presentations, for example. KOLs can act with clearer consciences if the substantial benefits they receive are seen as parts of scientific exchanges. The same may be true for physicians benefitting from continuing medical education courses or the attention of company representatives. But whether the ghost-managed medical science disguises pharma interests so that they *cannot* be seen, or simply so that they *need not* be seen, the result is often that they *are not* seen.

The ghostly work of pharma companies to produce, distribute and encourage the consumption of medical information is not merely a corporate use of the patina of science. In the ghost management of medical science by pharmaceutical companies, we have a new mode of science. This is corporate science, done by many unseen workers, performed for marketing purposes, skilfully communicated and disseminated, and drawing its authority from traditional academic science. However, this commercially driven science differs from academic science in the narrow interests behind it and the kinds of choices those narrow interests produce. Unlike most independent researchers, pharmaceutical companies have clear and strong interests in particular kinds of research, questions and outcomes. They want to build markets and increase sales.

The ancient Greek word 'pharmakon', I mentioned earlier, can be translated as either 'cure' or 'poison'. According to the 'inverse benefit law', the effort to enlarge the market for a drug is correlated with a decrease in the ratio of benefits to risks.[1] Increasing the number of people taking a drug decreases its average benefit, and may increase its average risk – adverse reactions to prescription drugs are currently the third or fourth leading cause of death in many countries.[2] The pharmakon becomes less cure and more poison.

If almost every decision in the research and publication process pushes the research even subtly in a consistent direction, then that is the direction in which the research will go. We can reasonably expect – and there is abundant evidence to support this – that the industry makes its choices to support its commercial interests. We know that pharma companies' research produces *results* that favour its products. We might care just as much about the more nebulous issues of how the *kinds of research* and *questions* that pharma supports shape medicine to favour its products.

Because assemblage marketing is a much larger activity than mere advertising, it changes the world in profound but subtle ways. In particular, pharma's assemblage marketing increases the burden of disease. To increase their markets, pharma-sponsored medical studies and guidelines tend to expand the definitions and prominence of specific diseases. This increases the number of people potentially affected. Pharma's selective but aggressive distribution of medical information promotes symptoms and diagnoses to physicians and patients. Patients present themselves to their doctors with complaints shaped by pharma promotion and readily available pharma-sponsored information. Physicians may then understand their patients, and patients may understand themselves, in terms laid out by the industry. Big pharma's invisible hands are making us more sick.

GHOST-MANAGED INTEGRITY

Medicine's close relationships with the pharmaceutical industry pose moral challenges. At the core of justifications of the connections between medicine and the pharmaceutical industry is the assumption that medicine has the integrity and rigour needed to keep control while welcoming pharma's invisible hands into its journals, conferences, clinics and more. Medicine and its regulators hope to use what pharma has to offer to improve medical science, education and care. They very rarely see the possibility of interested knowledge, the possibility that the careful deployment of science can support commercial over patient interests: science is taken as a guarantee that medicine can remain pure. This is even though the terms in which medicine evaluates science – and the resulting education and care – are influenced by pharma.

For example, we saw in Chapter 5 that KOLs, without any need for prompting, respond to conflict in their roles by drawing on a range of justificatory schemes, producing a range of moral microclimates.[3] The main sources of the justification they provide for working for pharma involve connected claims that they are contributing to patient health by educating other doctors, and that they stand behind their ghost-managed presentations and articles, believing in the products they promote. Their sense of independence or integrity is crucial. They can vigorously insist that they are not paid shills, paid stooges or paid monkeys, even though they *are* paid. They can focus on the fact that they believe what they say, that they see it as warranted, regulated and useful. If they can speak with conviction, they don't consider relevant any of the relationships that they might have with the sponsoring company. KOLs can cheerfully take the money, status and perks that pharmaceutical companies offer, believing that they are acting in the interests of health.

Similar things could be said about many of the other actors we've met. Doctors who see sales representatives are often confident of their ability to maintain their independence and their scientific standards, and to take advantage of what the reps have to offer, thus helping their patients.[4] While some patient advocacy organizations are simple pharma creations, other PAOs are or develop out of grassroots patient efforts, and join forces with pharma in order to conscientiously represent patient interests. Some of the interest in patient adherence is purely to increase sales, but some researchers approach the adherence issue from the position that doctors' prescriptions improve patients' health, and therefore that non-adherence is a health problem to be addressed. Even within pharma, publication planners, medical science liaisons, sales representatives and others often justify their actions in terms of communicating scientific truths.

But pharma companies go to some lengths to gain control over the actions, habits, beliefs and loyalties of the people with whom they engage. Relationships, and what those relationships are intended to achieve, are carefully managed, and in the process they are co-opted into promotional plans. By definition, pharma's careful management efforts impinge on medicine's actual independence, though medicine may not always be aware of it. People working in medicine may be misled by their sense of integrity, since they are not fully independent.

Not only does pharma put considerable effort into managing its relationships with medicine, but it also creates conflicts of interest. Publication planners, for example, are paid to create sound scientific articles reporting on clinical trials and other studies, and at the same time to help promote products by placing favourable articles in medical journals. It would be surprising if study results weren't sometimes bent to serve promotional goals. Meanwhile, the authors on those ghost-managed articles receive something for almost nothing: credit for scientific work in trade for their credibility. It would be surprising if they weren't inclined to accept pharma manuscripts more or less as they receive them, even if the results reported in those manuscripts are spun to serve companies' interests. KOLs' conflicts of interest, stemming from their payments for speaking engagements, not only make it more likely that they will give sales messages in their talks, but also make it more likely that they won't even recognize that this is what they are doing. Conflict of interest has powerful effects, in medicine as elsewhere.[5]

In addition, integrity does not address central issues in the political economy of medical knowledge. The industry provides roughly half of the funding for clinical trials, and sponsors a majority of the new trials initiated each year. As we've seen, pharmaceutical companies produce a significant portion of the scientific literature on in-patent prescription drugs. They and their agents shape these articles, and choose both their authors and the journals to which they are submitted. Companies' interests influence a myriad of legitimate choices in the design, implementation, analysis, description and publication of clinical trials. The result is still recognizably medical science, but it is science serving very particular and clear commercial goals. The influence goes on: when pharmaceutical companies get physicians and researchers to circulate information, it is the companies' preferred KOLs doing the circulation and the companies' preferred information being circulated. If seen as education, the form of continuing medical education in which KOLs participate is one thoroughly shaped by the interests of the companies that sponsor it; this is science chosen to help sell a product. Even if companies are not completely coherent actors, they are coherent enough in their goals that choices at all the different stages of research and communication can point in the same direction.

As a result, when physicians learn about conditions and treatments, they are often learning results created by agents of pharmaceutical companies and transmitted by other agents of those companies. In the end, it matters little what all the participants think they are doing, how honest they are, or how much they believe what they say. They are, inevitably and inescapably, part of large-scale, commercially driven efforts to shape the medical knowledge that physicians have and apply in practice. Where pharma is involved, research, education and marketing are everywhere fused by invisible hands.

LOOSENING THE GRIP

Pharma has achieved a considerable degree of hegemony over medical science and the practice of medicine. The industry has succeeded by applying its enormous resources where they can influence taken-for-granted medical knowledge, ordinary medical practice, policies and regulations, and attitudes toward the industry itself and its contributions to health. It is difficult to muster effective responses to the industry's actions, precisely because it commands so many resources. Attempts to reform pharma-haunted medicine are often met with very effective opposition.

In addition, pharma has so tightly insinuated itself into medicine that pharma appears essential to the functioning of medicine. How would new drugs be developed without the industry? How could medical research run without pharma funding? How would physicians stay up to date without presentations paid for by pharma companies? How would clinics run without the free lunches provided by sales reps? As a result of this infiltration, attempts at reform are often met with genuine opposition from within medicine. There is no point in giving moralizing sermons to physicians and researchers. Not only are sermons ineffective, but the industry is already easily able to counter them, pointing to how much it contributes to medicine and medical research.

Effective ways of addressing the haunted world of pharma should focus on correcting large imbalances in the current political economy of medical knowledge. Unfortunately, this way of understanding the problem doesn't lend itself to easy solutions. If pharmaceutical companies' substantial resources give them too much power to shape medical knowledge, solutions have to focus on reducing their resources or substantially redressing the balance of resources.

Given the scale and reach of the pharma industry's actions, no single solution will address all of the problems it creates, short of closing the industry down. So many reforms have been proposed, and even implemented, that I cannot discuss them here. Instead, I'll chart out approaches in very general terms.

Responses that challenge pharma tend to assume one of seven forms, not always cleanly distinct from each other: individual withdrawal, safeguarding the quality of information, increasing transparency, restricting pharma practices, applying monetary penalties for illegal actions and harms, promoting the independence of medicine and industry, and disrupting the industry as a whole. I discuss each of these in turn.

Individual Withdrawal

Perhaps the most straightforward, though modest, approach is for individual patients to cautiously and sensibly avoid taking more prescription drugs than necessary, and for physicians to avoid prescribing more drugs than necessary.

One of the starting points of this book is that information does not move on its own, but always requires a mover. I've argued that when it comes to medical information, pharmaceutical companies are some of the most important movers, though their efforts are often obscured. Most of us could be much more aware than we are that the health and drug information we receive – even the information that we appear to receive randomly – may have been shaped and transmitted by pharma. At the least, it is always worth asking whether and how much influence pharma has had.

Patients even need to ask this of the information they receive from their own doctors. With that in mind, we might try to avoid becoming patients in the first place by avoiding unnecessary tests, paying more attention to our bodies, using common sense and staying healthy in uncontroversial ways. (This is not an advertisement for 'alternative' treatments, which can be both controversial and also embedded in their own problematic political economies of knowledge.)

When we do become patients, we should press our doctors about whether there are alternatives to drug treatment, whether there are older, off-patent drugs – not only are they less expensive, but their effects and side-effects are better known and the interests in propping up a body of knowledge behind them are much smaller. We might also press our doctors to avoid long-term treatments, thinking of us as intrinsically healthy rather than intrinsically diseased. And finally, we should press them about exactly how they gained their knowledge.

For each of these points, there are analogous ones for physicians, who can actively work toward minimalist prescribing and generous de-prescribing.

Safeguarding the Quality of Medical Information

Many people take this issue to be one of ensuring that medical information is sound. Many regulators prevent pharma companies from off-label marketing – for example through their sales reps' and speaker bureau presentations – so the label reflects evidence that has gone through proper channels.

However, much of the information that pharma promotes is already ordinary. We shouldn't assume that well-educated and apparently honest physicians and researchers are routinely peddling falsehoods. Indeed, the kind of knowledge they share fits medical standards well, and passes many routine regulatory and scientific tests. It looks like mainstream medical science. This is why medical journals solicit pharma's articles and apply similar standards to them as they do to more independently produced articles.

Relatively few pharma medical journal articles have been shown to involve scientific fraud involving data or statistics (although of course there is widespread fraud in terms of authorship). For the cases of fraud, correctives to the medical literature can be very useful – seen in, for example, the recent initiative to 'restore invisible and abandoned trials'.[6] But without widespread dissemination, correctives can languish. Meanwhile, pharma companies are distributing their preferred parts of the medical science literature.

The fact that pharmaceutical companies go to such length to disguise their interests suggests that people are prepared to accept that even rigorous science can be affected by interests. At this point in the book, it might seem obvious that science can be shaped by interests, but that idea runs against the common view that pharma can be a valuable contributor to medicine as long as it respects common rules.

Medical journals could stop publishing pharma-sponsored research altogether. The twenty or so most important medical journals have such a lock on prestige that together they could step away from the pharmaceutical industry and show off their clean hands. A set of 'pharma-free journals' might even gain prestige.

Given this book's argument that pharma controls a shadowy economy of medical knowledge, we need to focus on *independent* quality information. Though they may not always do it, pharma's invisible hands are fully capable of producing what passes for good medical science, but it is *interested* medical science.

Transparency

Transparency, captured by the saying that 'sunlight is the best disinfectant', is a popular response to the shadowy aspects of pharma's actions.[7] Transparency is especially valuable to those studying pharma. This book has benefitted considerably from access to data – on clinical trials, on payments to physicians – made available through various public disclosures. This, however, is a very roundabout route for sunlight to take to become a disinfectant. Analyses based on disclosures come slowly, and people need to act on them.

Sometimes transparency affects behaviour more directly. The US Physician Payments Sunshine Act, which records all payments to physicians by pharmaceutical companies, had very minor effects on total payments.[8] However, it appears that the amount spent on speakers' fees dropped slightly in the first few years of the programme. And at conferences on managing speaker bureau programmes, I heard anecdotal evidence that the amount spent on speakers' fees plummeted immediately before the Act was implemented. This suggests that exposing payments was potentially embarrassing to at least some KOLs, or that the industry saw some payments as posing public relations problems.

There is some evidence that exposing conflicts of interest intensifies their effects – people declaring conflicts seem to feel licensed to act less in the public interest, but they are perceived as acting more in the public interest.[9] Even setting aside this concern, pharma funding of medical education and research is common; as a result, many people within the medical community evaluate information with industry origins or connections in the same ways they evaluate more independent information, and sometimes even value it more highly. For example, physicians know that sales reps have interests in promoting products, but many nevertheless welcome interactions with those reps.

Finally, transparency can be challenging to implement. Some shadowy practices can remain in the shadows. The industry can subvert efforts at transparency by making data take forms that ensure their uselessness.[10] It can also comply selectively, if the risk and consequences of being caught are low enough. For example, it appears that the industry does not fully comply with mandates for transparency around clinical trials, and doesn't even provide all trial data to regulators, despite legal requirements to do so.[11]

Restrictions on Pharma

Some strategies for reform simply focus on taking away some of the pharmaceutical industry's effective tools. In some places, pharma companies are prevented from (or have voluntarily stopped as a result of pressure) providing branded trinkets – Viagra pens, Abilify clipboards and the like. These apparently trivial gifts are effective, but can't be justified as contributing to medical care or education. In other jurisdictions, regulatory bodies have banned gifts above a certain value – golf trips, tickets to sporting events – that don't directly contribute to education. In most places, direct-to-consumer advertising is restricted.

All of these measures simply restrict effective sales techniques. However, they are almost always implemented in such a way that equally or more effective sales techniques bound up with education and medical care continue to be allowed. So, golf trips might be banned, but not free dinners accompanied by educational presentations. Branded prescription pads might be unacceptable, but not free samples of the drugs themselves. Direct-to-consumer advertising is restricted, except when it comes to disease awareness programmes. Building on the argument of this book, restrictions on pharma's effective marketing tools would have to extend to tools that also claim to contribute to medical research, education and care.

Monetary Penalties and Threats

Perhaps the most promising avenue for addressing pharma is through legal action. Leading the way, the Office of the Inspector General of the US has argued that, through illegal marketing, individual pharmaceutical companies have defrauded federal health care programmes. These suits have resulted in settlements, because none of the companies can afford to lose cases and then see their products become ineligible for purchase by Medicare, Medicaid, and other programmes. The settlements have put in place very wide-ranging procedures – called corporate integrity agreements – that temporarily limit some unethical and inappropriate actions. Among other things, these corporate integrity agreements often demand that companies establish firewalls between their commercial and their medical affairs departments.[12]

Therefore, though corporate integrity agreements may originate in complaints about illegal activity, they are sometimes able to effect safeguards that go beyond simply penalizing one-off instances of such activity. Nevertheless, they are only temporary agreements, and tend to cleave to the logics that accept the value of pharma companies contributing directly to medical research, education and care.

Separating Medicine and Industry

We can see some of the problems around pharma in terms of conflicts of interest, which appear to be handled particularly poorly.[13] In an earlier chapter I mentioned the revolving doors between regulators and the industry. The routine application of familiar conflict of interest rules should rule out such obvious problems. But they might also be applied to many other situations, including almost all payments and perks going to physicians. These payments put physicians in positions of conflicted interest with respect to their duties to their patients. Whether physicians recognize it or not, payments are inducements to prescribe. It is a testament to pharma's success at insinuating itself into medicine that it would be considered almost unthinkable to end all such payments.

One could respond to this book's account of KOLs with a limited proposal based on conflicts of interest and a separation of powers. There is no obvious public good served by physicians giving promotional talks. Even if there is educational value in promotional talks – a point debated even by the KOLs who give those talks – that value could be provided just as well by sales representatives as by physicians. It would make sense, then, to ban promotional talks by physicians. If promotional talks persisted, they would be given by sales representatives, whose promotional role is at least overt.[14]

A number of organizations provide independent sources of information about pharmaceuticals, often carefully reviewing the medical literature with highly critical eyes and a commitment to digging deep into the data. These are extremely useful ventures for those physicians and others who consult them. However, they run up against the same problem as corrective publications, namely, that pharma has much better resources for distributing its preferred medical information than have independent agencies.

Recognizing that the integration of pharmaceutical R&D and marketing doesn't serve the interests of the public, governments could force companies to split these functions – just as electricity generation and distribution are separated in many privatized markets, and, more informally, the editorial and advertising departments of newspapers are supposed to be separated. R&D firms would sell, in a well-regulated manner, their successful products to marketing firms, and so would have less incentive to carry out thorough assemblage marketing.[15]

Or, at the highest level, governments could separate drug research and marketing more firmly.[16] We can't assume that drug companies will end the integration of research and marketing on their own. A number of commentators have suggested that governments take clinical trials – at least those done for regulatory purposes – out of the hands of drug companies and fund necessary ones through taxes on those companies.[17] Such solutions would take an enormous political will that is currently nowhere in view, but might solve many problems.

Disrupting Pharma as a Whole

Other approaches are even more radical. They identify the problems with the pharmaceutical industry as rooted in a core conflict between capitalism and medicine. Seen in this way, real solutions must involve dramatic changes to how drugs are developed, produced and sold. A common proposal is to end patents on drugs, which would allow for broad competition on price and would reduce pharma's interest in creating markets for expensive treatments. Another proposal is to integrate pharmaceutical research, development and manufacturing into national health systems; this would, presumably, more closely link pharmaceuticals to pre-existing health needs in a context in which costs are contained.[18]

Perhaps, while researchers and governments work out how to completely reform the system, there could be a moratorium on new drug approvals – ten years would give some breathing space.

Obviously, if governments are mostly unwilling to separate drug research and marketing, they will be much less willing to consider radical disruptions of pharma more generally. At the highest level, governments are themselves highly conflicted, typically seeing the pharmaceutical sector as an important part of the new high-tech economies that they wish to establish.

Stepping Back

Reform should attempt to limit the sheer amount of influence that pharmaceutical companies have on medical opinion. A small number of companies with well-defined and narrow interests have inordinate influence over how medical knowledge is produced, circulated and consumed. The issue here, as in other cases of hegemony, is one of a few actors having accumulated the power to shape landscapes – in this case, some very important landscapes – on which many others base their decisions. And pharmaceutical companies not only shape taken-for-granted medical knowledge and opinions, but in many locations have also naturalized their presence and activities. Most physicians see the companies as playing legitimate roles in their offices, in creating and distributing medical research and in funding and providing medical education.

The high commercial stakes mean that all of the parties connected with pharma's presence in medicine can find reasons to participate, support and steadily normalize it. It seems that it is here to stay for a while.

ACKNOWLEDGMENTS

I HAVE BEEN DOING RESEARCH ON AND WRITING ABOUT THE PHARMACEUTICAL industry for so long that my acknowledgments here can't be even nearly complete. I started this research after hearing an excellent constellation of presentations by Jennifer Fishman, Jeremy Greene, David Healy and Andy Lakoff. They then introduced me to the area and some of the many other people working in it. I especially appreciated my conversations with Jeremy then and later – everybody working in this area can learn from him. Many of my other intellectual debts are in the footnotes, but I particularly want to acknowledge conversations and exchanges with Jill Fisher, Marc-André Gagnon, David Healy, C-F Helgesson, Sammi King, Joel Lexchin, Phil Mirowski, Maggie Mort, Marc Rodwin and Jamie Swift.

Upon entering the world of pharma, I was lucky to become part of a lively private listserv discussion of the pharmaceutical industry's practices. That discussion has informed my work in many intangible ways, and has given me a wealth of pharmaceutical knowledge that I've been able to use to support my research.

I was also lucky to be coming from the field of Science and Technology Studies. My background encouraged me to not naturalize existing or ideological boundaries of medicine, and led me to try to understand the processes and structures through which the pharmaceutical industry was acting. Altogether, this background led me to look for – and then find – things that many people coming from medicine, bioethics and other fields studying pharma often ignore.

Much-appreciated funding for this project came from grants from the Canadian Institutes of Health Research (#106892) and the Social Sciences and Humanities Research Council of Canada (#410-2010-1033). The publication of this book was also supported, in part, by on-going funding from Queen's University.

The first version of Chapter 3 was published as Sergio Sismondo, 'Ghosts in the Machine: Publication Planning in the Medical Sciences', *Social Studies of Science* 39, no. 2 (2009): 171–198; some of that material was used in later articles, including 'Pushing Knowledge in the Drug Industry: Ghost-Managed Science', in Sergio Sismondo and Jeremy Greene, eds, *The Pharmaceutical Studies Reader* (Malden, MA: Wiley-Blackwell, 2015), 150–164. Similarly, an early version of Chapter 5 was published as Sergio Sismondo, 'Key Opinion Leaders: Valuing Independence and Conflict of Interest in the Medical Sciences', in Isabelle Dussauge, C-F Helgesson and Francis Lee, eds, *Value Practices in the Life Sciences* (Oxford: Oxford University Press, 2015), 31–48. A portion of Chapter 5 also descends from Sergio Sismondo and Zdenka Chloubova, '"You're Not Just a Paid Monkey Reading Slides": How Key Opinion Leaders Explain and Justify Their Work', *BioSocieties* 11, no. 2 (2016): 199–219. Bits and pieces of the rest of the book are taken from a number of other articles and chapters, too numerous to mention.

The many audiences at presentations of early versions of some of these chapters, at excellent universities around the world, contributed important questions, comments and the occasional enthusiastic reception. I especially want to thank audiences at Berkeley, Copenhagen, Harvard, Leiden, Linköping, Northwestern, Pennsylvania, Vienna, York and a few annual meetings of the Society for Social Studies of Science. Students taking my courses have had to put up with my trying out different ideas and chapter theses, including some that did not make it out of the classroom and into the book.

The people interviewed for this project are owed enormous thanks for their time and thoughtfulness. If you were interviewed and you're reading this, I know that the results don't flatter your professions, but I hope that you find the results useful to think about.

On a few occasions, I hired or worked with research assistants or associates. Some whose work was particularly important to this book and who deserve special thanks are Zdenka Chloubova (who helped interview KOLs), Khadija Coxon, Elliot Ross and Jelena Subina, each of whom attended an industry conference and gave me detailed reports of the presentations there, and Heather Poechman, with whom I collaborated on most of the diagrams and who read the entire manuscript, helping with the formatting and checking it for spelling and grammar problems.

Over the past few years, weekly conversations and exercise with Luis Illas helped out tremendously. Christine Sismondo is an inspiration and always a fount of good sense: read her book *America Walks into a Bar*! I've also appreciated the tacit support, and sometimes more tangible help of Clara and Joe Sismondo. Phoebe distracted me as I was trying to pull the book together, but in the end she gave in to the fact that I was determined to spend a lot of time in front of the computer.

I very much appreciated close readings of the manuscript by two editors for Mattering Press, Uli Beisel and Endre Dányi; Endre also did an excellent job of shepherding the manuscript through to publication, providing excellent support and advice. Mattering Press has done a super job, and I would encourage other authors in Science and Technology Studies to consider it for their next book.

When I needed him, my good friend Alec Ross stepped up and read the book, making good suggestions throughout to make the prose less leaden. Alec had been hearing about and reading the central ideas and research here for a very long time, and I hope that the larger project has lived up to its promise. I was flattered when my friend and colleague Nicole Nelson insisted on reading a penultimate draft of the manuscript, and then provided many pages of incisive and generous comments. Read her recent book, too: *Model Behavior*.

Khadija Coxon read and/or helped with earlier versions of a number of these chapters, and had to put up with me working through the same constellation of ideas for far too long. The conversations we had about them improved my work in more ways than I can know. Thank you! And thank you all!

NOTES

1. POWER AND KNOWLEDGE IN DRUG MARKETING

1 This is true even in nearly ideal circumstances – for example, as part of the close communication between teachers and students who have incentives respectively to teach and to learn, and who have books and articles to support their communication. Much knowledge moves only with difficulty.

2 For a general overview of the field, see Sergio Sismondo, *An Introduction to Science and Technology Studies*, 2nd edn (Chichester: Wiley, 2010).

3 For a few key early works adopting this view, see David Bloor, *Knowledge and Social Imagery*, 2nd edn (Chicago: University of Chicago Press, 1991); H. M. Collins, *Changing Order: Replication and Induction in Scientific Practice*, 2nd edn (Chicago: University of Chicago Press, 1990); G. Nigel Gilbert and Michael Mulkay, *Opening Pandora's Box: A Sociological Analysis of Scientists' Discourse* (Cambridge: Cambridge University Press, 1984); Karin D. Knorr-Cetina, *The Manufacture of Knowledge: An Essay on the Constructivist and Contextual Nature of Science* (Oxford: Pergamon Press, 1981); Bruno Latour and Steve Woolgar, *Laboratory Life: The Construction of Scientific Facts*, 2nd edn (Princeton, NJ: Princeton University Press, 1986); Steven Shapin and Simon Schaffer, *Leviathan and the Air-Pump: Hobbes, Boyle, and the Experimental Life* (Princeton, NJ: Princeton University Press, 1985).

4 In a fascinating study, Harry Collins shows that technical knowledge moves much more easily when attempts at transmission include face-to-face contact than when they are conducted purely through written texts. This resonates with the pharmaceutical industry's use of key opinion leaders and sales representatives, as seen in Chapters 5 and 6 of this book. See H. M. Collins, *Changing Order: Replication and Induction in Scientific Practice*, 2nd edn (Chicago: University of Chicago Press, 1990). Bruno Latour argues that models of the movement of information in terms of 'translation' tell us much more than do models in terms of 'diffusion'. His point is essentially the same as mine on the quasi-substantiality of knowledge. See Bruno Latour, *Science in Action: How to Follow Scientists and Engineers through Society* (Cambridge, MA: Harvard University Press, 1987).

5 Even Wikipedia is not as egalitarian as it seems, though. See Heather Ford and Judy Wajcman, '"Anyone Can Edit", Not Everyone Does: Wikipedia's Infrastructure and the Gender Gap', *Social Studies of Science* 47, no. 4 (2017): 511–527.

6 These terms are borrowed from the sociologist Pierre Bourdieu, for example in 'The Specificity of the Scientific Field and the Social Conditions of the Progress of Reason', *Social Science Information* 14, no. 6 (1975): 19–47. There is no escaping the sciences' social structures, even as they remain within the sciences. As Bourdieu says, 'The "pure" universe of even the "purest" science is a social field like any other, with its distribution of power and its monopolies, its struggles and strategies, interests and profits'. Even the production of 'objective truth' requires social conditions. Moreover, action in a field is competitive, a struggle for limited capital among its members. This will be accentuated when some parties have access to considerably more resources for establishing scientific knowledge than have others. See also Pierre Bourdieu, *Language and Symbolic Power* (Cambridge, MA: Harvard University Press, 1981).

7 Antonio Gramsci, *Selections from the Prison Notebooks*, ed. and trans. Quinton Hoare and Geoffrey Nowell-Smith (New York: International Publishers, 1971). Gramsci's central concern was strategic: to displace conservative (in particular Fascist) hegemony over key institutions in favour of socialist hegemony. I hope that people will be able to use my work in this book in strategic ways, too: to displace pharmaceutical industry hegemony over key aspects of the medical world, in favour of a more democratic medicine.

8 Antonio Gramsci, *Selections from the Prison Notebooks*, ed. and trans. Quinton Hoare and Geoffrey Nowell-Smith (New York: International Publishers, 1971), 5 (emphasis in the original).

9 Therefore, my approach is quite different from that of, say, Ben Goldacre, who tends to focus on issues of truth and falsity in claims about efficacy and safety. This is not to dismiss his fine work: Ben Goldacre, *Bad Pharma: How Drug Companies Mislead Doctors and Harm Patients* (Toronto: McClelland & Stewart, 2012). See also, for example, John Abraham and Courtney Davis, 'Drug Evaluation and the Permissive Principle: Continuities and Contradictions between Standards and Practices in Antidepressant Regulation', *Social Studies of Science* 39, no. 4 (2009): 569–598; Jon N. Jureidini, Leemon B. McHenry, and Peter R. Mansfield, 'Clinical Trials and Drug Promotion: Selective Reporting of Study 329', *International Journal of Risk & Safety in Medicine* 20, no.1–2 (2008): 73–81; Bruce M. Psaty and Richard A. Kronmal, 'Reporting Mortality Findings in Trials of Rofecoxib for Alzheimer Disease or Cognitive Impairment: A Case Study Based on Documents from Rofecoxib Litigation', *Journal of the American Medical Association* 299, no. 15 (2008): 1813–1817.

10 Industry-sponsored studies appear to be as rigorous as other studies, even while sponsorship strongly shapes reported outcomes. For a recent meta-analysis, see Andreas Lundh, Sergio Sismondo, Joel Lexchin, Octavian A. Busuioc, and Lisa Bero, 'Industry Sponsorship and Research Outcome', *Cochrane Database of Systematic Reviews* 12 (2012). Two earlier meta-analyses came to similar conclusions: Joel Lexchin, Lisa A. Bero, Benjamin Djulbegovic, and Otavio Clark, 'Pharmaceutical Industry Sponsorship and Research Outcome and Quality: Systematic Review', *British Medical Journal* 326, no. 7400 (2003): 1167–1170; Justin E. Bekelman, Yan Li, and Cary P. Gross, 'Scope and Impact of Financial Conflicts of Interest in Biomedical Research: A Systematic Review', *Journal of the American Medical Association* 289, no. 4 (2003): 454–465.

11 Political economy has been an important lens through which the field of Science and Technology Studies has viewed biotechnology and pharmaceutical trials. See, for example, Melinda Cooper, 'Experimental Labour – Offshoring Clinical Trials to China', *East Asian Science, Technology and Society* 2, no. 1 (2008): 73–92; Jill Fisher, *Medical Research for Hire: The Political Economy of Pharmaceutical Clinical Trials* (New Brunswick, NJ: Rutgers University Press, 2009); Kaushik Sunder Rajan, *Biocapital: The Constitution of Postgenomic Life* (Durham, NC: Duke University Press, 2006); Catherine Waldby, *Tissue Economies: Organs and Cell Lines in Late Capitalism* (Durham, NC: Duke University Press, 2006). I am expanding that to pharmaceutical knowledge. Like economic markets, major knowledge markets have definite histories, are actively made, and are shaped by circumstances. For economic markets, see Naazneen H. Barma and Steven K. Vogel, eds, *The Political Economy Reader: Markets as Institutions* (New York: Routledge, 2008). Among those who have explicitly extended the point to knowledge markets is Steve Fuller, *The Knowledge Book: Key Concepts in Philosophy, Science and Culture* (New York: Routledge, 2014).

12 Alfred Chandler, Jr., *The Visible Hand: The Managerial Revolution in American Business* (Cambridge, MA: Harvard University Press, 1977).

13 Peter Gøtzsche has a similar attitude, but he sees the hidden actors in terms of organized crime. In a book structured around a great many anecdotes, he also explores how the pharmaceutical industry attempts to dominate medicine. See Peter C. Gøtzsche, *Deadly Medicines and Organised Crime: How Big Pharma Has Corrupted Healthcare* (London: Radcliffe Publishing, 2013).

14 See, for example, Stephan Erhardt, Lawrence J. Appel, and Curtis L. Meinert, 'Trends in National Institutes of Health Funding for Clinical Trials Registered in ClinicalTrials.gov', Journal of the American Medical Association 314, no. 23 (2015): 2566–2567.

15 Sergio Sismondo, 'Ghost Management: How Much of the Medical Literature is Shaped Behind the Scenes by the Pharmaceutical Industry?' *PLoS Medicine* 4, no. 9 (2007): e286.

16 MD NetGuide, 'The 'e'volution of Pharmaceutical Marketing' <http://www.mdnetguide.com/specialty_editions/marketer/v1n1/pharmmarket.htm> [accessed 13 August 2004].

17 Susanne L. Rose, Janelle Highland, Matthew T. Karafa, and Steven Joffe, 'Patient Advocacy Organizations, Industry Funding, and Conflicts of Interest', *JAMA Internal Medicine* 177, no. 3 (2017): 344–350.

18 David S. Hilzenrath, 'In FDA Meetings, "Voice" of the Patient Often Funded by Drug Companies', *Project On Government Oversight*, 1 December 2016 <http://www.pogo.org/our-work/reports/2016/in-fda-meetings-voice-of-the-patient-often-funded-by-drug-companies.html>.

19 For the television ad figure see Beth Snyder Bulik, 'With a Month Left to Go, Pharma's $3.2B TV Ad Spending Has Already Topped 2016', *FiercePharma* <https://www.fiercepharma.com/marketing/pharma-tv-ad-spending-tops-2016-total-one-month-left-led-by-abbvie-and-pfizer>[accessed 12 December 2017]. For approximate ratios of TV to other advertising see Julie Liesse, 'Healthcare Marketing', *Advertising Age*, 17 October 2016 <http://gaia.adage.com/images/bin/pdf/KantarHCwhitepaper_complete.pdf> [accessed 12 December 2017]. Medical journal ad spending is reported in Larry Dobrow, 'Medical Journal Ad Spend in H1 2017: All the Data in One Place', *Medical Marketing & Media*, 4 October 2017 <http://www.mmm-online.com/campaigns/medical-journal-ad-spend-in-h1-2017-all-the-data-in-one-place/article/696599/>.

20 There have been many studies of pharmaceutical advertising. For a few examples of different kinds of analyses, see: Peter Conrad and Valerie Leiter, 'From Lydia Pinkham to Queen Levitra: Direct-to-Consumer Advertising and Medicalisation', *Sociology of Health & Illness* 30, no. 6 (2008): 825–838; Barbara Mintzes, Morris L. Barer, Richard L. Kravitz, Arminée Kazanjian, Ken Bassett, Joel Lexchin, Robert G. Evans, Richard Pan, and Stephen A. Marion, 'Influence of Direct to Consumer Pharmaceutical Advertising and Patients' Requests on Prescribing Decisions: Two Site Cross Sectional Survey', *British Medical Journal* 324, no. 7332 (2002): 278–279.

21 See, for example, Statista, 'Revenue of the worldwide pharmaceutical market from 2001 to 2016 (in billion U.S. dollars)' <https://www.statista.com/statistics/263102/pharmaceutical-market-worldwide-revenue-since-2001/> [accessed 5 May 2018].

22 As long noted, firms rely on hierarchical organizations, rather than always outsourcing. In a classic paper, Ronald Coase argues that the reason for this was the possibility of reducing transaction costs within an organization, compared with between independent actors. See Ronald Coase, 'The Nature of the Firm', *Economica* 4, no. 16 (1937): 386–405. Coase's account has been challenged and supplemented by a number of others that emphasize other factors relevant to the rise and stability of

firms. See, e.g. Demetri Kantarelis, *Theories of the Firm,* 2nd edn (Geneva: Inderscience Publishers, 2014).

23 David J. Teece, Gary Pisano, and Amy Shuen, 'Dynamic Capabilities and Strategic Management', *Strategic Management Journal* 18, no. 7 (1997): 509–533.

24 Quoted in Stephen P. Dunn, 'Galbraith, Uncertainty and the Modern Corporation', in Michael Keaney, ed., *Economist with a Public Purpose: Essays in Honour of John Kenneth Galbraith* (New York: Routledge, 2001), 157–182.

25 I was introduced to the idea of channel marketing, and to the pharmaceutical industry as engaging in channel marketing, by Kalman Applbaum, 'Getting to Yes: Corporate Power and the Creation of a Psychopharmaceutical Blockbuster', *Culture, Medicine, and Psychiatry* 33, no. 2 (2009): 185–215.

26 There is a sense in which this is not unusual. The perceived validity of most knowledge, scientific and otherwise, ultimately rests on trust in its sources. See, e.g. Steven Shapin, 'Cordelia's Love: Credibility and the Social Study of Science', *Perspectives on Science* 3, no. 3 (1995): 255–275. However, medical practitioners may be more removed from core medical evidence than are many other experts.

27 Definition of Marketing', *American Marketing Association* <https://www.ama.org/AboutAMA/Pages/Definition-of-Marketing.aspx> [accessed 22 December 2017].

28 The term 'marketing era' and the starting point of my stance here are owed to Kalman Applbaum, *The Marketing Era: From Professional Practice to Global Provisioning* (New York: Routledge, 2004).

29 The theorist of marketing Peter Drucker, writing in the early 1970s, recognized the new marketing era: 'Selling and marketing are antithetical rather than synonymous or even complementary. There will always be, one can assume, a need for some selling. But the aim of marketing is to make selling superfluous. The aim of marketing is to know and understand the customer so well that the product or service fits her and sells itself. Ideally, marketing should result in a customer who is ready to buy'. Peter F. Drucker, *Management: Tasks, Responsibilities, Practices* (New York: Routledge, 1974), 64–65.

30 As many readers will recognize, the term 'assemblage' is taken from Gilles Deleuze and Félix Guattari, for example in their *A Thousand Plateaus: Capitalism and Schizophrenia* (London: Bloomsbury Publishing, 1988). However, my account of assemblage marketing owes more to Actor-Network Theory, perhaps because the construction and stabilization of actor-networks have been more clearly described than have the construction and stabilization of assemblages. For early articulations of Actor-Network Theory, see Bruno Latour, *Science in Action: How to Follow Scientists and Engineers through Society* (Cambridge, MA: Harvard University Press, 1987); Michel Callon, 'Some Elements of a Sociology of Translation: Domestication of the Scallops and the Fishermen of St. Brieuc Bay', in John Law, ed., *Power, Action and*

Belief (London: Routledge & Kegan Paul, 1986): 196–233; John Law, 'Technology and Heterogeneous Engineering: The Case of Portuguese Expansion', in Wiebe E. Bijker, T.P. Hughes and Trevor Pinch, eds. *The Social Construction of Technological Systems: New Directions in the Sociology and History of Technology* (Cambridge, MA: The MIT Press, 1987): 111–134.

31 There has been some fascinating work in Science and Technology Studies on the creation and development of markets. For example, markets require infrastructure to allow communication and exchange, as seen in the carefully constructed material and electronic structures of stock and commodity exchanges: e.g. Devin Kennedy, 'The Machine in the Market: Computers and the Infrastructure of Price at the New York Stock Exchange', *Social Studies of Science* 47 no. 6 (2017): 888–917; Caitlin Zaloom, *Out of the Pits: Traders and Technology from Chicago to London* (Chicago: University of Chicago Press, 2006). In particular, there is a thriving research programme studying how academic economics contributes to and shapes real markets. This is relevant to Chapter 5 of this book. See, e.g. Donald MacKenzie, Fabian Muniesa and Lucia Siu, eds, *Do Economists Make Markets? On the Performativity of Economics* (Princeton, NJ: Princeton University Press, 2007); Daniel Breslau, 'Designing a Market-Like Entity: Economics in the Politics of Market Formation', *Social Studies of Science* 43, no. 6 (2013): 829–851. Even demand has to be constructed, as shown in Franck Cochoy, *On Curiosity: The Art of Market Seduction* (Mattering Press, 2016). Other fields that study markets as institutions make some related points about the contingent structures of markets: See Naazneen H. Barma and Steven K. Vogel, eds, *The Political Economy Reader: Markets as Institutions* (New York: Routledge, 2008).

32 For example John Abraham, 'Pharmaceuticalization of Society in Context: Theoretical, Empirical and Health Dimensions', *Sociology* 44, no. 4 (2010): 603–622; Simon J. Williams, Paul Martin and Jonathan Gabe, 'The Pharmaceuticalisation of Society? A Framework for Analysis', *Sociology of Health & Illness* 33, no. 5 (2011): 710–725.

33 For a good overview of what is often called 'disease-mongering' or 'selling sickness', see Ray Moynihan and Alan Cassels, *Selling Sickness: How the World's Biggest Pharmaceutical Companies Are Turning Us All into Patients* (Vancouver: Greystone Books, 2005).

34 ExL Events, 'Disease Awareness Campaigns Forum' <http://exlevents.com/disease-awareness-campaigns-forum/> [accessed 6 April 2018].

35 David Healy, 'Shaping the Intimate: Influences on the Experience of Everyday Nerves', *Social Studies of Science* 34, no. 2 (2004): 219–245.

36 Lucie Gerber and Jean-Paul Gaudillière, 'Marketing Masked Depression: Physicians, Pharmaceutical Firms, and the Redefinition of Mood Disorders in the 1960s and 1970s', *Bulletin of the History of Medicine* 90, no. 3 (2016): 455–490.

37 For example, Robert Whitaker, *Anatomy of an Epidemic: Magic Bullets, Psychiatric Drugs, and the Astonishing Rise of Mental Illness in America* (New York: Random House, 2011).

38 Jeremy A. Greene, *Prescribing by Numbers: Drugs and the Definition of Disease* (Baltimore: Johns Hopkins University Press, 2007); Ray Moynihan and Alan Cassels, *Selling Sickness: How the World's Biggest Pharmaceutical Companies are Turning Us All into Patients* (Vancouver: Greystone Books, 2005). In addition, it is widely recognized that diseases change through time, because of interactions among patients, physicians and illnesses; see, e.g. Robert Aronowitz, *Making Sense of Illness: Science, Society, and Disease* (Cambridge: Cambridge University Press, 1998); Jacalyn Duffin, *Lovers and Livers: Disease Concepts in History* (Toronto: University of Toronto Press, 2005); Duffin's elegant account focuses on two very different diseases, lovesickness and hepatitis C.

39 Jeremy A. Greene, *Prescribing by Numbers: Drugs and the Definition of Disease* (Baltimore: Johns Hopkins University Press, 2007).

40 Anne Pollock, *Medicating Race: Heart Disease and Durable Preoccupations with Difference* (Durham, NC: Duke University Press, 2012).

41 This description owes much to the work of anthropologist Joseph Dumit, who approaches these changes as part of a new cultural logic around health. See Joseph Dumit, *Drugs for Life: How Pharmaceutical Companies Define Our Health* (Durham, NC: Duke University Press, 2012). Similar views have come out of the medical world itself, often focusing on over-diagnosis; see, e.g. H. Gilbert Welch, Lisa M. Schwartz and Steven Woloshin, *Over-Diagnosed: Making People Sick in the Pursuit of Health* (Boston: Beacon Press, 2011).

42 See, for example, Jon N. Jureidini, Jay D. Amsterdam, and Leemon B. McHenry. 'The Citalopram CIT-MD-18 Pediatric Depression Trial: Deconstruction of Medical Ghostwriting, Data Mischaracterisation and Academic Malfeasance', *International Journal of Risk & Safety in Medicine* 28, no. 1 (2016): 33–43; Adriane J. Fugh-Berman, 'The Haunting of Medical Journals: How Ghostwriting Sold "HRT"'. *PLoS Medicine* 7, no. 9 (2010): e1000335; Joseph S. Ross, Kevin P. Hill, David S. Egilman, and Harlan M. Krumholz, 'Guest Authorship and Ghostwriting in Publications Related to Rofecoxib: A Case Study of Industry Documents from Rofecoxib Litigation', *Journal of the American Medical Association* 299, no. 15 (2008): 1800–1812.

43 Promises are central to many aspects of business communication, and in some contexts can help to establish the very things promised, as explored in Mads Borup, Nik Brown, Kornelia Konrad, and Harro Van Lente, 'The Sociology of Expectations in Science and Technology', *Technology Analysis & Strategic Management* 18, no. 3-4 (2006): 285–298.

44 Helen B. Schwartzman, *The Meeting: Gatherings in Organizations and Communities* (New York: Plenum, 1989).

45 Josh Katz, 'Drug Deaths in America Are Rising Faster Than Ever', *New York Times*, 5 June 2017.

46 Centers for Disease Control and Prevention, 'Prescription Opioid Overdose Data', 1 August 2017 <https://www.cdc.gov/drugoverdose/data/overdose.html> [accessed 17 June 2017]. However, official statistics appear to underestimate overdose deaths, because death certificates often don't identify drugs; see Christopher J. Ruhm, 'Geographic Variation in Opioid and Heroin Involved Drug Poisoning Mortality Rates', *American Journal of Preventive Medicine* 53, no. 6 (December 2017): 745–753.

47 One study estimated that prescription opioid abuse cost the US economy roughly $500 billion in 2015 alone, although that figure mixes incompatible kinds of costs. Council of Economic Advisors, reported in: Lucia Mutikani, 'Opioid Crisis Cost U.S. Economy $504 Billion in 2015: White House', *Reuters*, 21 November 2017 <https://www.reuters.com/article/usa-opioids-cost/opioid-crisis-cost-u-s-economy-504-billion-in-2015-white-house-idUSL1N1NP0J7>.

48 For an excellent historical parallel, complete with fascinating analyses, see Nicolas Rasmussen, *On Speed: The Many Lives of Amphetamine* (New York: New York University Press, 2008). Rasmussen would argue that many of the structures described in this book were already nascent in the 1920s to 1950s, when amphetamines were developed and promoted.

49 Art Van Zee, 'The Promotion and Marketing of OxyContin: Commercial Triumph, Public Health Tragedy', *American Journal of Public Health* 99, no. 2 (February 2009): 221–227.

50 John Temple, 'DEA Secretly OKs Killer Quantities of Oxy and Morphine', *Daily Beast*, 21 October 2015 <http://www.thedailybeast.com/dea-secretly-oks-killer-quantities-of-oxy-and-morphine>.

51 Patrick Radden Keefe, 'The Family that Built an Empire of Pain', *The New Yorker*, 30 October 2017.

52 United States, Washington. U.S. General Accounting Office, 'Prescription Drugs: OxyContin Abuse and Diversion and Efforts to Address the Problem', GAO-04-110, 22 January 2004 <http://www.gao.gov/htext/d04110.html>. See also Art Van Zee, (2009) 'The Promotion and Marketing of OxyContin: Commercial Triumph, Public Health Tragedy', *American Journal of Public Health* 99, no. 2 (February 2009): 221–227.

53 United States, Washington. U.S. General Accounting Office, 'Prescription Drugs: OxyContin Abuse and Diversion and Efforts to Address the Problem', GAO-04-110, 22 January 2004 <http://www.gao.gov/htext/d04110.html>.

54 'About The Joint Commission', *The Joint Commission* <https://www.jointcommission.org/about_us/about_the_joint_commission_main.aspx>.

55 United States, Washington. U.S. General Accounting Office, 'Prescription Drugs:

OxyContin Abuse and Diversion and Efforts to Address the Problem', GAO-04-110, 22 January 2004 <http://www.gao.gov/htext/d04110.html>.

56 Theodore Cicero and Matthew S. Ellis, 'Roots of Opioid Epidemic Can be Traced Back to Two Key Changes in Pain Management', *The Conversation*, 17 March 2016 <https://theconversation.com/roots-of-opioid-epidemic-can-be-traced-back-to-two-key-changes-in-pain-management-50647> [accessed 21 July 2017].

57 David Armstrong, 'Secret Trove Reveals Bold "Crusade" to make OxyContin a blockbuster', *STAT News*, 22 September 2016 <https://www.statnews.com/2016/09/22/abbott-oxycontin-crusade/>.

58 Pamela T.M. Leung, Erin M. Macdonald, Irfan A. Dhalla, and David N. Juurlink, 'A 1980 Letter on the Risk of Opioid Addiction', *New England Journal of Medicine* 376, no. 22 (1 June 2017): 2194–2195.

59 Sanford H. Roth, Roy M. Fleischmann, Francis X. Burch et al., 'Around-the-Clock, Controlled-Release Oxycodone Therapy for Osteoarthritis-Related Pain: Placebo-Controlled Trial and Long-Term Evaluation', *Archives of Internal Medicine* 160, no. 6 (March 2000): 853–860.

60 United States of America v. The Purdue Frederick Company, Attachment 8 to Plea Agreement, Virginia, 12-13 (2007) <http://i.bnet.com/blogs/purdue-agreed-facts.pdf>.

61 Harriet Ryan, Lisa Girion, and Scott Glover, '"You Want A Description of Hell?" OxyContin's 12 Hour Problem', *Los Angeles Times*, 5 May 2016.

62 Harriet Ryan, Lisa Girion, and Scott Glover, '"You Want A Description of Hell?" OxyContin's 12 Hour Problem', *Los Angeles Times*, 5 May 2016.

63 Marion S. Greene and R. Andrew Chambers, 'Pseudoaddiction: Fact or Fiction? An Investigation of the Medical Literature', *Current Addiction Reports* 2, no. 4 (1 October 2015): 310–317 <http://dx.doi.org/10.1007/s40429-015-0074-7>.

64 Marion S. Greene and R. Andrew Chambers, 'Pseudoaddiction: Fact or Fiction? An Investigation of the Medical Literature', *Current Addiction Reports* 2, no. 4 (1 October 2015): 310–317 <http://dx.doi.org/10.1007/s40429-015-0074-7>.

65 Sheryl Ubelacker, 'Pain Course Revised Over Concerns About Drug Company Influence', *The Globe and Mail*, 26 March 2017 <https://www.theglobeandmail.com/news/national/pain-course-revised-over-concerns-about-drug-company-influence/article1321037/>.

66 John Fauber and Ellen Gabler, 'Narcotics Use for Chronic Pain Soars Among Seniors', *Milwaukee-Wisconsin Journal Sentinel*, 29 May 2012 <http://archive.jsonline.com/watchdog/watchdogreports/narcotics-use-for-chronic-pain-soars-among-seniors-kg56kih-155555495.html/>.

67 Dora H. Lin, Eleanor Lucas, Irene B. Murimi, Andrew Kolodny, Caleb Alexander, 'Financial Conflicts of Interest and the Centers for Disease Control and Prevention's

2016 Guideline for Prescribing Opioids for Chronic Pain', *The Journal of the American Medical Association Internal Medicine* 177, no. 3 (March 2017): 427–428.

68 Eric Eyre, 'Drug Firms Poured 780M Painkillers into WV amid Rise of Overdoses', *Charleston Gazette-Mail*, 17 December 2016 <http://www.wvgazettemail.com/news-health/20161217/drug-firms-poured-780m-painkillers-into-wv-amid-rise-of-overdoses>. There were also more than 550 million doses of hydrocodone shipped to West Virginia in this period.

69 Scott Higham and Lenny Bernstein, 'The Drug Industry's Triumph Over the DEA', *The Washington Post*, 15 October 2017.

70 Barry Meier, 'In Guilty Plea, OxyContin Maker to Pay $600 Million', *The New York Times*, 10 May 2007.

71 Philip J. Wininger, 'Pharmaceutical Overpromotion Liability: The Legal Battle Over Rural Prescription Drug Abuse', *Kentucky Law Journal* 93, no. 269 (2004-2005): 269.

72 David Herzberg argues that the US has had a number of pairs of addiction problems – to do with licit and illicit drugs – going along with pairs of responses. See David Herzberg, 'Entitled to Addiction? Pharmaceuticals, Race, and America's First Drug War', *Bulletin of the History of Medicine* 91, no. 3 (2017): 586–623.

73 United States, Washington. U.S. General Accounting Office, 'Prescription Drugs: OxyContin Abuse and Diversion and Efforts to Address the Problem', GAO-04-110, 22 January 2004 <http://www.gao.gov/htext/d04110.html>.

74 Scott Higham and Lenny Bernstein, 'The Drug Industry's Triumph Over the DEA', *The Washington Post*, 15 October 2017.

75 Don Winslow, 'El Chapo and the Secret History of the Heroin Crisis', *Esquire*, 9 August 2016 <http://www.esquire.com/news-politics/a46918/heroin-mexico-el-chapo-cartels-don-winslow/>.

76 Harriet Ryan, Lisa Girion, and Scott Glover, 'OxyContin Goes Global – "We're Only Just Getting Started"', *Los Angeles Times*, 18 December 2016.

77 Abby Zimet, 'OxyContin For Kids: What Could Possibly Go Wrong?', *Common Dreams*, 3 July 2012 <https://www.commondreams.org/further/2012/07/03/oxycontin-kids-what-could-possibly-go-wrong>.

78 Thomas Reuters, '6 Ex-Pharma Executives Arrested in U.S. in Fentanyl Bribe Case', *CBC News Health*, 8 December 2016 <http://www.cbc.ca/news/health/fentanyl-bribery-1.3887631>. For a rich account published well after this chapter was written, see Evan Hughes, 'The Pain Hustlers', *The New York Times*, 2 May 2018.

79 United States Department of Justice Drug Enforcement Administration, New Orleans Division News, 'Two Mobile Pain Doctors Convicted After Seven-Week Trial', 2 March 2017 <https://www.dea.gov/divisions/no/2017/no030217.shtml>.

80 John Hempton, 'Get Your Opiates for Free: Capitalism Meets the Zombie

Apocalypse', *Bronte Capital* (blog), 3 February 2014 <http://brontecapital.blogspot. ca/2014/02/get-your-opiates-for-free-capitalism.html>.

2. DATA EXTRACTION AT THE MARGINS OF HEALTH

1   Courtney Davis, Huseyin Naci, Evrim Gurpinar, Elita Poplavska, Ashlyn Pinto, and Ajay Aggarwal, 'Availability of Evidence of Benefits on Overall Survival and Quality of Life of Cancer Drugs Approved by European Medicines Agency: Retrospective Cohort Study of Drug Approvals 2009-13', *The British Medical Journal* 359 (4 October 2017): j4530. In a similar vein, the majority of the forty-eight new treatments for solid cancers approved by the US Food and Drug Administration (FDA) between 2002 and 2014 did not have meaningful health benefits, increasing survival by a median of only 2.1 months. Peter H. Wise, 'Cancer Drugs, Survival, and Ethics', *The British Medical Journal* 355 (9 November 2016): i5792.

2   On the effectiveness of statins, see, e.g. R. Chou, T. Dana, I. Blazina, M. Daeges, and T.L. Jeanne, 'Statins for Prevention of Cardiovascular Disease in Adults: Evidence Report and Systematic Review for the US Preventive Services Task Force', *JAMA* 316, no. 19 (15 November 2016): 2008–2024. For patients who have not suffered a heart attack, it is statistically unclear that taking statins delays death: Therapeutics Letter 77, 'Do Statins Have a Role in Primary Prevention? An Update', Therapeutics Initiative, 18 October 2010 <http://www.ti.ubc.ca/2010/10/18/ do-statins-have-a-role-in-primary-prevention-an-update-/>. The 2013 guidelines changed focus from cholesterol targets to risk factors. See Neil J. Stone, Jennifer Robinson, Alice H. Lichtenstein, C. Noel Bairey Merz, Conrad B. Blum, Robert H. Eckel, Anne C. Goldberg, David Gordon, Daniel Levy, Donald M. Lloyd-Jones, Patrick McBride, J. Sanford Schwartz, Susan T. Shero, Sidney C. Smith, Karol Watson, and Peter W.F. Wilson, '2013 ACC/AHA Guideline on the Treatment of Blood Cholesterol to Reduce Atherosclerotic Cardiovascular Risk in Adults', *American Heart Association Journal* 137, no. 2 (12 November 2013) <https://doi. org/10.1161/01.cir.0000437738.63853.7a>. Indefinitely increasing the number of people taking the drugs would make sense if there were no negative effects or other costs.

3   'Prescrire's Ratings: New Products and Indications over the Last 10 Years', *Prescrire in English*, last modified 1 May 2017 <http://english.prescrire.org/en/81/168/53056/0/ NewsDetails.aspx>.

4   Nortin Hadler, 'American Healthcare Rackets: Monopolies, Oligopolies, Cartels and Kindred Plunderbunds', *The Health Care Blog*, 25 November 2016 <http:// thehealthcareblog.com/blog/2016/11/25/american-healthcare-rackets-monopolies-oligopolies-cartels-and-kindred-plunderbunds/>.

5 Alan Cassels, 'More Cholesterol Craziness', *Common Ground*, 8 July 2017 <http://commonground.ca/category/drug-bust-by-alan-cassels/>.

6 For example, CenterWatch, *State of the Clinical Trials Industry: A Sourcebook of Charts and Statistics* (Boston, MA: CenterWatch, 2009).

7 Ian Hacking, '"Style" for Historians and Philosophers', *Studies in History and Philosophy of Science Part A* 23, no. 1 (1992): 1–20; Chunglin Kwa, *Styles of Knowing: A New History of Science from Ancient Times to the Present*, David McKay, trans. (Pittsburgh: University of Pittsburgh Press, 2011).

8 Arthur A. Daemmrich, *Pharmacopolitics: Drug Regulation in the United States and Germany* (Chapel Hill: University of North Carolina Press, 2004).

9 Harry M. Marks, *The Progress of Experiment: Science and Therapeutic Reform in the United States, 1900–1990* (Cambridge: Cambridge University Press, 1997).

10 Harry M. Marks, 'Trust and Mistrust in the Marketplace: Statistics and Clinical Research, 1945–1960', *History of Science* 38, no. 3 (2000): 343–355.

11 Ariel L. Zimerman, 'Evidence-Based Medicine: A Short History of a Modern Medical Movement', *AMA Journal of Ethics* 15, no. 1 (2013): 71–76.

12 G. Guyatt, J. Cairns, D. Churchill, et al., 'Evidence-Based Medicine: A New Approach to Teaching the Practice of Medicine', *Journal of the American Medical Association* 268, no. 17 (1992): 2420–2425.

13 E.g. John Worrall, 'Evidence in Medicine and Evidence-Based Medicine', *Philosophy Compass* 2, no. 6 (2007): 981–1002.

14 Stefan Timmermans and Marc Berg, *The Gold Standard: The Challenge of Evidence-Based Medicine and Standardization in Health Care* (Philadelphia: Temple University Press, 2003); David Healy, *Pharmageddon* (Bekeley: University of California Press, 2012).

15 Robin Bluhm, 'From Hierarchy to Network: A Richer View of Evidence for Evidence-Based Medicine', *Perspectives in Biology and Medicine* 48, no. 4 (2005): 535–547; Jason Grossman and Fiona J. Mackenzie, 'The Randomized Controlled Trial: Gold Standard, or Merely Standard?' *Perspectives in Biology and Medicine* 48, no. 4 (2005): 516–534.

16 Andreas Lundh, Sergio Sismondo, Joel Lexchin, Octavian A. Busuioc and Lisa Bero, 'Industry Sponsorship and Research Outcome and Quality (Review)', *The Cochrane Library* (12 December 2012) <doi 10.1002/14651858.MR000033>.

17 D. A. Tobbell, *Pills, Power, and Policy: The Struggle for Drug Reform in Cold War America* (Berkeley: University of California Press, 2012).

18 Daniel Carpenter, *Reputation and Power: Organizational Image and Pharmaceutical Regulation at the FDA* (Princeton, NJ: Princeton University Press, 2010).

19 Daniel Carpenter, *Reputation and Power: Organizational Image and Pharmaceutical Regulation at the FDA* (Princeton, NJ: Princeton University Press, 2010), 272.

20 'Obligatory point of passage' is Bruno Latour's term of art for an element required in order for others to form a network. In the case of drugs, we can see marketing as the formation of very large networks. See Bruno Latour, *Science in Action: How to Follow Scientists and Engineers through Society* (Cambridge, MA: Harvard University Press, 1987).

21 There are, nonetheless, complex relationships among in-patent, branded and generic drugs, with the generic often serving as a challenge to in-patent drugs: Jeremy A. Greene, *Generic: The Unbranding of Modern Medicine* (Baltimore, MD: Johns Hopkins University Press, 2014). Brands of generics sometimes themselves become markers of quality: see Cori Hayden, 'Generic Medicines and the Question of the Similar', in Sergio Sismondo and Jeremy A. Greene, eds, *The Pharmaceutical Studies Reader* (Chichester: John Wiley & Sons, 2015), 261–267; Kris Peterson, *Speculative Markets: Drug Circuits and Derivative Life in Nigeria* (Durham, NC: Duke University Press, 2014).

22 For example, Edward Nik-Khah, 'Neoliberal Pharmaceutical Science and the Chicago School of Economics', *Social Studies of Science* 44, no .4 (2014): 489–517.

23 For example, in recent years, challenges to a core piece of the 1962 Act have been slowly working their way through the US courts: drawing on the US's strong protection of freedom of speech, companies have been chipping away at the FDA's legal authority to regulate off-label marketing. Joshua M. Sharfstein and Alta Charo, 'The Promotion of Medical Products in the 21st Century: Off-label Marketing and First Amendment Concerns', *Journal of the American Medical Association* 314, no. 17 (2015): 1795–1796.

24 Courtney Davis and John Abraham, *Unhealthy Pharmaceutical Regulation: Innovation, Politics and Promissory Science* (Basingstoke: Palgrave MacMillan, 2013); Govin Permanand, *EU Pharmaceutical Regulation: The Politics of Policy-Making* (Manchester: Manchester University Press, 2006).

25 John Abraham and Tim Reed, 'Progress, Innovation and Regulatory Science in Drug Development: The Politics of International Standard-Setting', *Social Studies of Science* 32, no. 3 (2002): 337–369. 'ICH' now stands for the International Council for Harmonization.

26 Kaushik Sunder Rajan describes this as 'pharmocracy', and, like me, finds Gramsci's idea of hegemony valuable here. See Kaushik Sunder Rajan, *Pharmocracy: Value, Politics, and Knowledge in Global Biomedicine* (Durham, NC: Duke University Press, 2017)

27 Monique L. Anderson, Karen Chiswell, Eric D. Peterson, Asba Tasneem, James Topping, and Robert M. Califf, 'Compliance with Results Reporting at ClinicalTrials. gov', *New England Journal of Medicine* 372, no. 11 (2015): 1031–1039.

28 P. C. Gøtzsche, A. Hróbjartsson, H. K. Johansen, M. T. Haahr, D. G. Altman, and A. –W. Chan, 'Ghost Authorship in Industry-Initiated Randomised Trials', *PLoS Medicine* 4, no. 1 (2007): 47–52.

29 Kalman Applbaum, 'Getting to Yes: Corporate Power and the Creation of a Psychopharmaceutical Blockbuster', in Sergio Sismondo and Jeremy A. Greene, eds, *The Pharmaceutical Studies Reader* (Chichester: John Wiley & Sons, 2015), 133–149.

30 I am drawing on Edward Nik-Khah, 'Neoliberal Pharmaceutical Science and the Chicago School of Economics', *Social Studies of Science* 44, no. 4 (2014): 489–517.

31 Tufts Center for the Study of Drug Development, 'Research' <http://csdd.tufts. edu/research> [accessed 4 January 2018].

32 The CSDD also helped to support the idea that regulation created a 'drug lag', reducing the number of new drugs on the market. In addition to Edward Nik-Khah's work cited above, see Arthur Daemmrich, 'Invisible Monuments and the Costs of Pharmaceutical Regulation: Twenty-Five Years of Drug Lag Debate', *Pharmacy in History* 45, no. 1 (2003): 3–17.

33 Tufts Center for the Study of Drug Development, 'Cost to Develop and Win Marketing Approval for a New Drug Is $2.6 Billion', *MarketWired*, 18 November 2014 <http://www.marketwired.com/press-release/cost-develop-win-marketing-approval-new-drug-is-26-billion-according-tufts-center-study-1969439.htm>.

34 Jerry Avorn, 'The $2.6 Billion Pill – Methodologic and Policy Considerations', *New England Journal of Medicine* 372 (2015): 1877–1899.

35 Donald W. Light and Rebecca Warburton, 'Demythologizing the High Costs of Pharmaceutical Research', *BioSocieties* 6, no. 1 (2011): 34–50; Steve Morgan, Paul Grootendorst, Joel Lexchin, Colleen Cunningham and Devon Greyson, 'The Cost of Drug Development: A Systematic Review', *Health Policy* 100, no. 1 (2011): 4–17.

36 Vinay Prasad and Sham Mailankody, 'Research and Development Spending to Bring a Single Cancer Drug to Market and Revenues After Approval', *JAMA Internal Medicine* 177, no. 11 (2017): 1569–1575.

37 Fran Quigley, 'Escaping Big Pharma's Pricing with Patent-Free Drugs', *The New York Times*, 18 July 2017.

38 Ben Hirschler, 'GlaxoSmithKline Boss Says New Drugs Can Be Cheaper', Reuters, 14 March 2013 <https://www.reuters.com/article/us-glaxosmithkline-prices/glaxosmithkline-boss-says-new-drugs-can-be-cheaper-idUSBRE92D0RM20130314>.

39 Kaushik Sunder Rajan, *Biocapital: The Constitution of Postgenomic Life* (Durham, NC: Duke University Press, 2006); Stefan Helmreich, 'Species of Biocapital', *Science as Culture* 17, no. 4 (2008): 463–478.

40 Javier Lezaun and Catherine M. Montgomery, 'The Pharmaceutical Commons: Sharing and Exclusion in Global Health Drug Development', *Science, Technology, & Human Values* 40, no. 1 (2015): 3–29.

41 Alberto Cambrosio, Peter Keating, Thomas Schlich, and George Weisz, 'Regulatory Objectivity and the Generation and Management of Evidence in Medicine', *Social Science & Medicine* 63, no. 1 (2006): 189–199; Claes-Fredrik Helgesson, 'From Dirty

Data to Credible Scientific Evidence: Some Practices Used to Clean Data in Large Randomised Clinical Trials', in Catherine Will and Tiago Moreira, eds, *Medical Proofs, Social Experiments: Clinical Trials in Shifting Contexts* (New York: Routledge, 2016), 49–64.

42 Andreas Lundh, Sergio Sismondo, Joel Lexchin, Octavian A. Busuioc and Lisa Bero, 'Industry Sponsorship and Research Outcome and Quality (Review)', *The Cochrane Library* (12 December 2012) <doi 10.1002/14651858.MR000033>.

43 Jill Fisher, *Medical Research for Hire: The Political Economy of Pharmaceutical Clinical Trials* (New Brunswick, NJ: Rutgers University Press, 2009); Philip Mirowski and Robert Van Horn, 'The Contract Research Organization and the Commercialization of Scientific Research', *Social Studies of Science* 35, no. 3 (2005): 503–534.

44 Anu Gummerus, Marja Airaksinen, Mia Bengtström and Anne Juppo, 'Outsourcing of Regulatory Affairs Tasks in Pharmaceutical Companies – Why and What?', *Journal of Pharmaceutical Innovation* 11, no. 1 (2016): 46–52.

45 Outsourcing of the chemistry and the other laboratory studies is common enough that Pfizer had to employ 'queue management theory' and the 'Six Sigma' approach to factory production developed by Motorola, to make the work more efficient. See F. Christopher Bi, Heather N. Frost, Xiaolan Ling, David A. Perry, Sylvie K. Sakata, Simon Bailey, Yvette M. Fobian, Leslie Sloan, and Anthony Wood, 'Driving External Chemistry Optimization Via Operations Management Principles', *Drug Discovery Today* 19, no. 3 (2014): 289–294.

46 Adriana Petryna, *When Experiments Travel: Clinical Trials and the Global Search for Human Subjects* (Princeton, NJ: Princeton University Press, 2009), 17.

47 Melissa Cooper, 'Experimental Labour – Offshoring Clinical Trials to China', *East Asian Science and Technology Studies Journal* 2, no. 1 (2008): 73–79. Adriana Petryna, 'Clinical Trials Offshored: On Private Sector Science and Public Health', in Sergio Sismondo and Jeremy A. Greene, eds, *The Pharmaceutical Studies Reader* (Chichester: John Wiley & Sons, 2015), 208–221.

48 Ignatio Atal, Ludovic Trinquart, Raphaël Porcher, and Philippe Ravaud, 'Differential Globalization of Industry- and Non-Industry-Sponsored Clinical Trials', *PLOS On* (14 December 2015) <https://doi.org/10.1371/journal.pone.0145122>.

49 Johan P.E. Karlberg, *Globalization of Industry-Sponsored Clinical Trials* (Clinical Trial Magnifier Limited, 2014) <http://www.clinicaltrialmagnifier.org/Globalization/> [accessed 4 August 2017]; Tamara Lytle, 'Industry Struggles with Prospect of Trials Leaving U.S.', *CenterWatch Monthly* 19, no. 4 (April 2012): 14–20.

50 Johan P. E. Karlberg, 'Sponsored Clinical Trial Globalization Trends', *Clinical Trial Magnifier* 1, no. 2 (2008): 13–19; Adriana Petryna, 'Globalizing Human Subjects Research', in A. Petryna, A. Lakoff, and A. Kleinman, eds, *Global Pharmaceuticals: Ethics, Markets, Practices* (Durham, NC: Duke University Press, 2006), 33–60.

51 Sonia Shah, *The Body Hunters: Testing New Drugs on the World's Poorest Patients* (New York: New Press, 2006), 17.

52 Kaushik Sunder Rajan, 'The Experimental Machinery of Global Clinical Trials: Case Studies from India', in Sergio Sismondo and Jeremy A. Greene, eds, *The Pharmaceutical Studies Reader* (Chichester: John Wiley & Sons, 2015), 222–234.

53 Kaushik Sunder Rajan, 'Experimental Values: Indian Clinical Trials and Surplus Health', *New Left Review* 45 (2007): 67–88.

54 Sonia Shah, *The Body Hunters: Testing New Drugs on the World's Poorest Patients* (New York: New Press, 2006), 17; Kaushik Sunder Rajan, 'Experimental Values: Indian Clinical Trials and Surplus Health', *New Left Review* 45, (2007): 67–88.

55 C. Foster and A.Y. Malik, 'The Elephant in the (Board) Room: The Role of Contract Research Organizations in International Clinical Research', *The American Journal of Bioethics* 12, no. 11 (2012): 49–50 <doi 10.1080/15265161.2012.719267>.

56 Sonia Shah, *The Body Hunters: Testing New Drugs on the World's Poorest Patients* (New York: New Press, 2006), 117.

57 Kaushik Sunder Rajan, 'Experimental Values: Indian Clinical Trials and Surplus Health', *New Left Review* 45 (2007): 67–88.

58 Melissa Cooper, 'Experimental Labour – Offshoring Clinical Trials to China', *East Asian Science and Technology Studies Journal* 2, no. 1 (2007): 73–92.

59 Kaushik Sunder Rajan, 'The Experimental Machinery of Global Clinical Trials: Case Studies from India', in Sergio Sismondo and Jeremy A. Greene, eds, *The Pharmaceutical Studies Reader* (Chichester: John Wiley & Sons, 2015), 222–234.

60 Roberto Abadie, *The Professional Guinea Pig: Big Pharma and the Risky World of Human Subjects* (Durham, NC: Duke University Press, 2010).

61 Mark Schmukler, *Pharma Marketing News, Physician Education Special Supplement* (2006), 14–16.

62 Mark Schmukler, *Pharma Marketing News, Physician Education Special Supplement* (2006), 14–16.

63 John LaMattina, 'Does Marketing Have Too Much Control In Big Pharma Clinical Trials?', *Forbes*, 26 January 2016 <https://www.forbes.com/sites/johnlamattina/2016/01/26/does-marketing-have-too-much-control-in-big-pharma-clinical-trials/#79c744e557c>.

64 John LaMattina, 'Does Marketing Have Too Much Control In Big Pharma Clinical Trials?', *Forbes*, 26 January 2016 <https://www.forbes.com/sites/johnlamattina/2016/01/26/does-marketing-have-too-much-control-in-big-pharma-clinical-trials/#79c744e557c>.

65 M. T. Whitstock, 'Manufacturing the Truth: From Designing Clinical Trials to Publishing Trial Data', *Indian Journal of Medical Ethics* (14 November 2017): 1–11 <doi 10.20529/IJME.2017.096>.

66 Richard Smith, 'Lapses at the New England Journal of Medicine', *Journal of the Royal Society of Medicine* 99, no. 8 (August, 2006): 380–382 <doi 10.1258/jrsm.99.8.380>.

67 Clive Barker, *Books of Blood, vol. 1* (Hertford, NC: Crossroad Press, 2017).

68 Here I am drawing on the extensive work of Jill Fisher and Roberto Abadie, who have done excellent studies of Phase I trials and trial participants. See, e.g. Torin Monahan and Jill A. Fisher, '"I'm Still a Hustler": Entrepreneurial Responses to Precarity by Participants in Phase I Clinical Trials', *Economy and Society* 44, no. 4 (2015): 545–566; Jill A. Fisher, 'Feeding and Bleeding: The Institutional Banalization of Risk to Healthy Volunteers in Phase I Pharmaceutical Clinical Trials', *Science, Technology, & Human Values* 40, no. 2 (2015): 199–226; Roberto Abadie, *The Professional Guinea Pig: Big Pharma and the Risky World of Human Subjects*, (Durham, NC: Duke University Press, 2010). Abadie's study was of a number of frequent trial participants in Philadelphia, including a number of anarchists for whom trial income meant that they didn't have to maintain more permanent jobs. Fisher has interviewed hundreds of Phase I trial participants and dozens of staff at multiple clinics running the trials. Her work addresses day-to-day routines within the clinics, the attitudes and actions of frequent Phase I trial participants, and structures that shape the system. In addition, I have drawn on the systematic account of Phase I trial participation on the website Just Another Lab Rat!, last modified 26 January 2017 <http://www.jalr.org/about_just_another_lab_rat.html>, as well as a number of anecdotal accounts.

69 Again, I am following the insights of Jill Fisher here. See Jill A. Fisher, 'Feeding and Bleeding: The Institutional Banalization of Risk to Healthy Volunteers in Phase I Pharmaceutical Clinical Trials', *Science, Technology, & Human Values* 40, no. 2 (2015): 199–226.

70 See T.S. Eliot, *The Use of Poetry and the Use of Criticism* (Cambridge, MA: Harvard University Press, 1933). Bruno Latour and Steve Woolgar introduce the idea of an 'inscription device', which also focuses on the transformation of materials into ink. Laboratories are places where materials are manipulated, to be turned into written data. See Bruno Latour and Steve Woolgar, *Laboratory Life: The Construction of Scientific Facts*, 2nd edn (Princeton, NJ: Princeton University Press, 1986).

71 Jill A. Fisher, 'Feeding and Bleeding: The Institutional Banalization of Risk to Healthy Volunteers in Phase I Pharmaceutical Clinical Trials', *Science, Technology, & Human Values* 40, no. 2 (2015): 199–226.

3. GHOSTS IN THE MACHINE: PUBLICATION PLANNING 101

1 Andreas Lundh, Sergio Sismondo, Joel Lexchin, Octavian A. Busuioc, and Lisa Bero, 'Industry Sponsorship and Research Outcome', *Cochrane Database of Systematic Reviews* 12 (2012).

2   When I began looking at it, almost nobody had written about publication planning – indeed, it seemed that nobody outside the industry had even noticed its existence – but at around that time, several other researchers started publishing about it. In particular, Adrienne Fugh-Berman and Alistair Matheson published interesting analyses of the activity. See Adrienne Fugh-Berman and Susanna J. Dodgson, 'Ethical Considerations of Publication Planning in the Pharmaceutical Industry', *Open Medicine* 2, no. 4 (2008): e33–36; Adrienne Fugh-Berman, 'The Haunting of Medical Journals: How Ghostwriting Sold "HRT"', *PLoS Medicine* 7, no. 9 (2010): e1000335; Alastair Matheson, 'Corporate Science and the Husbandry of Scientific and Medical Knowledge by the Pharmaceutical Industry', *BioSocieties* 3, no. 4 (2008): 355–382; also Alastair Matheson, 'The Disposable Author: How Pharmaceutical Marketing is Embraced Within Medicine's Scholarly Literature', *Hastings Center Report* 46, no. 3 (2016): 31–37.

3   Wyeth, 'Publication Plan 2002 – Premarin/Trimegestone HRT Working Draft' <http://dida.library.ucsf.edu/tid/awb37b10>.

4   David Healy and Dinah Cattell 'Interface Between Authorship, Industry and Science in the Domain of Therapeutics' *British Journal of Psychiatry* 183: 22–27; Joseph S Ross, Kevin P. Hill, David S. Egilman and Harlan M. Krumholz, 'Documents from Rofecoxib Litigation Related to Rofecoxib: A Case Study of Industry Guest Authorship and Ghostwriting in Publications. *JAMA* 299, no. 15 (2008): 1800–1812.

5   David Healy and Dinah Cattell 'Interface Between Authorship, Industry and Science in the Domain of Therapeutics' *British Journal of Psychiatry* 183: 22–27.

6   Joseph S Ross, Kevin P. Hill, David S. Egilman and Harlan M. Krumholz, 'Documents from Rofecoxib Litigation Related to Rofecoxib: A Case Study of Industry Guest Authorship and Ghostwriting in Publications. *Journal of the American Medical Association* 299, no. 15 (2008): 1800–1812.

7   Alistair Matheson, personal communication. Though they are locally consistent, they may vary from country to country. See Andrew Lakoff, 'The Anxieties of Globalization: Antidepressant Sales and Economic Crisis in Argentina', *Social Studies of Science* 34, no. 2 (2004): 247–269.

8   Quintiles, 'Scientific Communication' <http://www.quintiles.com/services/brand-and-scientific-communication> [accessed 22 July 2016].

9   Documents related to Wyeth's campaign and PC(2) can be found in Prempro Products Liability Litigation, *Drug Industry Document Archive* <http://dida.library.ucsf.edu> [accessed 7 July 2011]. Quotes here are from those documents, unless otherwise noted.

10 Adrienne Fugh-Berman, 'The Haunting of Medical Journals: How Ghostwriting Sold "HRT". *PLoS Medicine* 7, no. 9 (2010): e1000335.

11 Natasha Singer and Duff Wilson, 'Menopause, as Brought to You by Big Pharma', *New York Times,* 12 December 2009.

12 E.g. Complete Healthcare Communication <http://www.chcinc.com/> [accessed 20 December 2006].

13 Speaker at TIPPA Midwest meeting, St. Louis, 2011. Data kindly provided by Elliot Ross.

14 Envision Pharma <http://www.envisionpharma.com/publicationsPlanning/> [accessed 20 December 2006]. Watermeadow Medical <https://www.ashfieldhealthcare. com/gb/healthcare-agency-gb/watermeadow-gb/> [accessed 21 March 2017]. Adis Communications <http://www.pharmalive.com/content/supplements/gpms/2004/ adis.cfm> [accessed 20 December 2006].

15 Most measurement of return on investment of publications is in terms of readership. Watermeadow Medical, for example, advertises, 'we employ unique alternative metrics to identify the most relevant communication channels and measure the true reach of your publications and data'. See Watermeadow Medical <https://www. ashfieldhealthcare.com/gb/healthcare-agency-gb/watermeadow-gb/> [accessed 21 March 2017].

16 Michael Oldani, 'Thick Prescriptions: Toward an Interpretation of Pharmaceutical Sales Practices', *Medical Anthropology Quarterly* 18, no. 3 (2004): 325–356.

17 Gardiner-Caldwell Group <http://www.thgc-group.com/> [accessed 29 November 2007].

18 Ariel L. Zimerman, 'Evidence-Based Medicine: A Short History of a Modern Medical Movement', *AMA Journal of Ethics* 15, no.1 (2013): 71–76.

19 Jon N. Jureidini, Jay D. Amsterdam, and Leemon B. McHenry, 'The Citalopram CIT-MD-18 Pediatric Depression Trial: Deconstruction of Medical Ghostwriting, Data Mischaracterisation and Academic Malfeasance', *International Journal of Risk & Safety in Medicine* 28, no. 1 (2016): 33–43 <doi 10.3233/JRS-160671>.

20 Jon N. Jureidini, Jay D. Amsterdam, and Leemon B. McHenry, 'The Citalopram CIT-MD-18 Pediatric Depression Trial: Deconstruction of Medical Ghostwriting, Data Mischaracterisation and Academic Malfeasance', *International Journal of Risk & Safety in Medicine* 28, no. 1 (2016): 33–43 <doi 10.3233/JRS-160671>, 37.

21 Jon N. Jureidini, Jay D. Amsterdam, and Leemon B. McHenry, 'The Citalopram CIT-MD-18 Pediatric Depression Trial: Deconstruction of Medical Ghostwriting, Data Mischaracterisation and Academic Malfeasance', *International Journal of Risk & Safety in Medicine* 28, no. 1 (2016): 33–43 <doi 10.3233/JRS-160671>, 35.

22 Christina Goetjen and Mary Prescott correspondence, 2001, <https://www. industrydocumentslibrary.ucsf.edu/drug/docs/#id=pymf0220> [accessed 4 January 2018].

23 Jon N. Jureidini, Jay D. Amsterdam, and Leemon B. McHenry, 'The Citalopram

CIT-MD-18 Pediatric Depression Trial: Deconstruction of Medical Ghostwriting, Data Mischaracterisation and Academic Malfeasance', *International Journal of Risk & Safety in Medicine* 28, no. 1 (2016): 33–43, at 38. The comment about the 'masterful stroke of euphemism' is in Charles Flicker, Amy Rubin and Paul Tiseo correspondence, 2000 <https://www.industrydocumentslibrary.ucsf.edu/drug/docs/#id=jjbn0225> [accessed 6 April 2018]; Jay Amsterdam drew my attention to this.

24 Jon N. Jureidini, Jay D. Amsterdam, and Leemon B. McHenry, 'The Citalopram CIT-MD-18 Pediatric Depression Trial: Deconstruction of Medical Ghostwriting, Data Mischaracterisation and Academic Malfeasance', *International Journal of Risk & Safety in Medicine* 28, no. 1 (2016): 33–43, at 40.

25 It was strategic decisions like these that led to the study being part of a lawsuit, and led to the interest in it and the manuscript by Jureidini and colleagues. The manuscript was published as Karen Dineen Wagner, Adelaide S. Robb, Robert L. Findling, Jianqing Jin, Marcelo M. Gutierrez and William E. Heydorn, 'A Randomized, Placebo-Controlled Trial of Citalopram for the Treatment of Major Depression in Children and Adolescents', *American Journal of Psychiatry* 161, no. 6 (2004): 1079–1083.

26 Leemon B. McHenry, 'Ghosts in the Machine: Comment on Sismondo', *Social Studies of Science* 39, no. 4 (2009): 943-947.

27 Jeffrey Lacasse and Jonathan Leo (personal communication) drew all of these comments to my attention, in the context of their work on rebuttals to accusations of ghostwriting. The Pfizer statement is quoted in Julie Steenhuysen, 'Drug Co. Paid Writers to Promote Hormone Therapy', *Reuters*, 8 September 2010 <https://uk.reuters.com/article/health-us-hormone-therapy/drug-co-paid-writers-to-promote-hormone-therapy-idUKTRE6874E220100908>. The University of Pennsylvania's statement is reported in Ellie Levitt, Psychiatry Chairman Faces Ghostwriting Accusations', *The Daily Pennsylvanian*, 3 December 2010 <http://www.thedp.com/article/2010/12/psychiatry_chairman_faces_ghostwriting_accusations>. MECC founder Thomas Sullivan defends the psychiatry textbook in Thomas Sullivan, 'New York Times: The Un-Ghost Writing of the Distant Past', *Policy and Medicine*, 2 December 2010 <http://www.policymed.com/2010/12/new-york-times-the-un-ghost-writing-of-the-distant-past.html>.

28 David Bloor, *Knowledge and Social Imagery* (London: Routledge & Kegan Paul, 1976).

29 For example, J.E. Bekelman, Y. Li, and C. Gross, 'Scope and Impact of Financial Conflicts of Interest in Biomedical Research: A Systematic Review', *Journal of the American Medical Association* 289, no. 4 (2003): 454–465; Joel Lexchin, Lisa Bero and Benjamin Djulbegovic, 'Pharmaceutical Industry Sponsorship and Research Outcome and Quality: Systematic Review', *British Medical Journal* 326, no. 7400

(2003): 1167–1170; Andreas Lundh, Sergio Sismondo, Joel Lexchin, Octavian A. Busuioc, and Lisa Bero, 'Industry Sponsorship and Research Outcome', *Cochrane Database of Systematic Reviews* 12 (2012).

30 See Retraction Watch <http://retractionwatch.com/> [accessed 8 January 2018].

31 Gardiner Harris, 'Doctor's Pain Studies were Fabricated, Hospital Says', *New York Times*, 10 March 2009.

4. HOSTS AND GUESTS IN THE HAUNTED HOUSE

1 Nikolaos Patsopoulos, John P.A. Ioannidis, A. Analatos Apostolow, 'Origin and Funding of the Most Frequently Cited Papers in Medicine: Database Analysis', *British Medical Journal* 332, no. 7549 (2006): 1061–1064. Philippe Gorry analyses a group of ninety-two articles known to be ghost-managed, identified in documents from three legal proceedings. Among other things, Gorry notes that ghost-managed articles were cited approximately ten times more often than were typical other articles in the same journals – and almost none of the difference is explained by a difference in the prestige of the authors (personal communication): Philippe Gorry, 'Medical Literature Imprinting by Pharma Ghost Writing: A Scientometric Evaluation' <https://pdfs.semanticscholar.org/5528/9bbf436abb9d1ecdd53ec8062a5d8918 8c60.pdf > [accessed 3 February 2018]. David Healy and Dinah Cattell had earlier analyzed a subset of that group, in David Healy and Dinah Cattell, 'Interface Between Authorship, Industry and Science in the Domain of Therapeutics', *British Journal of Psychiatry* 183 no. 1 (July 2003): 22–27. Unsurprisingly, the two studies come to some overlapping conclusions. Healy and Cattell compare their group of fifty-five ghost-managed articles on a particular drug with other articles on the same drug published in the same period: ghost-managed articles were cited between 2.4 and 2.9 times more frequently than matched counterparts.

2 Most self-citation involves authors citing their own work. Self-citation in this case is interesting because it is much more hidden.

3 Marilyn Larkin, 'Whose Article is it Anyway?', *The Lancet* 354, no. 9173 (1999): 136.

4 Richard Smith, 'Lapses at the New England Journal of Medicine', *Journal of the Royal Society of Medicine* 99, no. 8 (2006): 380–382.

5 Joel Lexchin and Donald W. Light, 'Commercial Bias in Medical Journals: Commercial Influence and the Content of Medical Journals', *British Medical Journal* 332, no. 7555 (2006): 1444.

6 Bob Grant, 'Merck Published Fake Journal', *TheScientist.com*, 30 April 2009.

7 Wiley, 'Wiley Resources for the Healthcare Industry' <http://eu.wiley.com/ WileyCDA/Section/id-310320.html> [accessed 19 July 2009].

8 ICMJE (International Committee of Medical Journal Editors), 'Defining the Role of Authors and Contributors' <http://www.icmje.org/recommendations/browse/roles-and-responsibilities/defining-the-role-of-authors-and-contributors.html> [accessed 4 February 2018].

9 Rebecca Kukla, '"Author TBD": Radical Collaboration in Contemporary Biomedical Research', *Philosophy of Science* 79, no. 5 (2012): 845–858; Mario Biagioli, 'Rights or Rewards', in Mario Biagioli and Peter Galison, eds, *Scientific Authorship: Credit and Intellectual Property in Science* (New York: Routledge, 2003), 253–280.

10 Mario Biagioli, 'The Instability of Authorship: Credit and Responsibility in Contemporary Biomedicine', *The FASEB Journal* 12, no. 1 (1998): 3–16.

11 In addition, because they are important participants in the world of medical research, journals typically want to make sure that researchers are receiving appropriate credit, even while they are concerned about undue influence. Promoting the right credit as a professional matter within medicine may push in opposite directions than does combatting hidden influence on medical journal articles.

12 Alistair Matheson, 'How Industry Uses the ICMJE Guidelines to Manipulate Authorship – And How They Should Be Revised', *PLoS medicine* 8, no. 8 (2011): e1001072.

13 Elliot Ross, 'How Drug Companies' PR Tactics Skew the Presentation of Medical Research', *The Guardian*, 20 May 2011.

14 US District Court, 'Deposition of Karen D. Mittleman in Re: Prempro Products Liability Litigation', 2006 <https://www.industrydocumentslibrary.ucsf.edu/drug/docs/#id=sqbw0217> [accessed 4 June 2017]. Mario Biagioli drew my attention to this document.

15 Tino F. Schwarz, Andrzej Galaj, Marek Spaczynski et al., 'Ten-Year Immune Persistence and Safety of the HPV-16/18 AS04-Adjuvanted Vaccine in Females Vaccinated at 15-55 Years of Age', *Cancer Medicine* 6, no. 11 (2017): 2723–2731. This was brought to my attention by my colleague Pierre Biron.

16 Aubrey Blumsohn, 'Authorship, Ghost-Science, Access to Data and Control of the Pharmaceutical Scientific Literature: Who Stands Behind the Word?' *AAAS Professional Ethics Report* 29, no. 3 (2006): 1–4.

17 Jennifer Washburn, 'Rent-a-Researcher: Did a British University Sell Out to Procter & Gamble?', *Slate*, 22 December 2005 <http://www.slate.com/articles/health_and_science/medical_examiner/2005/12/rentaresearcher.html>; the specific quotes are in an associated document file <http://www.fraudinscience.org/PG/20030424email.htm> [accessed 22 April 2017].

18 Aubrey Blumsohn, 'Authorship, Ghost-Science, Access to Data and Control of the Pharmaceutical Scientific Literature: Who Stands Behind the Word?' *AAAS Professional Ethics Report* 29, no. 3 (2006): 1–4.

19 A number of scholars have made more careful versions of Dr McGrath's argument, challenging the coherence of the idea of raw data. For an excellent set of articles on the issue, see Lisa Gitelman, ed., *Raw Data is an Oxymoron* (Cambridge, MA: MIT Press, 2015).

20 PhRMA, 'Principles on Conduct of Clinical Trials, Communication of Clinical Trial Results' (2009 <http://www.phrma.org/about/principles-guidelines/clinical-trials> [accessed 7 July 2011].

21 Pharma's adventures in medical research probably represent the most prominent and numerous connections between industry and the academy. Commercialized science has been of great interest to Science and Technology Studies in recent years, in a variety of contexts. In particular, analysts have explored the ways in which connections to industry are shaping academic cultures and the scientific knowledge they produce. See, e.g. Daniel Lee Kleinman, *Impure Cultures: University Biology and the World of Commerce* (Madison: University of Wisconsin Press, 2003); Grischa Metlay, 'Reconsidering Renormalization: Stability and Change in 20th-century Views on University Patents', *Social Studies of Science* 36, no. 4 (2006): 565–597; Sheila Slaughter and Gary Rhoades, *Academic Capitalism and the New Economy: Markets, State, and Higher Education* (Baltimore, MD: Johns Hopkins University Press, 2004).

22 A long tradition in Science and Technology Studies has emphasized the interpretive flexibility of methodological rules, data and objects. See, e.g. Harry M. Collins, 'Stages in the Empirical Programme of Relativism', *Social Studies of Science* 11, no. 1 (1981): 3–10; Trevor J. Pinch and Wiebe E. Bijker, 'The Social Construction of Facts and Artefacts: Or How the Sociology of Science and the Sociology of Technology Might Benefit Each Other', *Social Studies of Science* 14, no. 3 (1984): 399–441.

23 Formal objectivity is the kind of objectivity established by carefully defined procedures, even if those procedures deviate from what people would take to be the truth. See, e.g. Theodore M. Porter, *Trust in Numbers: The Pursuit of Objectivity in Science and Public Life* (Princeton, NJ: Princeton University Press, 1995); Lorraine Daston and Peter Galison, 'The Image of Objectivity', *Representations* 40 (Autumn, 1992): 81–128.

24 Ewen Callaway, 'Questions Over Ghostwriting in Drug Industry', *Nature*, 7 September 2010 <doi 10.1038/news.2010.453>.

25 The original article was Sergio Sismondo, 'Ghost Management: How Much of the Medical Literature is Shaped Behind the Scenes by the Pharmaceutical Industry?' *PLoS Medicine* 4, no. 9 (2007): e286; and the response is Larry Hirsch 'Response from the International Society for Medical Publication Professionals (ISMPP)' *PLoS Medicine* <http://journals.plos.org/plosmedicine/article/comment?id=10.1371/annotation/cd5a7a44-b33a-4560-8f5b-909f854066ac>.

5. POSSESSION: MAKING AND MANAGING KEY OPINION LEADERS

1 For example, Paul Lazarsfeld, 'The Election is Over', *Public Opinion Quarterly* 8 (1944): 317–330.

2 Elihu Katz and Paul Lazarsfeld, *Personal Influence: The Part Played by People in the Flow of Mass Communications* (Glencoe, IL: The Free Press, 1955).

3 James S. Coleman, Elihu Katz and Herbert Menzel, *Medical Innovation: A Diffusion Study* (Indianapolis, In: Bobbs-Merrill, 1966).

4 The industry had made use of opinion leaders prior to the 1950s, as shown by, for example, Nicolas Rasmussen, 'The Drug Industry and Clinical Research in Interwar America: Three Types of Physician Collaborator', *Bulletin of the History of Medicine* 79 (2005): 50–80. However, Katz and colleagues provided tools for thinking about how to use opinion leaders more systematically. An early effort at the concerted and systematic use of opinion leaders by the company Merck Sharp & Dohme, which may owe something to the Pfizer study, is discussed in Jeremy A. Greene, 'Releasing the Flood Waters: Diuril and the Reshaping of Hypertension', in Sergio Sismondo and Jeremy Greene, eds, *The Pharmaceutical Studies Reader* (Oxford: Wiley-Blackwell, 2015), 51–69.

5 Philip Topham, 'Quantity Does Not Equal Quality in Evaluating a Scientist's Real Importance as a Key Opinion Leader. lnx pharma whitepaper', 2010 <http://lnxpharma.com/images/pages/Lnx_Whitepaper_6.pdf> [accessed 29 March 2011].

6 Watermeadow, 'Rethinking the "KOL Culture"', *Next Generation Pharmaceutical* 4 (2007) <http://www.ngpharma.com/> [accessed 29 March 2011].

7 Alice Fabbri, Quinn Grundy, Barbara Mintzes, Swestika Swandari, Ray Moynihan, Emily Walkom, and Lisa Bero, 'A Cross-Sectional Analysis of Pharmaceutical Industry-Funded Events for Health Professionals in Australia', *BMJ Open* 7, no. 6: e016701. For a general account of speaker bureaus, and issues about their conflicts with professional ethics, see Lynette Reid and Matthew Herder, 'The Speakers' Bureau System: A Form of Peer Selling', *Open Medicine* 7, no. 2 (2013): e31.

8 Quoted in Ray Moynihan, 'Key Opinion Leaders: Independent Experts or Drug Representatives in Disguise', *British Medical Journal* 336 (2008): 1402–1403.

9 Daniel Carlat, 'Dr. Drug Rep', *The New York Times*, 25 November 2007.

10 Quoted in Ray Moynihan, 'Key Opinion Leaders: Independent Experts or Drug Representatives in Disguise', *British Medical Journal* 336 (2008): 1402–1403.

11 Wave Healthcare 2011

12 KnowledgePoint360, Promotional brochure, 2010.

13 Scott Hensley and Barbara Martinez, 'New Treatment: To Sell Their Drugs, Companies Increasingly Rely on Doctors', *Wall Street Journal*, 15 July 2005, p. A1.

14 It is interesting that in other contexts face-to-face communication is much more reliable than written texts at transmitting technical information. In the cases analysed in Science and Technology Studies, the reason for this is the transfer of tacit knowledge, rather than the modelling of behaviour. See, e.g. H.M. Collins, *Changing Order: Replication and Induction in Scientific Practice*, 2nd edn (Chicago: University of Chicago Press, 1990).

15 Scott Hensley and Barbara Martinez, 'New Treatment: To Sell Their Drugs, Companies Increasingly Rely on Doctors', *Wall Street Journal*, 15 July 2005, p. A1.

16 Adriane Fugh-Berman and Shahram Ahari, 'Following the Script: How Drug Reps Make Friends and Influence Doctors', *PLoS Medicine* 4, no. 4 (2007): e150.

17 Ed Silverman, 'Novartis Loses Battle with the Feds over Documents for 80,000 "Sham" Events' *STATnews*, 30 March 2017 <https://www.statnews.com/pharmalot/2017/03/30/novartis-feds-sham-events-doctors/> [accessed 11 May 2017]; *Policy and Medicine*, 'Novartis Kickback Case Will Continue, Rules Federal Judge; What We Can Glean from the Ruling, *Policy and Medicine*, 29 October 2014 <http://www.policymed.com/2014/10/judge-allows-novartis-sham-speaker-programme-kickback-case-to-continue.html> [accessed 15 May 2017].

18 United States Department of Justice, 'United States Files Complaint Against Novartis Pharmaceuticals Corp. for Allegedly Paying Kickbacks to Doctors in Exchange for Prescribing Its Drugs', *Justice News*, 26 April 2013 <https://www.justice.gov/opa/pr/united-states-files-complaint-against-novartis-pharmaceuticals-corp-allegedly-paying>.

19 Evan Hughes, 'The Pain Hustlers', *The New York Times*, 2 May 2018.

20 Ioannis A. Giannakakis and John P.A. Ioannidis, 'Arabian Nights—1001 Tales of How Pharmaceutical Companies Cater to the Material Needs of Doctors: Case Report', *British Medical Journal* 321, no. 7276 (2000): 1563–1564.

21 Thought Leader Select, Promotional brochure, 2010. See also Thought Leader Select, 'Our Services' <http://www.thoughtleaderselect.com/services/> [accessed 4 February 2018].

22 Lnx pharma, 'We Identify Truly Important Key Opinion Leaders and Undiscovered Connections' <http://lnxpharma.com/products/key-opinion-leaders/> [accessed 31 March 2011].

23 This was in a personal communication. The joking tone of the statement shouldn't be read as reducing its seriousness.

24 John Mack, 'Thought Leader Management – A Challenge Met', *Pharma Marketing News, Physician Education Special Supplement* (2006) 12–14.

25 Kimberly Cheryl, *Escape from the Pharma Drug Cartel* (Denver, CO: Outskirts Press, 2007), 71.

26 Ray Moynihan, 'Key Opinion Leaders: Independent Experts or Drug Representatives in Disguise?', *British Medical Journal* 336 (2008): 1402–1403.

27 Jim Zuffoletti and Otavio Freire, 'Marketing to Professionals: Key Opinion Control', *Pharmaceutical Executive,* 1 October 2006 <http://www.pharmexec.com> [accessed 28 March 2011].

28 Transparency laws differ widely from country to country, some building on industry self-regulation and some developing governmental structures. For a comparison of the transparency policies of nine European countries, see Alice Fabbri, Ancel.la Santos, Signe Mezinska, Shai Mulinari and Barbara Mintzes, 'Sunshine Policies and Murky Shadows in Europe: Disclosure of Pharmaceutical Industry Payments to Health Professionals in Nine European Countries', *International Journal of Health Policy and Management* (2018) <doi 10.15171/ijhpm.2018.20>.

29 Cutting Edge Information, *Thought Leader Fair-Market Value: Compensation Benchmarks and Procedures* (2009) <http://www.cuttingedgeinfo.com/thought-leader-fmv/> [accessed 3 October 2013]

30 InsiteResearch, 'Can KOL Management Generate a Return on Investment?' *Next Generation Pharmaceutical* 14 (2008) <http://www.ngpharma.com/> [accessed 28 March 2011].

31 Accreditation Council for Continuing Medical Education, 'Annual Report' (2012) <http://www.accme.org/sites/default/files/630_2012_Annual_Report_20130724_1.pdf > [accessed 3 October 2013].

32 Quoted in Howard Brody, *Hooked: Ethics, the Medical Profession, and the Pharmaceutical Industry* (Lanham, MD: Rowman & Littlefield Publishers, 2007), 208.

33 Quoted in Marcia Angell, *The Truth About the Drug Companies: How They Deceive Us and What to Do About It* (New York: Random House, 2005), 139.

34 Henryk Bohdanowicz, 'The Synergy of Public Relations and Medical Education' *Communiqué* 24 (2009): 14–16 <http://www.pmgrouplive.com/our_business/industry_sectors/pr/communique> [accessed 27 September 2009].

35 Jennifer Fishman, 'Manufacturing Desire: The Commodification of Female Sexual Dysfunction', *Social Studies of Science* 34, no. 2 (2004): 187–218.

36 InsiteResearch, 'Can KOL Management Generate a Return on Investment?' *Next Generation Pharmaceutical* 14 (2008) <http://www.ngpharma.com/> [accessed 28 March 2011].

37 We could read this claim in terms of an Actor-Network Theory account. See Bruno Latour, *Science in Action: How to Follow Scientists and Engineers through Society* (Cambridge, MA: Harvard University Press, 1987).

38 The term 'key opinion leader' ('KOL') remains the pharmaceutical industry's most commonly used term to describe influential doctors, preferred in 62% of companies, followed by 'thought leader' in 14%. Cision PR Newswire, 'Global Survey Reveals "Key Opinion Leader" (KOL) is the Most Commonly Used Term by Pharmaceutical

Industry', 19 September 2017, <http://www.prnewswire.com/news-releases/global-survey-reveals-key-opinion-leader-kol-is-the-most-commonly-used-term-by-pharmaceutical-industry-300521632.html>.

39 InsiteResearch, 'The Prescription for KOL Management', *Next Generation Pharmaceutical* 12 (2008), <http://www.ngpharma.com/> [accessed 28 March 2011].

40 David Healy, 'Shaping the Intimate: Influences on the Experience of Everyday Nerves', *Social Studies of Science* 34, no. 2 (2004): 219–245.

41 John Virapen, *Side Effects: Death – Confessions of a Pharma-Insider* (College Station, TX: virtualbookworm.com, 2010), 47.

42 Watermeadow Medical <http://www.watermeadowmedical.com/> [accessed 3 March 2009].

43 We might see a rough parallel to the supposed 'hostile worlds' of commerce and intimacy that, for example, Viviana Z. Zelizer describes in 'The Purchase of Intimacy', *Law & Social Inquiry* 25, no. 3 (2000): 817–848.

44 For a fuller account of these interviews, see Sergio Sismondo and Zdenka Chloubova, '"You're Not Just a Paid Monkey Reading Slides": How Key Opinion Leaders Explain and Justify Their Work', *BioSocieties* 11, no. 2 (2016): 199–219.

45 Emily Martin, 'Pharmaceutical Virtue', *Culture, Medicine and Psychiatry* 30, no. 2 (2006): 157–174, at 167.

46 Carl Elliott, *White Coat Black Hat: Adventures on the Dark Side of Medicine* (Boston: Beacon Press, 2010): 108.

47 Dr F, 'Comments on Dollars for Docs' <http://www.propublica.org/article/profiles-of-the-top-earners-in-dollar-for-docs> [accessed 31 March 2011].

48 A number of governments are in the process of regulating payments to physicians, which tends to lower payments to the level of 'fair market value'. Fair market value is a constant topic of discussion at industry conferences devoted to KOLs, and there are entire industry reports devoted to the topic. See, e.g., Cutting Edge Information 'KOL fair-market value and aggregate spend' <http://www.cuttingedgeinfo .com/thought-leader-fmv/> [accessed 3 October 2013]. The topic is important not because companies want to pay less, but because they want to avoid legally dubious payments that might be seen as inappropriate influence or even bribes.

49 Christophe Van den Bulte and Gary L. Lilien, 'Medical Innovation Revisited: Social Contagion versus Marketing Effort', *American Journal of Sociology* 106, no. 5 (2001): 1409–1435.

50 The phrase 'self-fulfilling prophecy' is owed to sociologist Robert K. Merton, 'The Self-Fulfilling Prophecy', *The Antioch Review* 8, no. 2 (1948): 193–210. Coincidentally, Merton worked closely with Paul Lazarsfeld, including on opinion leaders.

51 Besides Merton's 'self-fulfilling prophecy', there are a number of other recent accounts of this kind of 'performativity' of models. At issue are such things as 'looping effects' in medicine and the social sciences and 'bootstrapped induction'. See Ian Hacking, 'The Looping Effects of Human Kinds', in Dan Sperber, David Premack and Ann James Premack, eds, *Causal Cognition: A Multidisciplinary Debate* (New York: Oxford University Press, 1995), 351–394; Barry Barnes, 'Social Life as Bootstrapped Induction', *Sociology* 17, no. 4 (1983): 524–545. A prominent group of scholars has been examining how models in economics in general, and finance in particular, 'perform' themselves. See, e.g. Donald MacKenzie, Fabian Muniesa and Lucia Siu, eds, *Do Economists Make Markets? On the Performativity of Economics* (Princeton, NJ: Princeton University Press, 2007).

6. DRAINING AND CONSTRAINING AGENCY

1 Jamie Reidy, *Hard Sell: The Evolution of a Viagra Salesman* (Kansas City, MO: Andrews McMeel Publishing, 2005), 69. A number of former pharmaceutical sales reps have written books in a roughly confessional genre. Reidy's is the most cheerful, because he is trying to tell a story of himself as a likeable slacker who happened to land a golden opportunity. Others in the genre tend to be more angry, about either their authors' own mistreatment at the hands of pharma or about the misdeeds being done to patients, or both.

2 Michael Oldani, 'Thick Prescriptions: Toward an Interpretation of Pharmaceutical Sales Practices', *Medical Anthropology Quarterly* 18, no. 3 (2004): 325–356, at 334.

3 Michael Oldani, 'Thick Prescriptions: Toward an Interpretation of Pharmaceutical Sales Practices', *Medical Anthropology Quarterly* 18, no. 3 (2004): 325–356, at 335.

4 Kimberly Cheryl, *Escape from the Pharma Drug Cartel* (Denver, CO: Outskirts Press, 2007), 62.

5 Michael Oldani, 'Thick Prescriptions: Toward an Interpretation of Pharmaceutical Sales Practices', *Medical Anthropology Quarterly* 18, no. 3 (2004): 325–356, at 36.

6 Adriane Fugh-Berman and Shahram Ahari, 'Following the Script: How Drug Reps Make Friends and Influence Doctors', in Sergio Sismondo and Jeremy A. Greene, eds, *The Pharmaceutical Studies Reader* (Chichester, UK: Wiley Blackwell, 2015), 123–132.

7 Jamie Reidy, *Hard Sell: The Evolution of a Viagra Salesman* (Kansas City, MO: Andrews McMeel Publishing, 2005), 75.

8 Jamie Reidy, *Hard Sell: The Evolution of a Viagra Salesman* (Kansas City, MO: Andrews McMeel Publishing, 2005), 73.

9 A number of studies have shown that samples affect prescriptions, and tend to encourage the use of more expensive drugs. See, e.g. Richard F. Adair and Leah R. Holmgren, 'Do Drug Samples Influence Resident Prescribing Behavior? A Randomized Trial', *The American Journal of Medicine* 118, no. 8 (2005): 881–884.

10 Kimberly Cheryl, *Escape from the Pharma Drug Cartel* (Denver, CO: Outskirts Press, 2007), 42.

11 John Virapen, *Side Effects: Death – Confessions of a Pharma-Insider* (College Station, TX: virtualbookworm.com, 2010), 26.

12 Michael Oldani, 'Thick Prescriptions: Toward an Interpretation of Pharmaceutical Sales Practices', *Medical Anthropology Quarterly* 18, no. 3 (2004): 325–356, at 348.

13 Shubham Mod, 'A Medical Representative Faces These 6 Types of Doctors' <http://tips-for-medical-representative.blogspot.ca/2015/02/a-medical-representative-faces-these-6.html> [accessed 24 January 2018].

14 <https://womenslawproject.wordpress.com/2010/05/25/a-victory-for-female-employees-at-novartis/>.

15 Quoted in Adriane Fugh-Berman and Shahram Ahari, 'Following the Script: How Drug Reps Make Friends and Influence Doctors', in Sergio Sismondo and Jeremy A. Greene, eds, *The Pharmaceutical Studies Reader* (Chichester, UK: Wiley Blackwell, 2015), 123–132, at 128.

16 MedReps.com, 'The 6 Doctors You May Encounter During Sales Calls', 22 September 2014 <https://www.medreps.com/medical-sales-careers/the-6-doctors-you-may-encounter-during-sales-calls/>.

17 Kimberly Cheryl, *Escape from the Pharma Drug Cartel* (Denver, CO: Outskirts Press, 2007), 44.

18 John Virapen, *Side Effects: Death – Confessions of a Pharma-Insider* (College Station, TX: virtualbookworm.com, 2010).

19 Evan Hughes, 'The Pain Hustlers', *The New York Times*, 2 May 2018.

20 Adriane Fugh-Berman and Shahram Ahari, 'Following the Script: How Drug Reps Make Friends and Influence Doctors', in Sergio Sismondo and Jeremy A. Greene, eds, *The Pharmaceutical Studies Reader* (Chichester, UK: Wiley Blackwell, 2015), 123–132.

21 Michael Oldani, 'Thick Prescriptions: Toward an Interpretation of Pharmaceutical Sales Practices', *Medical Anthropology Quarterly* 18, no. 3 (2004): 325–356, emphasis removed.

22 Adriane Fugh-Berman and Shahram Ahari, 'Following the Script: How Drug Reps Make Friends and Influence Doctors', in Sergio Sismondo and Jeremy A. Greene, eds, *The Pharmaceutical Studies Reader* (Chichester, UK: Wiley Blackwell, 2015), 123–132.

23 Kimberly Cheryl, *Escape from the Pharma Drug Cartel* (Denver, CO: Outskirts Press, 2007), 18.

24 Kimberly Cheryl, *Escape from the Pharma Drug Cartel* (Denver, CO: Outskirts Press, 2007), 12.

25 Jamie Reidy, *Hard Sell: The Evolution of a Viagra Salesman* (Kansas City, MO: Andrews McMeel Publishing, 2005), 33.

26 Jamie Reidy, *Hard Sell: The Evolution of a Viagra Salesman* (Kansas City, MO: Andrews McMeel Publishing, 2005), 17.

27 Quoted in Melissa A. Fischer, Mary Ellen Keogh, Joann L. Baril, Laura Saccoccio, Kathleen M. Mazor, Elissa Ladd, et al., 'Prescribers and Pharmaceutical Representatives: Why Are We Still Meeting?', *Journal of General Internal Medicine* 24, no. 7 (2009): 795–801.

28 Blue Novius, 'Get your Sales Reps Back to Doctors' Offices' <https://www.bluenovius.com/healthcare-marketing/pharma-sales-reps-visit-doctors-office/> [accessed 28 January 2018].

29 Quoted in Melissa A. Fischer, Mary Ellen Keough, Joann L. Baril, Laura Saccoccio, Kathleen M. Mazor, Elissa Ladd, et al., 'Prescribers and Pharmaceutical Representatives: Why Are We Still Meeting?', *Journal of General Internal Medicine* 24, no. 7: 795–801, at 797.

30 Kimberly Cheryl, *Escape from the Pharma Drug Cartel* (Denver, CO: Outskirts Press, 2007), 62.

31 Quoted in Michael Oldani, 'Thick Prescriptions: Toward an Interpretation of Pharmaceutical Sales Practices', *Medical Anthropology Quarterly* 18, no. 3 (2004): 325-356, at 325.

32 For their general sense of immunity, see, e.g. Michael A. Steinman, Michael Shlipak and Stephen J. McPhee, 'Of Principles and Pens: Attitudes and Practices of Medicine Housestaff toward Pharmaceutical Industry Promotions', *The American Journal of Medicine* 110, no. 7 (2001): 551–557. For the correlation with contact with the industry, see Brian Hodges, 'Interactions with the Pharmaceutical Industry: Experiences and Attitudes of Psychiatry Residents, Interns and Clerks', *Canadian Medical Association Journal* 153, no. 5 (1995): 553–559.

33 Advertisement for 'Patient Adherence is the Next Best Thing in Healthcare', eyeforpharma, 19 September 2011. <https://social.eyeforpharma.com/commercial/podcasts/podcast-patient-adherence-next-big-thing-healthcare>.

34 Leslie R. Martin, Summer L. Williams, Kelly B. Haskard and M. Robin DiMatteo, 'The Challenge of Patient Adherence', *Therapeutics and Clinical Risk Management* 1, no. 3 (2005): 189–199.

35 Anthropologist Kalman Applbaum also attended an industry conference focused on patient adherence, very similar to the ones on which I report here. His observations are very similar. Kalman Applbaum, '"Consumers are Patients!" Shared Decision-making and Treatment Non-compliance as a Business Opportunity', *Transcultural Psychiatry* 46, no. 1: 107-130.

36 For example, Sandra van Dulmen, Emmy Sluijs, Liset van Dijk, Denise de Ridder, Rob Heerdink and Jozien Bensing, 'Patient Adherence to Medical Treatment: A Review of Reviews', *BMC Health Services Research* 7 (2007): 55.

37 Howard Brody and Donald W. Light, 'The Inverse Benefit Law: How Drug Marketing Undermines Patient Safety and Public Health', *American Journal of Public Health* 101, no. 3 (2011): 399–404. The inverse benefit law takes some inspiration from Hart's inverse care law: 'The availability of good medical care tends to vary inversely with the need for it in the population served'. See Julian Tudor Hart, 'The Inverse Care Law', *The Lancet* 297, no. 7696 (1971): 405–412.

38 Michelle Vitko, 'Is Technology the Solution to Patient Non-Adherence?', Cutting Edge Info, 2011 <http://www.cuttingedgeinfo.com/2011/technology-patient-adherence> [accessed 23 April 2012].

39 The speaker's slide indicates that he is here quoting Stanford University health economist Alan Garber.

7. SIRENS OF HOPE, TROLLS OF FURY AND OTHER VOCAL CREATURES

1 Steven Woloshin and Lisa Schwartz, 'US Food and Drug Administration Approval of Flibanserin: Even the Score Does Not Add Up', *JAMA Internal Medicine* 176, no.4 (2016): 439–442.

2 Jennifer Block and Liz Canner, 'The "Grassroots Campaign" for "Female Viagra" Was Actually Funded by Its Manufacturer', *New York Magazine*, 8 September 2016 <https://www.thecut.com/2016/09/how-addyi-the-female-viagra-won-fda-approval.html>.

3 Jacinthe Flore (2017) 'Intimate Tablets: Digital Advocacy and Post-Feminist Pharmaceuticals. *Feminist Media Studies* <doi 10.1080/14680777.2017.1393834>.

4 Quoted in Alycia Hogenmiller, Alessandra Hirsch and Adriane Fugh-Berman, 'The Score is Even', *The Hastings Center Report*, 14 June 2017 <https://www.thehastingscenter.org/the-score-is-even/>.

5 John Mack, 'Introduction', *Pharma Marketing News* 16, no. 2 (2017) <http://www.virsci.com/pmn/PMN1602-01patph.pdf>.

6 Judy Z. Segal, 'Sex, Drugs and Rhetoric: The Case of Flibanserin for "Female Sexual Dysfunction"', *Social Studies of Science*, forthcoming (2018).

7 Judy Z. Segal, 'The Rhetoric of Female Sexual Dysfunction: Faux Feminism and the FDA' *Canadian Medical Association Journal* 187, no. 12 (2015): 915–916.

8 Alycia Hogenmiller, Alessandra Hirsch and Adriane Fugh-Berman, 'The Score is Even', *The Hastings Center Report* 14 June 2017 <https://www.thehastingscenter.org/the-score-is-even/>. In late 2017, Valeant gave Sprout, including flibanserin, back to its original shareholders. The smaller company will attempt to restart the marketing of Addyi, paying only small royalties to Valeant if successful. See Jen Wieczner, 'Valeant Is Paying to Get Rid of Its $1 Billion "Female Viagra" Acquisition, *Fortune*, 7 November 2017 <http://fortune.com/2017/11/06/valeant-pharmaceuticals-sprout/>.

9 Quoted in Leela Barham, 'Market Access: How to Engage Emerging Stakeholders', *Eye for Pharma*, 6 November 2011 <http://social.eyeforpharma.com/print/58312> [accessed 11 November 2011].

10 For an excellent account of AIDS activism, see Steven Epstein, *Impure Science: AIDS, Activism, and the Politics of Knowledge* (Berkeley: University of California Press, 1996).

11 There has been an enormous amount of research on patient advocacy organizations, and I cannot canvass it here. For a comprehensive general overview, see: Steven Epstein, 'Patient Groups and Health Movements', in Edward J. Hackett, Olga Amsterdamska, Michael Lynch and Judy Wajcman, eds, *The Handbook of Science and Technology Studies* (Cambridge, MA: The MIT Press, 2008): 499–540. Much of the focus has been on how patient advocates contribute to medical research. For example, see: Pei P. Koay and Richard R. Sharp, 'The Role of Patient Advocacy Organizations in Shaping Genomic Science', *Annual Review of Genomics and Human Genetics* 14 (August 2013): 579-595; Vololona Rabeharisoa, Tiago Moreira, Madeleine Akrich, 'Evidence-Based Activism: Patients' Users' and Activists' Groups in Knowledge Society', *BioSocieties* 9, no. 2 (2014): 111–128.

12 Sarah Jane Tribble, 'Drugmakers Help Turn Patients With Rare Diseases Into D.C. Lobbyists', *Kaiser Health News*, 10 April 2017 <https://khn.org/news/drugmakers-help-turn-patients-with-rare-diseases-into-d-c-lobbyists/>.

13 Sarah Jane Tribble, 'Drugmakers Help Turn Patients With Rare Diseases Into D.C. Lobbyists', *Kaiser Health News*, 10 April 2017 <https://khn.org/news/drugmakers-help-turn-patients-with-rare-diseases-into-d-c-lobbyists/>.

14 DIA Patient Initiatives <http://www.diaglobal.org/en/get-involved/patients> [accessed 4 February 2018].

15 Aaron Fleishman, 'Part One: Insights Into The DIA's Patient Advocacy Programme', BBK Worldwide, 9 September 2013 <http://innovations.bbkworldwide.com/bid/186718/Part-One-Insights-Into-The-DIA-s-Patient-Advocacy-Program>.

16 Among other things, this patient advocate mentions 'enlightening educational sessions' and 'fascinating information about research positioning, study designs and precision medicine'. Colleen Zak, 'My Experience as a Patient Advocate Fellow', Global Forum 4, no. 4 <http://www1.diahome.org/en-US/Networking-and-Communities/~/media/News-and-Publications/Global-Forum/Patient_Perspective.ashx> [accessed 4 February 2018].

17 Leela Barham, 'Market Access: How to Engage Emerging Stakeholders', *eyeforpharma*, Nov. 6, 2011 <http://social.eyeforpharma.com/print/58312>.

18 Amber Spier and David Golub, 'Leveraging the Power of Patient Advocates in Drug Development', *Global Forum* 2, no. 5 (2010): 29–31 <http://rs.diaglobal.org/Tools/Content.aspx?type=eopdf&file=%2fproductfiles%2f19794%2fgf_11%2Epdf> [accessed 27 December 2017].

19 Redrawn from Amber Spier and David Golub, 'Leveraging the Power of Patient Advocates in Drug Development', *Global Forum* 2, no. 5 (2010): 29–31 <http://rs.diaglobal.org/Tools/Content.aspx?type=eopdf&file=%2fproductfiles%2f19794%2fgf_11%2Epdf> [accessed 27 December 2017].

20 Sharon Batt, *Health Advocacy, Inc.: How Pharmaceutical Funding Changed the Breast Cancer Movement* (Vancouver: UBC Press, 2017). The quote is from activist Pat Kelly, on page 194.

21 Sharon Batt, *Health Advocacy, Inc.: How Pharmaceutical Funding Changed the Breast Cancer Movement* (Vancouver: UBC Press, 2017), 234–235.

22 The phrase is from Janice E. Graham, 'Harbinger of Hope or Commodity Fetishism: "Re-cognizing" Dementia in an Age of Therapeutic Agents', *International Psychogeriatrics* 13, no. 2 (2001): 131–134. Graham observes that patient advocates' hope can change how scientists understand and evaluate the phenomena, in this case dementia. In another analysis focused on hope, Carlos Novas describes how patient advocacy, especially by groups representing patients with particular genetic conditions, creates medical identities, and facilitates medical research. He argues that patient organizations can shape medical futures by mobilizing hope. Carlos Novas, 'The Political Economy of Hope: Patients' Organizations, Science and Biovalue', *BioSocieties* 1, no. 3 (2006): 289–305.

23 The phrase 'magic bullet' is owed to immunologist Paul Ehrlich. See, e.g. Robert S. Schwartz, 'Paul Ehrlich's Magic Bullets', *New England Journal of Medicine* 350 (11 March 2004): 1079–1080.

24 For discussions of how patients should be involved in regulatory decisions, see, e.g. Michael K. Gusmano, 'FDA Decisions and Public Deliberation: Challenges and Opportunities', *Public Administration Review* 73, no. S1 (2013): S115-S126; Barbara von Tigerstrom, 'The Patient's Voice: Patient Involvement in Medical Product Regulation', *Medical Law International* 16, no. 1-2 (2016): 27–57.

25 For the largest PAOs, see Matthew S. McCoy, Michael Carniol, Katherine Chockley, John W. Unwin, Ezekiel J. Emanuel and Harald Schmidt, 'Conflicts of Interest for Patient-Advocacy Organizations', *The New England Journal of Medicine* 376 (2 March 2017): 880–885. The more general statistics can be found in Susannah L. Rose, Janelle Highland, Matthew T. Karafa and Steven Joffe, 'Patient Advocacy Organizations, Industry Funding, and Conflicts of Interest', *JAMA Internal Medicine* 177, no. 3 (2017): 344–350. As this book is going to press, Kaiser Health News is launching a database of US pharmaceutical companies' payments to PAOs, finding, for example, that companies spend more on PAOs than they do on direct lobbying of governments; see Emily Kopp, Sydney Lupkin and Elizabeth Lucas, 'Patient Advocacy Groups Take in Millions From Drugmakers. Is There a Payback?' Kaiser Health News, 6 April 2018 <https://khn.org/news/patient-advocacy-groups-take-in-millions-from-drugmakers-is-there-a-payback/>.

26 Sheila M. Rothman, Victoria H. Raveis, Anne Friedman, and David J. Rothman, 'Health Advocacy Organizations and the Pharmaceutical Industry: An Analysis of Disclosure Practices', *American Journal of Public Health* 101, no. 4 (2011): 602–609.

27 David S. Hilzenrath, 'In FDA Meetings, "Voice" of the Patient Often Funded by Drug Companies', Project on Government Oversight, 1 December 2016 <http://www.pogo.org/our-work/reports/2016/in-fda-meetings-voice-of-the-patient-often-funded-by-drug-companies.html>.

28 Ian Sample, 'Big Pharma Mobilising Patients in Battle Over Drugs Trials Data', *The Guardian*, 21 July 2013.

29 For a tremendously insightful account of this conflict, see Stefan Ecks, 'Global Pharmaceutical Markets and Corporate Citizenship: The Case of Novartis' Anti-Cancer Drug Glivec', in Sergio Sismondo and Jeremy A. Greene, eds, *The Pharmaceutical Studies Reader* (Chichester: John Wiley & Sons, 2015), 247–260.

30 Tom Jefferson, 'The UK Turns to Witty, Vallance, and Van Tam for Leadership: Revolving Doors?' *The BMJ Opinion*, 6 December 2017 <http://blogs.bmj.com/bmj/2017/12/06/tom-jefferson-the-uk-turns-to-witty-vallance-and-van-tam-for-leadership-revolving-doors/>.

31 Corporate Europe Observatory, 'Ex-Head of Europe's Drug Regulator Set Up Consultancy While Still in Office', 19 December 2011 <https://corporateeurope.org/pressreleases/2011/12/ex-head-europe-drug-regulator-set-consultancy-while-still-office>.

32 Sydney Lupkin, 'Big Pharma Greets Hundreds of Ex-Federal Workers at the "Revolving Door"', *STAT News*, 25 January 2018 <https://www.statnews.com/2018/01/25/pharma-federal-workers-revolving-door/>.

33 Robert Yapundich, 'How Pharma Sales Reps Help Me Be a More Up-to-Date Doctor', *STAT News*, 1 September 2017 <https://web.archive.org/web/20170901111434/https://www.statnews.com/2017/09/01/doctor-pharma-sales-reps/>.

34 Kevin Lomangino, 'Tone Deaf Again on Pharma Conflict of Interest: STAT Piece Praising Drug Reps Fails to Disclose Industry Payments', *HealthNewsReview.org*, 5 September 2017 <https://www.healthnewsreview.org/2017/09/tone-deaf-pharma-conflict-interest-stat-piece-praising-drug-reps-fails-disclose-industry-payments/>.

35 Mary Chris Jaklevic, 'Non-Profit Alliance for Patient Access Uses Journalists and Politicians to Push Big Pharma's Agenda', *HealthNewsReview.org*, 2 October 2017 <https://www.healthnewsreview.org/2017/10/non-profit-alliance-patient-access-uses-journalists-politicians-push-big-pharmas-agenda/>.

36 Kevin Lomangino, '"A Blow to [STAT's] Credibility": MD Listed as Author of Op-Ed Praising Drug Reps Didn't Write It. Ghostwriting/PR Influence', *HealthNewsReview.org* <https://www.healthnewsreview.org/2017/09/a-blow-to-

stats-credibility-public-relations-firm-may-have-ghostwritten-op-ed-praising-drug-reps/> (accessed 4 February 2018).

37 For example, in the midst of a public outcry over steep drug price hikes, the Alliance for Patient Access wrote a blog post on the need for a 'comprehensive dialogue', especially focused on how insurers should cover full costs of drugs: Amanda Conschafter, 'Rx Cost Debate Overlooks Patient Access Issues', *Institute for Patient Access*, 3 November 2015 <http://allianceforpatientaccess.org/rx-cost-debate-overlooks-patient-access-issues/>. When discussions at a United Nations panel on access to medications turned to the exorbitant prices allowed by patents, the Alliance wrote a blog post on how patents make access possible: 'Rx Pricing, Patents & Patient Access', *Institute for Patient Access* <http://allianceforpatientaccess.org/rx-pricing-patents-patient-access/> [accessed 24 May 2018].

38 Global Colon Cancer Association (and others), Letter to Secretary of State John F. Kerry, 6 September 2016 <http://docs.wixstatic.com/ugd/21cfdb_658604e96b 1040beaf243554d6c6f354.pdf>.

39 For example, see the organization Patients for Affordable Drugs <https://www.patientsforaffordabledrugs.org/> [accessed 4 February 2018] which sees the problem of drug pricing as created primarily by the pharmaceutical industry.

40 The original is Cary P. Gross and Abbe R. Gluck, 'Soaring Cost of Cancer Treatment: Moving Beyond Sticker Shock', *Journal of Clinical Oncology*, published online before print, 13 December 2017 <doi 10.1200/JCO.2017.76.0488>.

41 Robert Goldberg, 'CMPI Awards Billy Madison Pharma Idiocy Award to Yale University Professors', DrugWonks.com, 3 January 2018 <http://drugwonks.com/blog/cmpi-awards-billy-madison-pharma-idiocy-award-to-yale-university-professors> [accessed 5 January 2018].

42 Cathy Jones (as told to Wency Leung), 'What It's Like to Speak Out About Vaginal Atrophy', *The Globe and Mail*, 24 March 2017 <https://www.theglobeandmail.com/life/health-and-fitness/health/what-its-like-to-have-vaginal-atrophy/article31990317/>.

43 This story was brought to my attention when I was contacted by Kelly Crowe of CBC News, asking if I would be interviewed for it. The quotes by Jones and the CGI Group contact are taken from Kelly Crowe, 'Ads Disguised as News: A Drug Company's Stealth Marketing Campaign Exposed', *CBC News*, 5 October 2016 <http://www.cbc.ca/news/health/vaginal-atrophy-analysis-1.3786547>.

CONCLUSION: THE HAUNTED PHARMAKON

1 Howard Brody and Donald W. Light, 'The Inverse Benefit Law: How Drug Marketing Undermines Patient Safety and Public Health', *American Journal of Public Health* 101, no. 3 (2011): 399–404.

2 See, e.g. Donald W. Light, Joel Lexchin and Jonathan Darrow, 'Institutional Corruption of Pharmaceuticals and the Myth of Safe and Effective Drugs', *Journal of Law, Medicine & Ethics* 14, no. 3 (2013): 590-610; Jacoline C. Bouvy, Marie L. De Bruin and Marc A. Koopmanschap, 'Epidemiology of Adverse Drug Reactions in Europe: A Review of Recent Observational Studies', *Drug Safety* 38, no. 5 (2015): 437–453.

3 The phrase 'moral microclimates' is Emily Martin's. For Martin, these moral microclimates operate as spaces from which pharmaceutical employees are able to actively engage in defining the meaning of their own work. See Emily Martin, 'Pharmaceutical Virtue', *Culture, Medicine and Psychiatry* 30, no. 2 (2006): 157–174. Our interviews with KOLs, and the justificatory schemes they use, are presented in more detail in Sergio Sismondo and Zdenka Chloubova, '"You're Not Just a Paid Monkey Reading Slides": How Key Opinion Leaders Explain and Justify Their Work', *BioSocieties* 11, no. 2 (2016): 199–219.

4 As I mentioned before, doctors who see sales reps frequently are more confident of their ability to remain independent than are those who avoid seeing them. Brian Hodges, 'Interactions with the Pharmaceutical Industry: Experiences and Attitudes of Psychiatry Residents, Interns and Clerks', *Canadian Medical Association Journal* 153, no. 5 (1995): 553–559.

5 Marc Rodwin, *Conflicts of Interest and the Future of Medicine: The United States, France and Japan* (Oxford: Oxford University Press, 2011).

6 Peter Doshi, Kay Dickerson, David Healy, S. Swaroop Vedula and Tom Jefferson, 'Restoring Invisible and Abandoned Trials: A Call for People to Publish the Findings', *British Medical Journal* 346 (2013): f2865.

7 The phrase stems from the US Supreme Court justice Louis Brandeis, who wrote that '[s]unlight is said to be the best of disinfectants; electric light the most efficient policeman'. See Louis D. Brandeis, *Other People's Money – And How Bankers Use It* (New York: F.A. Stokes, 1914).

8 Jeanne Lenzer, 'Two Years of Sunshine: Has Openness About Payments Reduced Industry Influence in Healthcare?', *British Medical Journal* 354 (2016): i4608.

9 Jason Dana and George Loewenstein, 'A Social Science Perspective on Gifts to Physicians from Industry', *Journal of the American Medical Association* 290, no. 2 (2003): 252–255.

10 I owe this point to Shai Mulinari, who is studying transparency as applied to pharma in a number of European countries.

11 Lars Jørgensen, Peter C. Gøtzsche and Tom Jefferson, 'Index of the Human Papillomavirus (HPV) Vaccine Industry Clinical Study Programs and Non-industry Funded Studies: A Necessary Basis to Address Reporting Bias in a Systematic Review', *Systematic Reviews* 7, no. 1 (2018): 8.

12 See, e.g. Office of the Inspector General, 'Health Care Fraud and Abuse Control Program Report' <http://oig.hhs.gov/reports-and-publications/hcfac/index.asp#pdf> [accessed 14 July 2011].

13 For some excellent overviews of conflicts of interest between the pharmaceutical industry and medicine, see Joel Lexchin, *Doctors in Denial: Why Big Pharma and the Canadian Medical Profession Are Too Close for Comfort* (Toronto: James Lorimer, 2017); Marc Rodwin, *Conflicts of Interest and the Future of Medicine: The United States, France and Japan* (Oxford: Oxford University Press, 2011).

14 A related proposal is made by Lynette Reid, and Matthew Herder, 'The Speakers' Bureau System: A Form of Peer Selling', *Open Medicine* 7, no. 2 (2013): e31.

15 A version of this proposal was put forward by Stan Finkelstein and Peter Temin to address another problem: drug pricing. See Stan Finkelstein and Peter Temin, *Reasonable Rx: Solving the Drug Price Crisis* (Upper Saddle River, NJ: FT Press, 2008).

16 For example, Arthur Schafer 'Biomedical Conflicts of Interest: A Defence of the Sequestration Thesis – Learning from the Cases of Nancy Olivieri and David Healy', *Journal of Medical Ethics* 30 (2004): 8–24; Marcia Angell, *The Truth About the Drug Companies: How They Deceive Us and What to Do About It* (New York: Random House, 2005).

17 For example, Marcia Angell, *The Truth About the Drug Companies: How They Deceive Us and What to Do About It* (New York: Random House, 2005).

18 For example, James Robert Brown, 'Medical Market Failures and Their Remedy', in Martin Carrier and Alfred Nordmann, eds, *Science in the Context of Application*, (Dordrecht: Springer Publishing, 2011), 271–281.

MATTERING PRESS TITLES

CPSIA information can be obtained
at www.ICGtesting.com
Printed in the USA
FSHW01n0542160818
51479FS